Activity, Incomes and Social Welfare

To Asghar,

It was nice meeting you
after such a long time — and
attending your most interesting
lecture on AIP.

     Best regards,

       Tim

       31/3/2015

Public Policy and Social Welfare
A Series Edited by the European Centre

 European Centre Vienna

Volume 33

The book relies on research supported by the project "Competitive Pressure and its Social Consequences in EU Member States and in Associated Countries" (COMP-PRESS, HPSE-CT-2002-00149) within the Fifth Framework Programme of the European Commission.

Tine Stanovnik acknowledges the financial support received from ARRS contract no. P5-0161c.

Manuela Sofia Stănculescu / Tine Stanovnik (Eds.)

Activity, Incomes and Social Welfare

A Comparison across Four New EU Member States

ASHGATE

Published by

Ashgate Publishing Limited
Wey Court East
Union Road
Farnham
Surrey GU9 7PT
United Kingdom

Ashgate Publishing Company
Suite 420
101 Cherry Street
Burlington, VT 05401-4405
USA

Copy-editing and DTP: Willem Stamatiou
European Centre for Social Welfare Policy and Research
Berggasse 17, 1090 Vienna, Austria

British Library Cataloguing-in-Publication Data. A catalogue record for this book is available from the British Library.

ISBN 978-0-7546-7777-2

Printed by Facultas Verlags- und Buchhandels AG, Vienna, Austria

Contents

Chapter 4

Changes in Income, Income Inequality and Poverty:

György Molnár / Viktoria Galla

Chapter 5

The Transition Process and Changes in Income,

Manuela Sofia Stănculescu / Lucian Pop

8

List of Figures and Tables

Figures

Chapter 1: The changing landscape: demography and activity

*Chapter 2: Changes in household income, income inequality and poverty:
    a comparative overview*

Chapter 6: The transition process and changes in income,
*   income inequality and poverty: the case of Slovenia*

List of Tables

Introduction

Chapter 1: The changing landscape: demography and activity

Chapter 2: Changes in household income, income inequality and poverty: a comparative overview

Chapter 3: The transition process and changes in income,
*   income inequality and poverty: the case of Bulgaria*

Chapter 4: Changes in income, income inequality and poverty: the case of Hungary

Chapter 5: The transition process and changes in income, income inequality and poverty: the case of Romania

Chapter 6: The transition process and changes in income, income inequality and poverty: the case of Slovenia

Introduction

Michael F. Förster[1]

The issues at stake

On 1st May 2004, Hungary and Slovenia, together with six other former centrally planned economies in Central Eastern Europe joined the European Union. Bulgaria and Romania followed less than three years later. As recent as 20 years ago, such a rapid process of integration would have been regarded by many as improbable, or even impossible. This process was accompanied by profound economic, political and social changes in each of these countries. Those had a direct impact on labour markets and labour market behaviour, on household incomes and poverty risks and, finally, on social policy responses. However, only a few generalized patterns emerge and most developments have been country-specific, not least due to differing "starting positions", economic as well as political.

This book is about changes in household structure, activity and income distribution during the transition period in four countries: Bulgaria, Hungary, Romania and Slovenia. It closes important gaps in many aspects of our knowledge of the transition process and its outcomes in these countries. First, it draws on these country-specific experiences to proceed to a true comparative analysis. It covers two countries of the first wave of EU enlargement and two countries of the most recent wave – at first sight, covering two sides of the prosperity spectrum of countries in the Central Eastern European region. Second, it looks at a longer time span, covering the almost 20 years since transition to market economies started. Third,

---

1   Michael Förster is a social policy analyst at the OECD Directorate for Employment, Labour and Social Affairs, and formerly for half a decade Research Fellow at the European Centre for Social Welfare Policy and Research, Vienna. The opinions expressed are those of the author and do not engage the OECD or its Member Countries.

while providing some basic comparative macro-economic background, it focuses on a perspective "from below", i.e. on labour market behaviour of people and income developments of households. Fourth, it relates these developments on a micro-economic level to social policy reforms.

In the early years of economic transition, the social insurance based systems in the four countries were under severe strain due to an unprecedented increase in beneficiaries and an erosion of the contribution base. Social policies reacted with *ad-hoc* measures to ensure the financial viability of the system: in Bulgaria and Romania, for instance, pensions were increased on a discretionary basis and not fully price-indexed until the late 1990s. In Hungary, a switch to an unfavourable calculation of the pension base in the early 1990s reduced the value of real pensions. And in Slovenia, pension indexation was discontinued for a short period around 1990/1991.

Starting in the mid-1990s, all four countries witnessed the search for more structural social policy reforms. Bulgaria introduced a new family allowances system in 2002, linking payment to household income and including means-testing while at the same time increasing level of benefit. The coverage of family benefits therefore sank from 95 to 72%. From 2004, family benefits are no longer paid to the employer but to the family directly. These reforms are aiming to increase the targeting features. Entitlement to unemployment benefits was restricted in 1997, especially for long-term unemployed and young first-job seekers, concerning about half of the registered unemployed. The Bulgarian pension system was reformed in 1999/2000, introducing a three-pillar system and increasing the standard retirement age to reach 60/63 in 2009.

The Hungarian reforms culminated in the so-called Lajos Bokros package, which was an overall package including new taxation and devaluating the Hungarian Forint. It also brought about a narrowed access to most social benefits. Family benefits became means-tested in 1995 but with a high income threshold – the philosophy being to "exclude the rich" rather than "targeting the poor" families. After 1998, the nominal value of the income-independent part of family benefits did not change and was replaced by a tax allowance which can be drawn only above a given income threshold. However, family benefits returned to universal coverage in 2000. The 1997 pension reform reduced the first pay-as-you-go pillar and comprised a new funded second pillar, while the statutory pension age was raised. A new pension indexation was introduced at the same time as "Swiss indexation" (half prices half real wage growth).

Unlike other Central Eastern European countries, Romania made only very modest efforts in social protection for a longer period and therefore did not compensate for the social costs of transition during much of the 1990s. Locally financed social aid was introduced in 1995 but its value decreased enormously until 2000. It was replaced by a guaranteed minimum income in 2002 (with a benchmark minimum revenue set at 36% of the minimum wage). In 2004, a means-tested support allowance for single parents was introduced. A pension reform took place in 2001, introducing a new calculation method aimed at reducing the enormous differences between high and low pensions, and a special social allowance for single old-age persons introduced in 2004 should improve the situation further. A new mechanism to recalculate all pre-2001 pensions was installed in 2004, and the legal retirement age was increased to 60/65.

In Slovenia, large legislative steps were taken in 1994 and 1996 to increase the coverage of child benefits to make it more universal. At the same time, parental allowances were expanded and a special allowance for families with three or more children was introduced in 2001. The unemployment benefit reform in 1998 brought a cut in duration, lower minimum amounts and changes in the basis for benefit calculation. The fairly stable expenditures on pensions resulted from a gradual decrease in the ratio between pensions and wages. This was mostly caused by the pension reform introduced in 2000, which decreased the pension rights not only of new entrants – i.e. future pensioners – but also for the current stock of pensioners – a rather unusual feature when compared to other countries.

All these structural policy reforms in these four countries took place in the context of huge shifts in income and household structure and the emergence of new groups at risk of poverty. It is tempting to compare the developments in the four countries with more global trends in the OECD world. The OECD recently released a major study on an issue entitled "*Growing Unequal?*" (OECD, 2008). This study finds that inequalities have increased over the past 20 years. The rise was moderate but significant and widespread, in that it concerned more than three quarters of OECD countries. At the same time, the study concludes that this trend had nothing inevitable and that policies can make a difference. Social policies, active labour market policies and fiscal policies can cushion and even reverse very high levels of market income inequality.

When put in such an international context, the reported levels of income inequality and poverty would place Hungary and Slovenia somewhat below OECD average, in the range of most Continental European countries, Romania above average – especially concerning poverty – with Bulgaria occupying an intermediate position. It should be noted, however, that these levels – due to a broader income definition (except for Slovenia) – are very likely to be underestimated. That said, the ranking *among* the four countries still prevails.

The micro data analysis in this book covers the period between the early/mid-1990s[2] and the early/mid-2000s[3]. Over the whole period, income inequality and poverty appeared rather stable, with smaller increases in Bulgaria and Hungary. As in many OECD countries, income from wages is more unequally distributed than most other sources of income, and increasingly so. On the other hand, there are other income sources shaping the distribution in the four countries which are of much less importance in OECD countries, notably farming income, income from self-consumption and inter-family transfers such as remittances. Interestingly, one of the few generalized patterns across the four countries which emerge from the analyses mirrors the experience in a great majority of OECD countries, namely a change in poverty risk groups. Older people experienced a fall in their exposure to income poverty while, at the same time, child poverty increased considerably.

Table 1: Age-specific risk of relative income poverty, trends over time. Income poverty rates of the entire population in each year = 100[a]

	Children			Older People		
	mid-1980s	early/mid-1990s	early/mid-2000s	mid-1980s	early/mid-1990s	early/mid-2000s
Bulgaria	-	102	120	-	135	47
Hungary	-	120	174	-	43	26
Romania	-	140	157	-	79	57
Slovenia	-	92	97	-	172	138
OECD	109	116	120	154	136	118

Note: a) Risk of relative income poverty is the age-specific poverty rate divided by the poverty rate for the entire population times 100. The poverty threshold is set at 50% of national median income of the entire population in each year. Children defined as persons below age 18 for OECD figures and persons below age 15 for the other countries. Older people defined as persons above age 65 for OECD figures and persons above age 60 for the other countries.

Source: OECD (2008) and country chapters in this book.

---

2   1992 for Bulgaria, 1993 for Hungary and Slovenia and 1995 for Romania.
3   2001-03 for Slovenia, 2002 for Bulgaria and Hungary and 2004 for Romania.

Contents of chapters

In Chapter 1, Manuela Sofia Stănculescu describes the macro-economic frame in which the four countries evolved in the past two decades. Almost all key macro indicators suggest that the two "old new" EU members have been performing better than the two "new new" EU members. The first three to four years after 1989 brought by a "transitional recession" during which output levels fell by as much as 20 to 25%. However, while Hungary and Slovenia saw steady growth after that period, Bulgaria and Romania experienced a second period of recession toward the later 1990s. Since 2000 and until 2007, all four countries have annual GDP growth rates above EU and OECD average, in the order of 4 to 5%. Today, real GDP levels in Hungary and Slovenia exceed the 1989 levels by 40-45%, while they are just one tenth higher in Romania and barely exceed the 1989 level in Bulgaria. This means that absolute differentials between the countries accentuated. Slovenia achieved the most in closing the gap to other EU countries, its GDP per capita level is only little below the EU-27 average, somewhere between the Greek and Portuguese level. Hungary is more than one third below EU-average, a bit above the levels in the Baltic countries and close to the Slovak one. And GDP per capita levels in Bulgaria and Romania are both still almost two thirds below the EU average and by far the lowest levels across EU-27.

Like in other European countries, the four countries are experiencing an ageing of the population. The share of people over 65 in the population now stands at 15-17%. At the same time, the share of children decreased from one fifth (one fourth in Romania) in 1989 to 14-16% today. The change in the population structure occurred thus much faster than in the "old" EU member countries. The structural population changes were exacerbated by emigration in Bulgaria and Romania where the total population shrank by 13% and 6%, respectively. Among the young, enrolment in general secondary education and tertiary education increased at a fast pace in all four countries.

Economic and population changes had serious repercussions on the labour market, but not necessarily the ones that were "expected". Stănculescu describes patterns of "jobless growth", especially in Romania and Hungary. Employment rates fell steeply at the beginning of the transition. After that they continued to fall in Romania and increased only slightly in the other three countries. In terms of levels, Slovenia developed very closely to the EU average, reaching a current employment level of about 65% while employment rates in the other three countries are very far from the Lisbon target of 70% – at about 56-58%. In Hungary, the agriculture's share in employment fell and in Slovenia it remained broadly stable while it actually increased in Bulgaria and Romania. Stănculescu suggests that agricultural employment acted as a coping strategy for the unskilled in these two countries, especially Romania.

After an initial upsurge of open unemployment at the beginning of the 1990s, the unemployment rate remained below the EU-average during the past decade in Hungary, Romania and Slovenia and above it in Bulgaria – though approaching the EU-level recently. At the same time, all four countries share the problem of very high long-term unemployment. Equally worrisome is the increase in the economically inactive population. The share of pensioners increased at a much faster rate than the share of elderly, due to a rise in early retirement, and also in disability pensions which in many cases acted as an alternative pathway into early retirement.

Chapter 2 by Tine Stanovnik and Nataša Kump turns the attention to the micro level: trends in household incomes and their elements and in the socioeconomic structure of households. Labour earnings are the most important source of income. The growth in real gross wages mirrored the development of real GDP per capita only partly: they increased steadily in Slovenia (since 1992) and Hungary (since 1996), to reach about 140% of their 1992 level by 2003. On the other hand, they increased at a much slower pace than GDP (and only since 1997) in Romania and only marginally in Bulgaria, suggesting a decreasing wage share in GDP in these countries. Except in Bulgaria, the growth of real pensions was less than that of wages, leading to a gradual decrease in the pension/wage ratio. This development was brought about by policies (Bokros austerity package in Hungary in 1996/97, Slovenian pension reform 1999) or had structural reasons (unfavourable system dependency ratio in Romania).

Apart from wages, agricultural income is particularly important in Bulgaria and Romania, accounting for one fifth of total household income. The lion's share, some 80%, constitutes in-kind agricultural income. The share of self-employed people increased in all four countries, but in Romania and Slovenia the share of self-employed income decreased – suggesting existence of "coping strategies", with employees and unemployed moving into low-productive self-employment activities.

Stanovnik and Kump juxtapose the traditional unemployment figures (based on the ILO definition) with estimates derived from household budget surveys and based on self-declaration. The latter are considerably higher than the former and did not decrease over time (except in Hungary). The authors take this as an indication that restructuring is not over yet and that there is a poor matching between the skills of the unemployed and the jobs offered. The share of very young and old dependants (people without own income resources) has decreased; for the latter, this is due to increased coverage of pensions. At the same time, the share of younger adults who are dependants has increased due to higher enrolment for tertiary education.

It is interesting to look at the distribution of main socioeconomic groups and corresponding income aggregates across income deciles. For instance, the share of wages as well as of workers increases monotonically with income. However, this pattern is much less pronounced in Bulgaria indicating a fairly high share of working poor. The distributional patterns for pensions are different. In Hungary and Romania, the distributions of pensions and pensioners is middle-class biased, i.e. they follow an inverted U-shaped curve. In Bulgaria and Slovenia, pensions have a tendency to decrease with higher deciles while the share of pensioners is pretty stable across the income spectrum. The patterns for the third important income source, agricultural income, are very country-specific: in Bulgaria, its shares in household income are increasing with higher income and they are high (10-30%) despite a low share of people active in agriculture, indicating a very large extent of agriculture as a secondary activity. In Hungary, income shares are lower but still sizeable (7-10%), especially in higher deciles which the authors take as indicating market-oriented agricultural activities. Romania is the only country with a higher share of persons in agriculture particularly in the lower deciles pointing to a large extent of subsistence farming. In Slovenia, the share of persons active in agriculture as well as agricultural income is very small but concentrated in the lowest deciles.

Stanovnik and Kump also examine trends in the coverage of public social benefits. For the financing side, they show that the covered wage bill (the amount of wages upon which social contributions are levied) is still very low in some countries: measured as a percentage of the actual wage bill, it is close to 80% in Hungary and Slovenia, but only 60% in Bulgaria and 45% in Romania. This suggests the persistence of a large informal sector and results in a weaker social protection system in the latter countries. As concerns the recipiency side, pension coverage increased while coverage of unemployment benefits decreased, except in Hungary. In addition, the average replacement rate of unemployment benefits fell in all four countries, from a 50-60% to a 30-40% range. Trends in the coverage of family benefits were subject to repeated regulatory changes. Currently, this coverage is rather high, in the 80-100% range.

How did the changes in income and household structure translate into income inequality and poverty? Surprisingly, the authors find little change in inequality of disposable household income between the early/mid-1990s and early/mid-2000s: a slight increase in Bulgaria and Hungary, stability in Romania and a slight decrease in Slovenia. Of course, this might hide significant changes which happened in the very early years of transition (as the authors suspect) but unfortunately no comparable data are available for this early period. There is more of a systemic evidence for income poverty trends. First, poverty incidence increased in the first sub-period, the mid- to late 1990s and decreased thereafter. Only in Romania, it remained at the same level throughout, significantly higher than in the other three countries. Second, the composition of poverty changed. In all four countries, the relative poverty risk of pensioners fell while that of children increased. Another group whose position worsened during the transition process and now records poverty rates twice to three times the country averages are the unemployed.

The subsequent chapters examine developments in the four countries in turn. In the country chapter on Bulgaria, Chapter 3, Silviya Nikolova analyses inequality and poverty against the backdrop of the transformational recession of the early 1990s and the severe financial crisis 1996/97. During the latter, social protection expenditure shares in GDP fell considerably, in particular pension expenditures. After this second recession, the number of regular old-age pensioners slightly decreased to 1.7 million, while the one of invalidity pensioners almost doubled and the one of social pensioners increased by a factor of 7 (both now account for 0.5 million people each). Nikolova describes this as coping strategy to escape open unemployment and as an inroad into early retirement.

Household incomes did not keep pace with GDP growth. The latter increased continuously since 1997 to reach in 2002 the level recorded one decade before. Net household incomes, however, stagnated since 1998 at around 60% of their level of the early 1990s. This had to do with a shift in the household income structure away from labour income coupled with a drop in average real wage. Indeed, the share of all labour income taken together fell from over two thirds to some 60% while that of transfers increased from one fourth to over 30%. Interestingly, the pattern was the inverse for low-income households, suggesting a growth in the number of working poor.

Nikolova looks at trends in coverage and adequacy of selected transfer payments. Family allowances have been universal in Bulgaria until 2002 when they became income-tested. The average recipiency rate among house holds with children thus fell from about 90% to 70%. Nonetheless, this rate did not vary by income decile. The author relates this to the fact that allowances are granted on the basis of "insured" (rather than real) income and concludes that "the targeting of family allowances needs further improvement". As for unemployment benefits, the percentage of households with unemployed members receiving this form of compensation fell from 33 to 14%, mainly due to cuts in eligibility. In fact, by 2002 just 19% of the 0.6 million registered unemployed received benefits, compared to 40% ten years earlier. The percentage of households receiving social assistance decreased while they became more strongly targeted. Taking incidence and targeting features of all cash social transfers together, Nikolova reports that these reduce poverty by about one third. This figure needs to be compared with the 60% reduction (50% among the working-age population) recorded on average in OECD countries (OECD, 2008).

A number of noteworthy changes in the socioeconomic structure happened in Bulgaria between 1992 and 2002: the concentration of self-employed in agriculture shifted from higher to lower income deciles while the concentration of non-agricultural self-employed in the highest deciles increased. Pensioners' concentration shifted from the lowest to the middle income deciles while children made the inverse move.

The distribution of incomes became slightly and that of consumption expenditures more significantly more unequal. The main contributing factors to income inequality during the period 1992-2002 were wages and salaries and income from agriculture. Similarly, relative income poverty – defined at several thresholds – slightly increased, whereby a stronger increase has been recorded in the first half of the 1990s. Throughout the whole period, unemployed persons recorded one of the highest poverty risks. Child poverty increased, especially for children in single-parent and large households and those with very young mothers. By contrast, pensioners' poverty decreased from above to below-average levels.

Nikolova devotes a separate section on the very high poverty risks experienced by the Roma population. It is estimated that the majority of this population lives below a poverty threshold, be it defined in relative or absolute terms, based on income or expenditure. The risk is therefore 7 to 10 times higher than for the rest of the population. The author relates this to

the extremely high incidence of unemployment (itself related to low education and loss of opportunities for low-skilled agricultural jobs) and lack of
access to basic services. Clearly, the Roma population was hit hardest by
the economic transformation.

In Chapter 4 György Molnár and Viktoria Galla analyse the development in Hungary which was characterized by an early transition recession
between 1988 and 1993 after which growth first resumed and then accelerated since 1997. This was not the case of employment which continued
decreasing until 1997 and barely took up since then. Many working-age
people went into inactivity through the pathway of early retirement or
disability pensions – their growth largely exceeded that of regular old-age
pensions. In Hungary, over half of all households receive some form of
pension income.

Nevertheless, labour income remained the most important source of
household income in Hungary and its share even increased from 57% to 60%
between the early 1990s and early 2000s, whereby a fall in agricultural income
was compensated for by a rise in self-employment and occasional work income (in the case of the first, particularly among wealthy households; in the
case of the latter, among poor households). The share of pensions increased,
too. This happened as the share of working-age benefits (unemployment,
family and other) was more than halved, from 13% to 6%. This significant
fall is not due to a decline in the unemployed and children population but
to shrinking average benefits and a somewhat stronger targeting.

That said, coverage of family benefits followed the legislative changes in
Hungary: quasi-universal coverage in 1993, 70% to 90% for the richest three
deciles in 1997 and return to quasi 100% by 2002. Coverage of unemployment benefits (that is the share of households with unemployed members
receiving benefits) fell from four fifths to two thirds in the mid-1990s but
returned to four fifths by 2002. At the same time, the replacement rate for
unemployment benefits strongly declined over the whole period, except for
the years between 1997 and 1999. Coverage of other social benefits (mainly
income support) decreased significantly.

Molnár and Galla look at the changes in the socioeconomic household
structure along the income ladder. They find that the relative position of the
(diminishing) unemployed population has worsened, related to a reduction in the insurance-part of unemployment benefits. The relative income
position of pensioners improved only slightly in the first half of the 1990s
and their majority is clustered around the middle deciles. By contrast, the
position of children has worsened.

Income inequality in Hungary increased between 1993 and 2002. In the first period, until 1997, this was due to a deterioration in the relative position of low-income households ("poor getting poorer") whereas in the more recent period, which was characterized by overall income growth, the position of high-income households improved ("rich getting richer"). Analysing the distributive patterns of the different household income elements, Molnár and Galla report a very high and increasing concentration of capital and non-agricultural self-employment income (though those account for just some 8% of total income). Wages are highly concentrated, too, but this somewhat smoothened over the years. On the other hand, unemployment and family benefits became increasingly concentrated towards the poorest households and are thus acting as "income inequality equalizers".

Overall income poverty increased between 1993 and 1997 and remained roughly stable since then. Among groups at risk, the unemployed are particularly exposed; their poverty rate was about three times the country average in 1993 and four times as high in 2002. A second group at risk of increasing poverty rates are children, especially younger children (i.e. during parents' child care leave); children in single-parent families and families with unmarried couples; and children in large households.

Chapter 5 by Manuela Sofia Stănculescu and Lucian Pop is devoted to Romania. This country experienced a deep recession between 1988 and 1992 and a second one between 1997 and 1999. Real wages have grown since then but, by 2004, are still 20% below their 1990 level. Employment, on the other hand, kept falling even after 2000. This led to a significant fall in the contribution of wages to total household incomes which was only partly compensated for by social benefits. A serious problem arose for the value of pensions and sustainability of the system: the total number of pensioners almost doubled to more than 6 million people between 1990 and 2004, while the number of employees declined, from over 8 million to about 6 million, of which only about 4.5 million were contributing to the system. The real average pension in 2004 was 40% below its 1990 level.

Stănculescu and Pop analyse the changes in the socioeconomic structure of households between 1995 and 2004. Employees are increasingly concentrated in high-income groups while farmers are persistently and unemployed increasingly concentrated in the lowest income groups. The non-farming self-employed display a U-shaped distribution and pensioners an inverted U-shape, i.e. they are concentrated in middle income classes.

Although on a falling trend, labour incomes taken together – be it wages, self-employment or agriculture – are the main contributors to the total household budget for poorer and affluent households alike, accounting for little above two thirds. Interfamily transfers (which notably include remittances from abroad) had a small contribution to the total household disposable income but still exceed that of income for capital, even for the most affluent households for whom this income source is particularly important. In 2004, the share of these transfers in household income was higher than that of family and unemployment benefits together. Stănculescu and Pop construct an indicator of "protection balance" which divides state protection (the sum of all public benefits in household income) by self-protection (the sum of agricultural income and interfamily transfers in household income). This is taken to indicate to which extent the state or else people's efforts for self-protection (by growing their own food and by investing in social networks) help cushioning the population against the transition shock. In Romania this indicator displays an inverse U-shape across the distribution implying higher state efforts only for middle classes. In Bulgaria, for comparison, this indicator is monotonically falling with higher income. The authors explain this as particularly strong kinship networks in Romania which had developed already before the transition as a response to the state socialist economy of shortage.

Stănculescu and Pop look at the changes in coverage of the main social benefits and conclude that (i) old-age related social risks have been tackled rather well by pensions; (ii) the unemployment benefit system reduced its protection function during the period; (iii) child allowances had an impact on absolute child poverty alleviation and (iv) social assistance significantly increased coverage and targeting after 2002.

Income inequality slightly decreased between 1995 and 1997, i.e. just before the second recession, and then slightly increased until 2004. Levels are relatively high but would be considerably higher if self-consumption would not be counted within income. Stănculescu and Pop demonstrate that this would increase the quintile share ratio from about 4 to about 7 and the Gini coefficient from 0.31 to 0.36. The first levels are close to the average across OECD countries (which do not account for self-consumption), the second ones correspond to levels found in Poland, Portugal and the United States. Looking at different income components, wages and capital income became increasingly concentrated while the inverse was the case for self-employment and farming income. The concentration of interfamily transfers was as high as the one for wages. Both unemployment and family benefits have negative concentration coefficients throughout the period, i.e. the poor received a larger part of them, but values changed little over the period, i.e. they did not become much more or less targeted.

Differences in returns to education between attainment levels have been large and growing. The relative income of people with tertiary education increased to almost double the overall level while relative incomes of all other attained educational levels decreased. Since 1995 the rural-urban education gap has widened which explains the significant poverty risks of the rural population. People active in agriculture and the unemployed are the population subgroups with the highest poverty risk in Romania – about 1.5 times the country average. Next exposed to risk come children, and particularly those living in single-parent families. Older people and pensioners, on the other hand, have below-average poverty rates. This gap between social groups tended further to increase since 1997. Stănculescu and Pop also look at the specific situation of the Roma population. These accumulate several risk factors: low education, high unemployment, low pension coverage and living in rural areas and large families. This is also the case in Bulgaria, where the Roma population faces huge risks of poverty. The authors estimate that half of Romanian Roma live below 40% of median income and four fifths below 60% of it.

The final chapter, by Tine Stanovnik and Mitja Čok, examines the development in Slovenia. Economic growth resumed earlier than in the other three countries, namely from 1992, and so did real average wages and pensions. Only overall employment kept on falling until 1996. The social protection system proved to be remarkably "accommodating" in adapting to the large increase in beneficiaries. Despite this, the share of social expenditure and its components in GDP remained fairly stable throughout the whole period.

Labour income represented a stable two thirds of household income in Slovenia throughout the years, while total transfers somewhat increased from 25 to 30%. Capital income remained marginal. Interfamily transfers and other income sources declined. But the development was not the same for poor and rich households: for the poor, labour income (mainly wages) decreased and among transfers, pensions decreased but family benefits increased considerably. For the rich, pension income increased.

In terms of transfer coverage, the share of families with children receiving family benefits increased from one fifth to four fifths between the early 1990s and the early 2000s. On the other hand, the share of households with unemployed members receiving unemployment benefit fell from half to one third.

The main changes in the socioeconomic structure in Slovenia were decreasing numbers of workers but also pensioners in the lowest decile and increasing numbers among the richest decile. The move was inverse for dependents, i.e. mainly children, and also unemployed. Stanovnik and Čok demonstrate that the latter include a large and increasing share of "discouraged" unemployed, i.e. those who are no longer actively seeking for work. Returns to education increased, especially in the early phase of transition, although differences in the relative position across educational levels appear not as stark as for instance in Romania.

Slovenia is the only country among the four where household income inequality slightly decreased with all of this decrease happening around the mid-1990s. This was due to the richest 20% losing significant income shares while the remaining 80% gained. This happened despite wages – with 60% the most important income source – becoming more concentrated during the same period, a period characterized by absence of wage regulation. This concentration was driven by the top 5% of wage-earners. By contrast, self-employment income became less concentrated over the period. Stanovnik and Čok explain this by the increase in the number of self-employed in the 1990s, often caused by redundancies and thus somewhat involuntary. Pensions became somewhat more concentrated though they are still much more equally distributed than wages. In line with policy changes, the concentration coefficient of family benefits moved from a high negative value to close to zero, implying that all people receive about the same amount.

Income poverty rates remained broadly stable over the period but the composition changed. For the period from the early to later 1990s, Stanovnik and Čok report trends observed in the other countries: pensioners' poverty moving from above to below-average values and child poverty moving in the inverse direction. However, in the early 2000s, Slovenia stands out in that child poverty decreased and pensioners' poverty increased again, though not reaching the levels of the early 1990s. In all years, unemployed persons faced the highest poverty risks, some three to four times the country average. Particularly worrisome is the high percentage of unemployed below the lowest poverty thresholds.

Outlook

The book reviews changes in household activity, household structures and incomes after the transition shock had taken place and stops around the time of the EU accession. A first imminent question is how the first years of membership in the European Union impacted on households' behaviour and income distribution in Bulgaria, Hungary, Romania and Slovenia. Did the economic integration bring about growth which trickled down to household incomes? What was the impact of the EU structural funds? During the process of political integration, were social norms changed, or new ones created? And did the social policy reforms undertaken in the late 1990s and early 2000s prove to be sustainable?

This could well be the issues of a new book to be written. But perhaps time has already run out to restrict us to this type of analysis. The first signs of a worldwide recession in late 2008 are prospected to lead to huge increases in unemployment and restrictions of income opportunities. In the OECD countries, the past period of economic and employment growth did not result in reductions of income inequality and relative poverty. As Sir Tony Atkinson put it when commenting on the OECD study, *"if a rising tide does not lift all boats, how will they be affected by an ebbing tide?"* The outlook for a second and, in the case of Bulgaria and Romania, third profound recession within less than two decades will put an extraordinary challenge to social policy makers in all four countries, if the progress which has been made in terms of policy reforms on the one hand, and living standards of households on the other, shall not be put at stake. The experiences and lessons resumed in this book will be a valuable element of help in this undertaking.

Reference

OECD (2008) *Growing Unequal? – Income Distribution and Poverty in OECD Countries*. Paris: OECD.

33

Chapter 1

The Changing Landscape: Demography and Activity

Manuela Sofia Stănculescu[1]

This chapter provides an overview of the main macro-economic tendencies that characterized the four transition countries studied in this book after 1990: Bulgaria, Hungary, Romania and Slovenia. The approach is comparative. The analysis focuses on the main demographic and labour market tendencies. It is based on time-series data (1989/90-2004/05), which were derived from a large variety of statistical sources, both national and international.

Table 1:   The four countries at a glance

	Bulgaria	Hungary	Romania	Slovenia
PPS GDP per capita in 2005:	7,900	14,500	7,700	19,400
PPS GDP per capita in 2005 (EU-27=100):	35	62	33	83
Average GDP growth rate 2000-2005:	5.3%	4.5%	5.1%	3.7%
Wages as % of GDP in 2003:	34.8%	35.1%	34.6%	46.1%
Inflation rate in 2005:	6.0%	3.5%	9.1%	2.5%
Population on January 1, 2005 (million):	7.76	10.09	21.66	1.99
Population in 2005 as % of 1989:	86.4%	95.4%	93.7%	100.1%
Net migration (including corrections):	-	+	-	+
Employment in 2005 (thousand):	2981.9	3901.5	9114.6	949.2
Total employment rate of persons 15 years and over in 2005:	42%	46.3%	59.9%	53.4%
Share of employees in total employment in 2005:	85.7%	86.3%	64.6%	84.9%
Share of total employment in agriculture in 2005:	8.9%	4.9%	32.3%	9.1%
ILO unemployment rate in 2005:	10.1%	7.2%	7.2%	6.5%
Share of the long-term unemployment in 2005:	59.8%	45.0%	56.3%	47.3%

Source: Eurostat, http://epp.eurostat.ec.europa.eu/portal/ (2007), and Country Statistical Yearbooks.

---

1   I should like to thank a few people who helped in writing this chapter. Mitja Čok, Viktoria Galla and Silviya Nikolova provided the country data and useful comments. Tine Stanovnik and Michael Förster acted as reviewers and offered helpful comments and suggestions.

The objective of this chapter is describing the context, which is basic for the comprehension of the subsequent country chapters. The analysis is organized in five sections. The first section refers to national income dynamics. The second presents demographic change, whereas the third section analyses the main trends of the economically active and inactive population. The fourth and the fifth section analyse the elderly and pensioners, and youth in education, respectively.

1   National income dynamics

By 1990, all four countries were already in a decline. This decline was not temporary, as all countries in transition experienced a depression for at least three consecutive years. Thus, Romania experienced a decline for five years (1988-1992), and the other three countries for six years (Bulgaria and Hungary between 1988-1993; Slovenia between 1987 and 1992).

Figure 1:   Real GDP (1989=100)

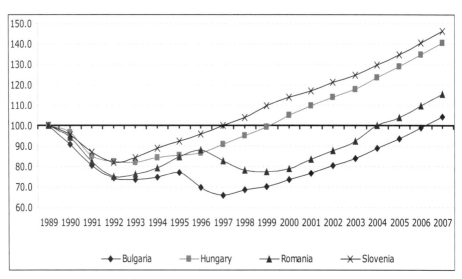

Source: For 1990-1998, computations based on Table EBRD in UNICEF, Innocenti Social Monitor 2004; for 1999-2007, Table a_gdp_k, Eurostat, 2005 for Bulgaria and 2006-2007 for all countries are forecasts.

In Slovenia, the economy did pick up as soon as in 1992, and Hungary has posted positive economic growth since 1993. By contrast, Bulgaria and

Romania faced a subsequent drop of the real GDP during 1996-1997, and 1997-1999 respectively. Recovery started only in 1998 in Bulgaria and in 2000 in Romania.

Figure 1 shows the trends in real GDP. Slovenia was above the 1989 GDP level in 1997, the Hungarian GDP recovered in 1999, whereas in Romania and Bulgaria GDP reached the 1989 level only in 2004 and 2006, respectively.

Slovenia and Hungary have performed best among the CEE countries, with growth from the mid-1990s compensating for early transition shocks. By contrast, the early transition shocks resulted in a large decline of the national GDP between 1989 and 1998 in Bulgaria (by 32% relative to 1989), which was not fully compensated by a 20% increase in GDP between 1998 and 2004. Romania's GDP also experienced a sharp fall between 1989 and 1998 (by 22% relative to 1989), which however was compensated in the following five years as the GDP increased by 22% between 1998 and 2004.

According to the Eurostat Structural Indicators database (2007 edition), during the entire period, Slovenia and Hungary have had a gross national income (GNI) per capita consistently higher than all other countries in the region, while the levels for Bulgaria and Romania have been well below any of the EU-25 member states. Thus, in 2005, the volume index of GDP per capita in PPS,[2] expressed in relation to the European Union (EU-27) average (which is set at 100), was 83 for Slovenia, 62 for Hungary, and only 35 for Bulgaria and 33 for Romania.

As an indicator of monetary stabilization, inflation was reduced to single-digit levels by 1996 in Slovenia, since 2000 in Bulgaria and Hungary and only by 2005 in Romania.

The massive dislocations associated with the transition to market economy have had huge social costs in the entire region: jobs destroyed, higher inequality, lower incomes, and, consequently, greater poverty. As economies declined in the early 1990s, both employment and real wages fell. When economic growth picked up, real wage increased, but the rise in employment followed suit only in some countries in the region. For example, Romania's rapid growth in output after 2000 was documented by various authors as "jobless growth" (e.g. CASE, 2004; Jackman, 2005).

37

---

2   Purchasing Power Standards (PPS) represents a common currency that eliminates the difference in price levels between countries allowing meaningful volume comparisons of GDP between countries.

2 Population

After 1990, the population decline became a major social cost related to transition in the entire region. According to the Eurostat database, between 1989 and 2004, Bulgaria lost almost 1.19 million persons, Hungary about 472 thousand, and Romania lost about 1.40 million persons. The population of Slovenia remained fairly constant.

Figure 2: Total population (beginning-of-year, in thousand persons)

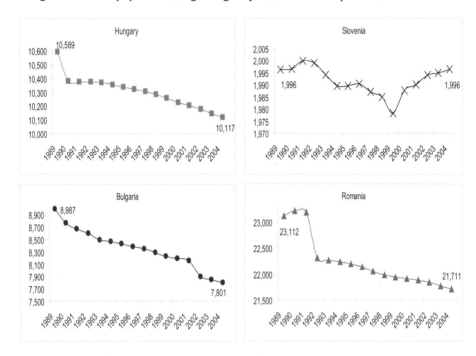

Source: Eurostat, http://epp.eurostat.ec.europa.eu/portal/ (2007).

The main causes of population decline were the large decrease in fertility, but also external migration[3] in Romania and Bulgaria. The net migration has been positive in Hungary during the entire period after 1990. In Slovenia, the net migration has become positive beginning with 1999 (Eurostat, 2007).

---

3   The 2002 Census in Romania revealed a "loss" of about 600,000 persons due to the unregistered external migration (Ghețău, 2003). Official data, however, do not include the informal emigrants left temporary to work abroad, which were estimated to more than 1 million persons in 2004. According to the most recent study on the economic migration of Romanians, between 1990 and 2005, at least 10% of the adult population worked temporary abroad (Sandu, 2006).

Fertility decline has started in Hungary since the late 1960s, in Bulgaria since the middle of the 1970s, and in Slovenia since the early 1980s. In Romania the fertility rate dropped steeply only after 1989, mainly caused by the abolition of the coercive pro-natalist policy promoted during the communist regime.

Figure 3: Population by age categories and by country (in per cent), 1990-2005

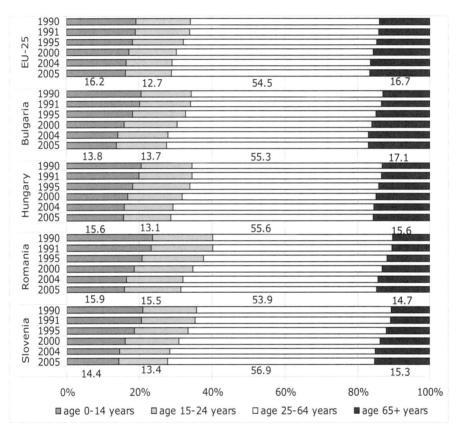

Source: Eurostat (2006).

The population structure has consequently changed: the proportion of the working-age category (15-64 years) has slightly increased, the proportion of children (0-14 years) has considerably decreased, whereas the share of elderly (65 years and over) has been continuously increasing (Figure 3). For example, between 1990 and 2005, the proportion of children decreased from 21% to 16% in Hungary, from 21% to 14% in Slovenia and Bulgaria, and from 24% to 16% in Romania, compared with the decrease from 19% to 16% in the EU-25 states. According to various demographic projections (e.g. Eurostat, UN Population Division), over the 2010-2050 period, the working-age population will begin to fall and the number of children will continue to decline, whereas the population 65 years and over will continue to grow.

Consequently, while the youth dependency ratio diminished, the "grey dependency" increased considerably (Figure 4). The ageing process is most accentuated in Bulgaria (with an ageing index[4] of 124, compared to the EU-25 average of 103 in 2005), somewhat less pronounced in Slovenia and Hungary (with levels comparable with the EU-25 average), and, at present, relatively modest in Romania. In Hungary (as in EU-25) the ageing trend has slowed down compared with the other three countries.

Figure 4:   Dependency ratios by country

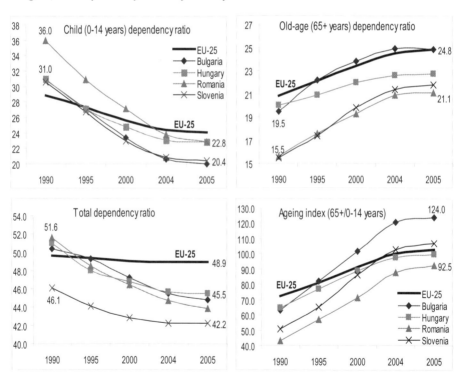

Source: Computations based on Eurostat (2006), Tables youngdep1 and olddep1.

---

4   The ageing index is the ratio between the population aged 65 years or more and children (0-14 years). The old-age dependency ratio is the ratio between the population aged 65 years or more and the population aged 15 to 64 years. The child dependency ratio is the ratio between the population aged 0 to 14 years and the population aged 15 to 64 years.

Changes at the population level have serious effects on the labour market, which are analysed in the next sections. In all four countries the proportion of the inactive population has exceeded the proportion of the economically active in the total population, which has had a direct impact on the social and income policies of these countries.

3 Working-age population

3.1 Labour force participation of the population aged 15 to 64 years

In the pre-transition period, all CEE countries had comparatively high activity rates due to the socialist policies, which focused on formal employment of all individuals. The large decline in the working population in the early 1990s[5] represented a great shock to societies that were used to the security of permanent working places and relatively substantial social benefits.

Figure 5:   Activity rates (employment and unemployment as percentage of total population 15-64 years), 1996-2005

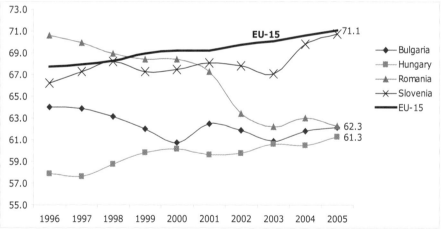

Source: Eurostat (2006), http://epp.eurostat.ec.europa.eu/portal.

After 1996, the activity rate was rather stable in Bulgaria, had a slightly growing trend in Slovenia and Hungary (comparable with the situation of the EU-15 member states), whereas in Romania it continued falling (Figure

---

5   By 1993, in all four countries, the labour force participation rate for those aged 15-64 years was 15-20 percentage points lower than the high levels of the pre-transition period.

5). By 2005, Slovenia's activity rate was comparable with the EU-15 rate, whereas the activity rates in the other three countries were considerably lower.

3.2 Employment

During the first years of transition "from plan to market", employment dropped steeply while unemployment increased substantially. In the period 1990-2005, the overall decline in employment rates of the working-age population reached its peak of 24.4 percentage points in Romania and was the lowest in Slovenia, only 5.9 percentage points (Table 2).

Table 2: Employment rates (in per cent) and employment loss (in percentage points) of the working-age population, 1990-2005

	1990	2000	2005	2005-1990
Bulgaria	63.1	50.4	55.8	-7.3
Hungary	69.9	54.5	56.5	-13.4
Romania	82	63.2	57.6	-24.4
Slovenia*	71.9*	64.2	66	-5.9

Source: Bulgaria – Eurostat (2006); Hungary – Hungarian Labour Market Review; Romania – Statistical Yearbook; Slovenia – Statistical Yearbook. * Data for 1987.

After the first shock, employment followed different patterns in the four countries, as seen from Figure 6.

Figure 6: Total employment rate of persons aged 15 to 64 years (in per cent), 1996-2005

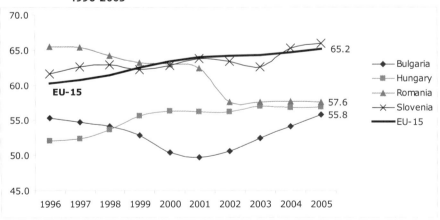

Source: Eurostat (2006), http://epp.eurostat.ec.europa.eu/portal. The indicator is based in the EU LFS.

In Slovenia and Bulgaria the employment rates decreased considerably during the economic recession and started increasing as the economy recovered. However, the employment decline was much larger and lasted longer in Bulgaria as compared to Slovenia. The contrast between the resumption of output growth and the absence of any corresponding growth in employment is very conspicuous in Hungary and especially in Romania, where employment has actually been falling as the economy recovered. This is evocative of the syndrome, which was said to characterize Western European countries in the 1980s and 1990s, known as "jobless growth".

In 2004/5 the employment rates of the working-age population, except for Slovenia, were still below 60%, as against the "Lisbon target" for the EU countries of 70%.

In all four countries, similar to the EU countries,[6] the female employment rate is significantly lower than the male employment rate (Table 3). During the period 1990-2005, the changes in employment rates and the gender differentials varied among the four countries. In Slovenia, the employment rate for men dropped more than that of women; in Hungary the relative employment losses were about the same, whereas in Romania and, to a lesser extent, Bulgaria, men experienced a smaller employment loss as compared to women.

Table 3:   Employment rates (in per cent) and employment loss (in percentage points) of the working-age population, by gender, 1990-2005

	Females				Males			
	1990	2000	2005	2005-1990	1990	2000	2005	2005-1990
Bulgaria	62.4	46.3	51.7	-10.7	63.9	54.7	60.0	-3.9
Hungary	60	49.7	51.0	-9.0	75	63.1	63.1	-11.9
Romania	79	57.5	51.5	-27.5	85	68.6	63.7	-21.3
Slovenia	63.4*	58.4	61.3	-2.1	80.5*	67.2	70.4	-10.1

Source: For 1990, *Country Statistical Yearbooks*; * Data for 1987; for 2000 and 2005, Eurostat (2006), http://epp.eurostat.ec.europa.eu/portal. The indicator is based on the EU LFS.

Structural adjustments, which occurred during the transition period, substantially changed the employment structure by sectors (Table 4). In the entire region, a shift from manufacturing to services occurred between 1989 and 2004. In other words, employment in industry diminished considerably, while employment in services sharply increased.

---

6   In 2005, the EU-15 average employment rate was 73% for men and 57% for women.

Agriculture was hardest hit by the transformation-related crisis in Hungary, where employment in agriculture decreased from 19% in 1989 to 4% of the labour force in 2004. In Slovenia the decline of employment in agriculture was much smaller. In contrast, in Bulgaria and particularly in Romania, despite the very large fall in agricultural production, employment in agriculture grew substantially: to 26% in Bulgaria and 43% in Romania in 2000. Subsequently, it fell but has still remained much higher than the EU-15 average.

Table 4: Structure of total employment (15+ years) by sector (in per cent) and changes in structural shares (in percentage points)

	1989	1997	2000	2004	2004-1989
EU-15					
Industry-excluding construction	22.5*	21.7	21.0	19.1	-3.4
Construction	7.8*	7.8	7.8	7.9	0.1
Services	64.3*	65.3	66.5	69.0	4.7
Agriculture, fishing and forestry	5.1*	4.9	4.3	3.8	-1.3
	100	100	100	100	
Bulgaria					
Industry-excluding construction	37.7	27.6	24.0	23.1	-14.6
Construction	8.3	4.4	4.3	4.5	-3.8
Services	35.4	42.7	45.5	47.5	12.1
Agriculture, fishing and forestry	18.7	25.3	26.2	25.0	6.3
	100	100	100	100	
Hungary					
Industry-excluding construction	35.1	28.9	28.9	26.6	-8.5
Construction	5.4	5.5	6.4	7.3	1.9
Services	40.1	56	59.5	62	21.9
Agriculture, fishing and forestry	19.4	9.6	5.2	4.1	-15.3
	100	100	100	100	
Romania					
Industry-excluding construction	38.1	26.3	22.4	26.0	-12.1
Construction	7	4.2	3.7	5.2	-1.8
Services	27.3	30.5	31.0	37.2	9.9
Agriculture, fishing and forestry	27.9	39.0	42.8	31.6	3.7
	100	100	100	100	
Slovenia					
Industry-excluding construction	38.7**	34.5	32.2	30.6	-8.2
Construction	5.5**	6.1	5.4	5.8	0.3
Services	45.1**	47.2	52.8	53.9	8.8
Agriculture, fishing and forestry	10.7**	12.1	9.6	9.7	-0.9
	100	100	100	100	

Source: EU-15 – EU LFS data extracted from Eurostat (2007); Bulgaria, Hungary, Slovenia – Country Statistical Yearbook (various editions); Romania – RLFS data in NIS, Social Trends (2005). * Data for 1995; **Data for 1993.

Due to the change of the ownership structure, particularly over the agricultural land, and the general shift from manufacturing to services, the number of private enterprises and self-employed increased. At the same time, the share of employees in total employment declined, particularly in Romania.

Table 5 shows that Bulgaria, Hungary and Slovenia have a structure of total employment by professional status rather similar to the one of the EU-15 member states. That is, employees (wage or salary earners) account for about 85% of total employment, employers for 4-5%, self-employed for about 5-10%, while unpaid family workers are only marginal, representing 5% at most. Romania makes a distinctive case. In Romania, the share of employees in total employment, although steadily increasing since 2001, reached only 66% in 2004. Employers represented only a mere 2% of total employment. The largest deviations for Romania, however, concern self-employed and unpaid family workers, which in 2004 represented as much as 18%, and 14% respectively. The shares of both self-employed and unpaid family workers in total employment increased until 2000, afterwards steadily declining as the economy recovered. Noteworthy, during the entire period, about 90% of the Romanian self-employed[7] (1.72 million out of 1.95 million, in 2004) and 95-96% of the Romanian unpaid family workers lived in rural areas and worked in agriculture.

The rise in the number of entrepreneurs in Central and Eastern Europe is often interpreted as a temporary response to the transformational recession: during the hard times many people started a business temporarily and "unwillingly" because it was difficult to find wage work. In 1999, the hypothesis of self-employed as "disguised unemployed" was refuted for the Hungarian case but confirmed for the Romanian self-employment in agriculture. Research by Köllő and Vincze (1999) revealed for the period 1993-1996 for Romania larger flows into self-employment, subsistence farming and black market in regions hit hard by the transition shock. At the same time, no net flows from self-employment back to paid work were observed in the

---

7   According to the official methodology, within a farmer household the person declared "head of the household" is recorded as self-employed whilst the other members of the family, performing the same agricultural activity (work on own plot), are recorded as "unpaid family workers". Accordingly, in 2004, most of the self-employed were men (69.7%) of 50 years or over, whereas most of the unpaid family workers were the wives, sons and daughters of the self-employed persons, 71.3% women and 61% younger than 49 years old.

few Romanian regions where the demand for labour was rising. A similar conclusion was reached by Ciupagea (2000) for the period 1993-1998.

Table 5:   Total employment (15 + years) by professional status
(annual average)

	1992	1995	1998	2000	2002	2004
EU-15						
Persons in employment (thou. persons), out of which (%):		148,728	153,252	158,730	162,690	164,907
Employees		82.6	83.3	84.0	84.2	83.9
Self-employed – TOTAL		15.0	14.7	14.3	14.1	14.7
- Individual private entrepreneurs		5.6	5.6	5.7	5.5	4.9
- Self-employed		9.4	9.2	8.6	8.6	9.8
Unpaid family workers		2.3	1.9	1.7	1.6	1.3
Bulgaria						
Persons in employment (thou. persons), out of which (%):	2,994*	2,984	3,035	2,797	2,739	2,922
Employees	88.7*	88.9	86.1	84.8	85.3	84.8
Self-employed – TOTAL	9.8*	9.9	12	13.2	12.8	13.1
- Individual private entrepreneurs			2.1	2.4	3.3	3.8
- Self-employed			9.9	10.8	9.5	9.3
Unpaid family workers	1.4*	1.1	1.6	1.5	1.6	1.9
Hungary						
Persons in employment (thou. persons), out of which (%):	4,026	3,623	3,675	3,856	3,871	3,900
Employees	85.1	84.6	85.6	85.9	86.8	85.8
Self-employed – TOTAL	13.7	14.3	13.6	13.4	12.6	13.7
- Individual private entrepreneurs	6.5	4.6	3.6	3.4	2.9	3.7
- Self-employed	7.2	9.7	10	10	9.7	10
Unpaid family workers	1.2	1.1	0.8	0.7	0.6	0.5
Romania						
Persons in employment (thou. persons), out of which (%):	9,602	9,493	10,845	10,764	9,234	9,158
Employees	79.9	60.6	59.4	56.1	61.7	65.9
Self-employed – TOTAL	15	22	21.1	24.2	23	20.1
- Individual private entrepreneurs	0.3	1.3	1.2	1.1	1.5	1.7
- Self-employed	14.7	20.7	19.9	23.1	21.5	18.4
Unpaid family workers	2.1	13.4	16.4	19.3	15.0	13.9
Slovenia						
Persons in employment (thou. persons), out of which (%):	845*	882	907	894	922	946
Employees	87.7*	85.5	84.0	83.9	83.8	84.4
Self-employed – TOTAL	12.2*	12.2	12.5	11.2	11.7	10.1
Unpaid family workers	3.2*	4.6	6.6	4.8	4.6	5.5

Source: EU-15 – EU LFS data extracted from Eurostat (2007); Bulgaria – BLFS; Hungary – Hungarian Labour Market Review (2006); Romania – Census 1992 and RLFS (2005); Slovenia – Statistical Yearbook (various editions 2000-2005). * Data for 1993.

Notes: 1) Bulgaria – Sum by column is less than 100, the difference represents the category of "others".
2) Romania – Self-employed includes persons performing professional services as well as farmers. Sum by column is less than 100, the difference represents members of agricultural associations. In 2002, the Romanian National Institute for Statistics changed the LFS methodology in accordance with the 2002 Census.
3) Slovenia – In 1997 the Statistical Office of the Republic of Slovenia introduced methodological changes to the monitoring of employment in companies and other organizations. It started to include data on private companies with one or two employees. Since 1997, the source of data on self-employed persons (except farmers) and persons employed by the self-employed has been the Statistical Registry of Persons in Employment, and for farmers the Labour Force Survey.

Thus, in Romania, during the "transformational recession", self-employment has been mainly agricultural self-employment and did not behave like a pool of unemployed workers normally does. In contrast, in Slovenia, both the number and the share of agricultural self-employed have been low and have continuously decreased since 1989. In Hungary, according to some authors (Kopasz, 2003), agricultural self-employment is underestimated by the HLFS data because persons without a tax identification number are not registered by the official statistics. A recent survey showed that 27% of the total self-employment performs in agriculture (Sik and Nagy, 2003). However, various studies (i.e. Köllő and Vincze, 1999 or EBRD, 2000) demonstrated that in Hungary the increase in the number of self-employed is mainly the result of widening business opportunities, self-employment representing a creative labour market strategy and not a coping strategy for the unskilled. In Bulgaria, self-employment has also increased from less than 1% in 1990 to 9.3% in 2004. The share of the self-employed in rural areas is more than three times higher than in urban areas (20.6% of the rural employment versus 5.7% of the urban one, in 2004), as is the share of unpaid family members (4.9% of the rural employment versus 1% of the urban employment). Thus, in Bulgaria, self-employment in agriculture is important, yet its share in total employment is much lower than in Romania.

3.3   Unemployment

During the socialist era there was no official unemployment, except for Slovenia, where official unemployment was recognized throughout the socialist period, and Hungary, where unemployment was officially recognized in the late 1980s. There was, however, hidden unemployment in all of these countries. At the beginning of the 1990s, unemployment was officially acknowledged also in Bulgaria and Romania.

The economic transformations resulted in an increase in open un-employment. In all four countries, the rate of registered unemployment[8] reached its peak between 1992 and 1994: 12.3% in Hungary (in 1992), 16.4% in Bulgaria and 14.4% in Slovenia (in 1993), and 10.9% in Romania (in 1994). The fall in the registered unemployment rate started in 1997 in Hungary and in 1998 in Slovenia. In Romania, it dropped until 1996 and rose again during the second recession period. Since 2000, it has started to decrease as GDP growth has resumed. In Bulgaria the unemployment rate increased considerably up to 2000. Afterwards, it started decreasing, as a result of a new law on unemployment benefits and active labour market measures introduced in 2000.

Data on registered unemployment do not necessarily provide an ac-curate picture of the unemployment phenomenon; the decrease in regis-tered unemployment in the late 1990s was also caused by a "cleansing" of registries, i.e. by applying more strict conditions for registered unemployed persons. Therefore, we also analyse the ILO unemployment.

The unemployment rates derived from Labour Force Surveys con-ducted on the basis of the ILO definition (Table 6) differ from the previous indicator as it measures a different, though partly overlapping, population group. If the ILO definition of unemployment is used, during the entire period 1996-2005, the unemployment rate is lower than the EU-15 average in Hungary, Romania and Slovenia; it is higher than the EU-15 average in Bulgaria. In 2004, the ILO unemployment rate was 6.1% in Hungary, 6.3% in Slovenia, 8.1% in Romania, and 12% in Bulgaria, compared to the EU-15 average of 8% (Eurostat, 2006).

The young (15-24 years) have had a relatively higher risk of being unemployed, as their unemployment rate is higher than the unemployment rate of the total labour force in all four countries. The youth unemployment rate is comparable with the EU-15 average only in Slovenia, while in Bul-garia, Hungary and Romania it is higher (19-22% compared to about 16%). With respect to the youth unemployment trend, none of the four countries followed the trend of the EU-15 rate, which decreased between 1997 and 2000 and afterwards varied in the narrow band of 14-16%. In Slovenia, the youth unemployment rate remained fairly constant after 1997. In Hungary, it decreased from 16.9% in 1997 to 10.7% in 2001, and subsequently increased to 19.4% in 2005. Bulgaria followed a reverse trend: youth unemployment

---

8   Source: Bulgaria and Hungary – *Country Statistical Yearbooks*, Romania – NIS, *Social Trends* (2002, 2005), Slovenia – ESS, *Annual Report* (2004, 2005). In Slovenia data represent annual averages. In the other three countries data refer to the end of the year.

peaked at 39.3% in 2001 and then continually decreased. In Romania, the youth unemployment rate grew until 2002 and after that it stabilized at 20-22%.

Table 6:   ILO unemployment rates (in per cent)

	1997	2000	2001	2002	2003	2004	2005
EU-15							
Total unemployment rate	9.8	7.7	7.2	7.6	7.9	8.0	8.1
- 15-24 years	21	16	14	14.6	15.2	15.8	16.5
- 50 years and over	8.1	6.6	5.6	5.7	5.9	6.3	6
- women	11.2	8.9	8.3	8.5	8.7	8.9	8.9
- low secondary school at most*	13.8	11.4	9.9	10.4	10.7	11.1	11.2
Long-term unemployment (12 + months) as share of the total unemployment	47.8	45.5	44	40.1	41.4	41	42
Bulgaria							
Total unemployment rate	15	16.4	19.5	18.1	13.7	12.0	10.1
- 15-24 years	33	33.3	39.3	35.6	27.1	24.5	22.3
- 50 years and over	:	12.9	17	14.5	11.2	9.6	8.4
- women	15.3	16.2	18.6	17.3	13.2	11.5	9.8
- low secondary school at most*	:	25.1	33.3	29.8	24.8	21	19.6
Long-term unemployment (12 + months) as share of the total unemployment	56	58.7	63.1	65.5	66.9	57.4	59.8
Hungary							
Total unemployment rate	9.0	6.4	5.7	5.8	5.9	6.1	7.2
- 15-24 years	16.9	12.3	10.7	11.4	12.9	14.4	19.4
- 50 years and over	6.1	3.8	3.8	3.5	3.5	3.5	4.5
- women	8.1	5.6	5	5.4	5.6	6.1	7.4
- low secondary school at most*	15.3	11.5	11.2	11.4	12.3	12.4	14.3
Long-term unemployment (12 + months) as share of the total unemployment	48.7	47.8	44.8	44.7	40.5	45	45
Romania							
Total unemployment rate	5.3	7.2	6.6	8.4	7.0	8.1	7.2
- 15-24 years	17.4	17.8	17.6	22.2	19.5	22.3	20.2
- 50 years and over	1.1	1.6	1.7	2.6	2.4	3.8	2.9
- women	5.7	6.4	5.9	7.7	6.4	6.9	6.4
- low secondary school at most*	4	4.2	4.3	6.2	5.8	8.3	6.7
Long-term unemployment (12 + months) as share of the total unemployment	48	49.2	48.6	56.5	61.5	59	56.3
Slovenia							
Total unemployment rate	6.9	6.7	6.2	6.3	6.7	6.3	6.5
- 15-24 years	16.3	16.4	15.7	14.8	15.3	14	15.9
- 50 years and over**	2.4	6.3	3.7	3.8	3.8	4.1	3.8
- women	7.1	7	6.8	6.8	7.1	6.8	7
- low secondary school at most*	8.5	10.8	9.1	8.7	10.5	9.5	9.5
Long-term unemployment (12 + months) as share of the total unemployment	51.9	62.7	63.3	54.7	56.6	53.1	47.3

49

Source: Eurostat (2006), http://epp.eurostat.ec.europa.eu/portal. * ISCED 1997 levels 0-2; ** unreliable or uncertain data.

Only in Slovenia, women have a higher risk of unemployment as compared to men, as in the EU-15 member states. In the other three countries, the female unemployment rates are lower or equal to the male rates. In Bulgaria, the female and the male unemployment rate had the same trend and they both almost halved between 2001 and 2005. In Hungary, the women's situation on the labour market has somewhat deteriorated since 2001. The female unemployment rate increased, but still remained lower than the EU-15 rate and is equal to the male rate. After 1997, the female unemployment rate in Romania remained rather stable and at a level lower than the EU-15 average; since 1998 it became lower than the unemployment rate for men.

Education is an important factor, determining the "employability" of a person. Unemployed people with higher levels of education find it easier to obtain work, while persons with few qualifications are not in demand on the labour market and remain unemployed for longer periods of time. Nevertheless, this broad rule has certain nuances. Whereas in Romania most unemployed had a high school diploma, in the other three countries the majority of unemployed had attained only primary or low secondary vocational education.

Due to employment opportunities in agriculture, unemployment in Romania and Bulgaria has been much higher in urban than in rural areas.

Of special concern is long-term unemployment, particularly in Bulgaria and Romania. In 2005, the share of unemployed for over one year in total unemployment was comparable with the EU-15 average (42%) in Hungary and Slovenia, but much higher in Romania (56%) and Bulgaria (60%). Furthermore, over the period 1997-2005, while long-term unemployment in Slovenia and Hungary decreased, in Bulgaria and Romania it increased until 2003 and started decreasing only in 2004.

3.4 Economically inactive population aged 15 to 64 years

The total economically inactive population comprises three categories, namely students, pensioners, and other inactive. The situation of the young in education is discussed in the last section of this chapter. Here, we present only the situation of pensioners and other inactive aged 15-64 years.

The total economically inactive population has had a dynamic reversed to that of the economically active population. Thus, as the active population decreased, the inactive population increased.

Early retirement[9] represented an alternative to massive redundancy, therefore the proportion of pensioners in the working-age population significantly increased after 1990, much more in Bulgaria compared with the other three countries. In addition, the share of disability pensioners in the working-age population also increased considerably. The growth of disability pensions[10] is considered to be "artificial" as it has been mainly determined by the "control and sanctions deficit" (Preda et al., 2004). In fact, in the turbulent context of social transformations, it functioned as "disguised early retirement". As the pension systems were reformed and pensioning policies changed, the share of working-age retired persons started to decrease in all four countries.

The category "other inactive" includes mainly housewives. After 1989, the share of this category in the working-age population increased in Hungary and Romania to 16-18%,[11] because retreating in the household niche was the only alternative for many women (mostly aged 40-50 years) that lost jobs and were too young for pensioning and too old for gaining a new job.

In contrast, in Bulgaria "other inactive" account for a very low share of the working-age population (BHBS data), decreasing from a low 2.7% in 1992 to 1.3% in 2002 (out of which women account for more than 70%). As most women were active before 1989, data indicate that most women that lost their job either succeeded immediately after 1990 to obtain a pension (women account for 65% of the working-age pensioners) or were unemployed. After 1992, the decline of the female employment was mirrored in the increase of unemployment and not in the rise of housewives or other inactive women.

---

9   Some professions have lower retirement ages (i.e. miners' retirement age is 45 years in Romania if the condition of 20 years on the job is fulfilled). In the transition years, these people have been retired immediately after they met the legal requirements either for ensuring working places for the young or, more often, for restructuring the sector (as in the mining sector in Romania).

10   In 2002, disability pensioners accounted for more than a quarter of total pensioners in Hungary and about a fifth in Slovenia, while the corresponding share was only 12% both in Bulgaria and Romania; however, it rose to 16.4% and 13.5% respectively in 2004. These differences between countries should be carefully considered as in some countries (for example, in Slovenia) disability pensioners remain in this status till death, while in other countries (such as Romania) they change their status in old-age pensioners as soon as they reach the retirement conditions.

11   Data from: Hungary – *Hungarian Labour Market Review* (2006); Romania – Census (1992) and RLFS (2000-2006).

4   Elderly and pensioners

The rising share of the elderly in the total population is a demographic trend common to all four countries. However, there are quite large differences between countries in the share of working elderly (65 years and over) in total employment. So, during the transition period, the share of elderly in total employment in Hungary and Bulgaria followed a U-shaped curve (decreasing and then increasing). In Romania, the curve had an inversed U-shape (increasing and then decreasing). In spite of this decrease, in 2004, the share of people 65 years and over in total employment was still a rather high 5.1% in Romania. It was lower (4.2%) in Hungary and only 1.6% in Bulgaria. Noticeably, the great majority of working elderly is concentrated in rural areas, working in agriculture.

Table 7:   Total number of pensioners by country (in thousands, annual average)

Year	Bulgaria	Hungary	Romania	Slovenia
1990	2273	2229.2	3365	384.1
1991	2374	2380.8	3813	418.9
1992	2443	2494.4	3975	448.8
1993	2439	2578.7	4313	457.5
1994	2423	2640.3	4837	458.1
1995	2409	3026	5106	460.3
1996	2381	2697.3	5264	463.3
1997	2391	2731.9	5431.4	468.2
1998	2387	2786.4	5605.9	472.4
1999	2380	2719.9	5787.7	476.4
2000	2375	2785.9	5997.2	482.2
2001	2369	2788.1	6192.4	492.5
2002	2344	2771	6212.3	509.1
2003	2330	2730.6	6141.5	517.8
2004	2320	2716.6	6069.8	523.9

Source: Bulgaria – National Social Security Institute (2005); Hungary and Romania – Country Statistical Yearbooks (various editions); Slovenia – Pension Insurance Fund, Monthly Statistical Survey, April 2006.

Since 1990, the number of pensioners has increased in all four countries (Table 7). Two main factors contributed to this: the ageing process and the policy of early retirement applied as an alternative to unemployment. The highest increase in the number of pensioners took place in Romania, where between 1990 and 2004 the number of pensioners increased from 3.37 to over 6 million. In the other countries the rise in the number of pensioners was much lower: in Bulgaria it increased from 2.27 million in 1990 to 2.32 million in 2004, in Hungary from 2.23 million in 1990 to 2.72 million in 2004, and in Slovenia from 384 thousand in 1990 to 524 thousand in 2004.

Figure 7: **Share of pensioners and share of population aged 65 years or more in the total population (in per cent), 1990-2004**

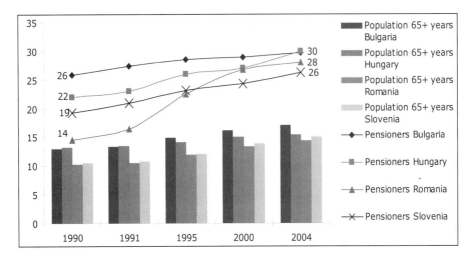

Source: Country Statistical Yearbooks (various editions).

The share of pensioners in the total population increased much more than the shares of the population aged 65 or more (Figure 7). This is mainly the effect of the various pensioning policies applied in the context of economic restructuring. Thus, although the majority of pensioners receive old-age social insurance pensions, the proportions of pensioners with an incomplete due status and disability pensioners increased significantly. Farmer pensioners constitute a distinct case.[12] In 2002, they accounted for more than a quarter (27%) of all pensioners in Romania, whereas in Slovenia and Bulgaria they were rather marginal, with shares of about 2%.

53

---

12   The special farming schemes differ from one country to another and have been closed at different times.

5   The young in education

After 1990, the enrolment in general secondary education has increased considerably in all countries (Table 8). However, in Romania in 2004, the enrolment rate in general upper secondary education of the population aged 15-18 was only 26.5%, which is much lower than the rates of the other three countries, which are situated in the band between 39 and 41%.

Table 8:   General (upper) secondary and technical vocational secondary education (gross enrolment rates as percentage of population aged 15-18)

	1990	1991	1993	1999	2000	2001	2002	2003	2004	2005
General secondary enrolment (ISCED 1997, level 3A)										
BG	29.8	28.9	30	32.6	33.1	35	38.3	40	41.2	42.3
HU *	17.6	18.2	20.8	27.8	34.3	35.4	36.5	38.1	39	39.6
RO	11.5	15.9	18.6	26.3	26.1	26.3	26.2	26.2	26.5	27.7
SI	-	-	19.5	28.9	31.6	34.5	36.4	37.3	38.5	-
Technical vocational secondary enrolment (ISCED 1997, level 3B/3C)										
BG	47.2	45.4	42.2	41.5	42.3	44.1	47.3	49.8	49.3	49
HU *	55.8	55.8	58.8	68.5	69.2	70.4	71.1	61.2	61.5	61
RO	78.4	57.9	45.6	43.9	46.1	46.9	47.4	48.3	49.7	51.2
SI	-	-	61	66.5	65.5	63.7	62.8	62.3	62	-
Total upper secondary enrolment (ISCED 1997, level 3)										
BG	77	74.3	72.2	74.1	75.4	79.1	85.6	89.8	90.5	91.3
HU *	73.4	74	79.6	96.3	103.5	105.8	107.6	99.3	100.5	100.6
RO	89.9	73.8	64.2	70.2	72.2	73.2	73.6	74.5	76.2	78.9
SI	-	-	80.5	95.4	97.1	98.2	99.2	99.6	100.5	-

Source: UNICEF, TransMONEE 2005 and Innocenti Social Monitor 2007. Data normally refer to 4-year programmes. * Children aged 14-17.

The relatively low gross enrolment ratio in total secondary education for Romania – 76.2% in 2004 compared to the ratios of 90% or more of the other three countries – is an effect of the very low access of the rural youth to these forms of education. Nearly all institutions providing secondary education are located in cities, and the rural young, particularly the poor ones, cannot afford commuting, accommodation and other education-related costs.

Table 9:   Tertiary education – ISCED 1997, levels 5 and 6 (gross enrolment rates as percentage of the population aged 19-24)

	1991	1999	2000	2001	2002	2003	2004	2004 as % of 1991	2004 as % of 1999
BG	31.1	45.7	44.5	42.5	39.8	40.8	41.1	132	90
HU *	14.0	33.2	36.7	40.3	44.7	51.9	59.6	426	180
RO	9.7	21.8	24.1	28.5	31.7	36.5	40.2	415	184
SI	23.8	52.8	56.0	61.4	67.4	70.1	73.7	309	140

Source: UNESCO Institute for Statistics, http://www.uis.unesco.org. * Data for those aged 18-23.

Enrolment in tertiary education (ISCED 5 and 6) increased in all four countries after 1990 (Table 9). Compared to 1991, the tertiary education gross enrolment in 2004 was three times larger in Slovenia, more than four times higher in Hungary and Romania and only 1.32 times larger in Bulgaria. Nonetheless, Bulgaria had a tertiary enrolment rate similar to Romania (about 40% of the population 19-24 years), whereas Hungary and particularly Slovenia had much higher rates (about 60 and 74% respectively). A major problem in Bulgaria and Romania is the concentration of students in urban areas, with rural young people having an extremely low access to higher education. Finally, with the exception of Bulgaria, the other three countries experienced further large increases in enrolment in tertiary education between 1999 and 2004.

55

6   Final remarks

In all four countries the transformation shock after 1990 resulted in more unemployed persons, more pensioners, less persons in employment, and particularly less employees (wage or salary earners).

Romania has accumulated more and deeper negative effects: there is a substantially lower share of wage-earners, and a higher share of pensioners, children and other inactive persons as compared to the other three countries. In addition, most of the self-employed are in fact "disguised unemployed" engaged in subsistence agriculture on small plots. Bulgaria is in a better position compared to Romania, yet it is still characterized by high unemployment, a high share of pensioners, and to a large extent its self-employment represents a coping strategy for the unskilled. In addition, in order to cope with the transition hardship, there is a greater reliance on own production from a small plot: 52.5% of the Bulgarian households produce various goods at home (Kovacheva and Pancheva, 2003).

The Hungarian and particularly the Slovenian economy have done better, recovered sooner, have better educated young people, and in relative terms are "work-rich".

7 References

CASE (Center for Social and Economic Research) (2004) *Operationalizing Pro-Poor Growth. Case of Romania*. Warsaw: World Bank Report.

Central Statistic Office of Hungary *Yearbook of Social Statistics* (various editions). Budapest.

Ciupagea, Ct. (2000) 'Rigidities of the Labour Market in a Transition Economy: The Case of Romania', *Romanian Journal of Economic Forecasting*, 3-4/2000: 29-57.

Employment Service of Slovenia (2004, 2005) *Annual Report*. Ljubljana.

EBRD (2000) *Transition Report 2000*. U.K., London.

EUROSTAT (2006 and 2007 editions) http://epp.eurostat.ec.europa.eu/portal/ page?_pagei d=1090,30070682,1090_33076576&_dad=portal&_schema=PORTAL

Ghețău, V. (2003) *2050: Will Romania's Population Fall Below 16 Million Inhabitants?*. Bucharest: Romanian Academy, Population Research Center Vladimir Trebici.

Institute of Economics (2002-2005) *Hungarian Labour Market Review*. Budapest: Hungarian Academy of Sciences.

Jackman, R. (2005) 'Competitiveness through low wages versus higher wages for stimulating demand', Paper presented to Conference on *Extending EU Labour Markets Eastward*, Bucharest, November 24-26, 2005, www.fes.ro.

Köllő, J./Vincze, M. (1999) 'Self-employment and unemployment: Lessons from Regional Data in Hungary and Romania', *Romanian Economic Research Observer* No.5/1999.

Kopasz, M. (2003) 'Hungary Country Contextual Reports', pp. 199-238 in: Wallace, C. (ed.) *Research Report #2. Country Contextual Reports. Demographic trends, labour market and social policies*. HWF Research Consortium, www.hwf.at. Vienna: Institute for Advanced Studies.

Kovacheva, S./Pancheva, T. (2003) 'Bulgaria Country Contextual Reports', pp. 239-294 in Wallace, C. (ed.) *Research Report #2. Country Contextual Reports. Demographic trends, labour market and social policies*. HWF Research Consortium, www.hwf.at. Vienna: Institute for Advanced Studies.

National Institute for Statistics from Romania, *Statistical Yearbook* (various editions), *Social Trends* (2002 and 2005), *Romanian Labour Force Survey* (various editions) Bucharest.

National Social Security Institute of Bulgaria (2005) *Demography, Economy and Social Insurance 1984-2004*. Sofia.

National Statistical Institute of Bulgaria, *Statistical Yearbook* (various editions). Sofia.

Pension Insurance Fund of Slovenia (April 2006) *Monthly Statistical Survey*. Ljubljana.

Preda, M. (coord.)/Dobos, C./Grigoras, V. (2004) *Romanian Pensions System during the Transition: Major Problems and Solutions*, Pre-Accession Impact Studies II, European Institute of Romania, www.ier.ro.

Sandu, D. (coord.) (2006) *Locuirea temporară în străinătate. Migrația economică a românilor: 1990-2006 (Living temporary abroad. The economic migration of the Romanians: 1990-2006)*. Bucharești Open Society Foundation

Sik, E./Nagy, I. (2003) 'HWF Hungary Country Survey Reports', pp. 297-340 in: Wallace, C. (ed.) *Research Report #3. HWF Survey: Country survey reports*. HWF Research Consortium, www.hwf.at. Vienna: Institute for Advanced Studies.

Statistical Office of the Republic of Slovenia, *Statistical Yearbook* (various editions), *Rapid Reports* (various editions). Ljubljana.

UN Population Division (2001) *World Population Prospects. The 2000 Revision*. New York.

UNESCO Institute for Statistics (2007 edition) http://www.uis.unesco.org.

UNICEF (2004) *Social Monitor 2004*, Innocenti Social Monitor CEE/CIS/Baltic States.

UNICEF (2005) *TransMonee 2005. Statistical Tables*, Innocenti Research Centre.

UNICEF (2007) *Social Monitor 2007*, Innocenti Social Monitor CEE/CIS/Baltic States.

57

Chapter 2

Changes in Household Income, Income Inequality and Poverty: A Comparative Overview

Tine Stanovnik / Nataša Kump

1   Introduction

Chapter 1 provided an overview of the dynamics of national income, the demographic situation and the activity rates during the 1990s and early 2000s. In this sense it "sets the stage" for a more detailed analysis, based on household budget surveys. As reliable household survey data for the pre-transition period do not exist for all of these countries, our analysis of household data starts with years that are well in the midst of the transition process: 1992 (for Bulgaria), 1993 (for Slovenia and Hungary) and 1995 (for Romania). We note that methodological issues and definitions adopted are all relegated to the technical annex.

Section 2 provides an overview of the dynamics of the two most important income sources – wages and pensions; these are not household survey data, but data collected by the statistical offices by other means. This overview is complemented with data from the household budget surveys, showing the changing structure of household income. Section 3 presents the changes in the socioeconomic structure of households, whereas section 4 provides a more detailed analysis of the more important income sources and the main socioeconomic groups (employees, pensioners, persons active in agriculture), showing the large differences in the income structure and socioeconomic structure between rich and poor households. Section 5 presents a brief comparative analysis of the coverage of two types of social benefits – unemployment benefits and family benefits. Income inequality is analysed in section 6, followed by the analysis of income poverty. Section 8 provides some concluding remarks.

2 Incomes at the national and household level

Before proceeding to the analysis using household survey data, we observe some trends based on statistical sources other than household budget surveys. These depict the dynamics of the most important income sources at the national level. We start with wages, and though there is no perfect correspondence between wage dynamics and the dynamics of household income, the trend in the most important household income source is indicative of what has been happening with total household income. The dynamics of wages are shown in Figure 1.

Figure 1: Growth of average real wages (1992=100)

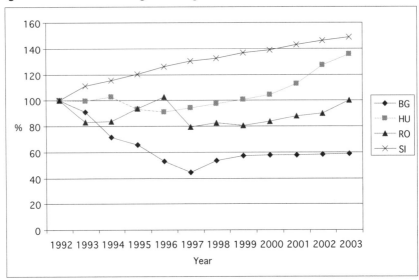

Source: Country studies.

As seen from Figure 1, national experiences are quite varied: in Slovenia real wages have been steadily increasing since 1992, in Hungary the steady increase started in 1996, whereas in Bulgaria and Romania wages declined up to 1997. After 1997, wages started to increase, though with quite different rates. Bulgaria, Hungary and Romania also had very "bumpy" years even after the initial transformation depression. These were the "crisis" years of 1996-1997 in Bulgaria, marked by hyperinflation; the Bokros (austerity) package in Hungary in 1995-1997, and the period of the second depression (1997-1999) in Romania.

In all the four countries, the growth of wages did not follow the pace of GDP growth, suggesting a "restructuring" of GDP, i.e. a decreasing share of wages in GDP; this in fact has been particularly visible in Bulgaria and Romania, and to a much lesser degree in Hungary and Slovenia.

The second most important income source for households is pensions. The relative importance of pensions, measured as percentage of GDP, shows remarkable stability in the four countries, and decreases in certain years can be explained by deliberate government policy. Thus, the drop in pension expenditures in Bulgaria in 1995 was due to poor indexation of pensions in a period of high inflation, whereas the decline in Hungary in the 1995-97 period was caused by the Bokros austerity package.

Figure 2:   Pension expenditures as percentage of GDP

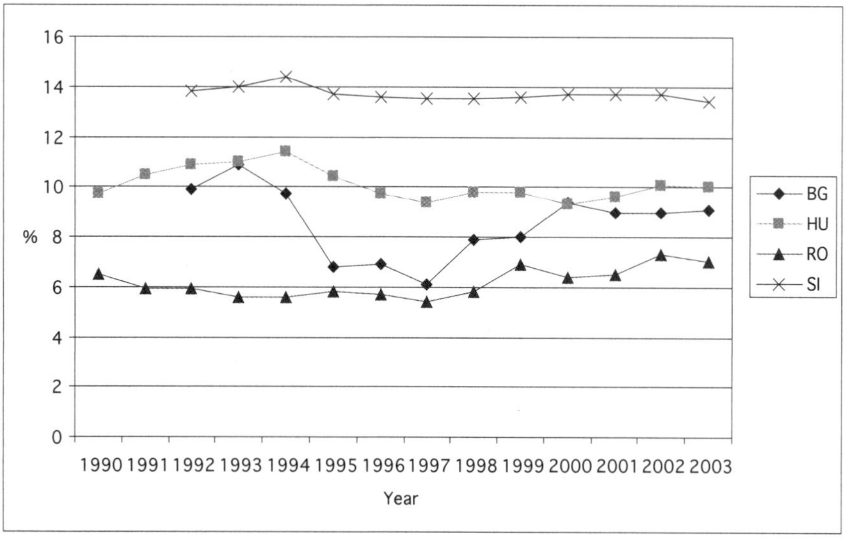

Source: Country studies.

As seen from Figure 3, the growth of real pensions follows a trend similar to that of real wages. However, with the exception of Bulgaria (where since 1999 pension growth surpassed wage growth), the growth of pensions did not quite follow the growth of wages. The "net" result is an overall gradual decrease in the pension/wage ratio, as seen from Figure 4.

Figure 3: Growth of average real pensions (1992=100)

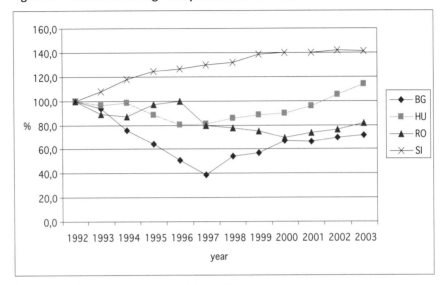

Notes: Romania: Average real pension of state social insurance pensioners.

Source: Country studies.

Here, there were specific country features that shaped these trends. For example, in Hungary the 1996 and 1997 slide in the pension/wage ratio was caused by the Bokros austerity package which reduced the real value of most social benefits. In Slovenia the 1999 pension reform caused the gradual decrease of the pension/wage ratio from 2000 onward.[1] The very low values of the pension/wage ratio for Bulgaria[2] and Romania are doubtlessly caused by the extremely unfavourable system dependency ratio, i.e. the ratio between pensioners and active insured persons. In the 1990s, the increase in the number of pensioners was particularly pronounced in Romania and Slovenia (see Chapter 1, Table 7). Also, comparing the early 1990s and early 2000s, the number of employees, i.e. active insured persons, has not changed much in Bulgaria, Hungary and Slovenia, but has substantially decreased in Romania.

---

1   The 1999 pension reform decreased the pensions not only for new entrants, but also for existing pensioners.

2   One must bear in mind that the ratio for Bulgaria is gross, i.e. average gross pension/ average gross wage. The net ratio is higher, as no social contributions are levied on pensions, and very little income tax.

Figure 4: Pension/wage ratio

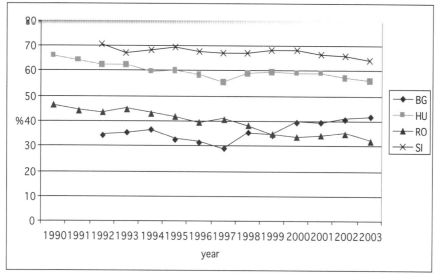

Notes: Bulgaria: average gross pension as % of average gross wage; Hungary: average net pension as % of
average net wage; Romania: average social insurance pension (all types) as % of average net wage;
Slovenia: average net pension as % of average net wage.

Source: Country studies.

Of course, a decrease in the pension/wage ratio does not necessarily imply a worsening of the income position of pensioners at the household level. One must bear in mind that in a period when household composition has been changing and the size of other vulnerable groups has been increasing, the relative "repositioning" of certain socioeconomic groups (here: pensioners) cannot be assessed only on the basis of a single aggregate indicator. We thus turn to the analysis of household income, its structure and changes since the early 1990s.[3]

Wages and salaries are clearly the most important income source, accounting for some 36% of household income in Bulgaria, 43% in Romania, 45% in Hungary and 62% in Slovenia. As for other primary incomes, in Bulgaria, Hungary and Romania income from agriculture is second in importance, with a particularly high share in Bulgaria and Romania, where it accounts for more than 20% of total household income. The fact that in

---

[3]   As already mentioned, all methodological and definitional issues are explained in the technical annex. Here we only mention that „household income" refers to household net income. We also use the synonymous term household disposable income. For Bulgaria, Hungary and Romania it also includes some types of income in kind.

Slovenia consumption in kind is not included in household income contributes to the very low share of agricultural income in Slovenia in household income. On the other hand the in-kind part of agriculture income accounts for more than 80% of agricultural income in Bulgaria, around two thirds in Hungary and some 80% in Romania.

Table 1:   The changing structure of household income

	Bulgaria		Hungary		Romania		Slovenia	
	1992	2002	1993	2002	1995	2004	1993	2002
Wages and salaries	41.7	36.4	41.8	44.9	45.5	42.9	62.4	62.0
Self-employment income	2.0	3.6	2.7	6.3	5.8	5.2	6.3	5.1
Income from agriculture	23.7	21.4	12.5	8.5	25.0	20.1	2.8	1.1
Capital income	0.2	0.8	2.6	2.0	0.4	0.8	0.1	0.4
Pensions	20.0	23.6	24.0	27.4	15.9	19.1	21.1	25.2
Unemployment benefits	0.5	0.8	3.0	0.8	1.4	0.9	1.4	0.9
Family benefits	2.5	0.8	8.4	4.2	1.5	1.6	0.7	3.0
Other social benefits	0.8	1.5	1.4	1.1	0.7	1.7	1.4	1.7
Interfamily transfers	2.6	4.4	2.6	4.2	2.5	3.2	2.0	0.3
Other income	6.0	6.7	0.9	0.6	1.3	4.6	1.7	0.2
Total	100.0	100.0	100.0	100.0	100.0	100.0	100.0	100.0

Notes: Hungary and Slovenia: Income from occasional work included in wages and salaries.
Source: Country studies.

The share of self-employment income in total household income has increased in Bulgaria and Hungary, and somewhat decreased in Romania and Slovenia; this in spite of the fact that the number of self-employed increased in the latter two countries (see Table 3). There is strong evidence that in Romania and to a lesser degree in Slovenia, the increase in the number of self-employed was the result of the "coping strategy", with employees and unemployed persons moving into low-productive self-employment activities.

The share of capital income has been increasing in all countries (except in Hungary), and this increase is due to the completion (or near-completion) of the privatisation process, with a larger share of the population possessing ownership shares or renting tangible property.

Pensions represent the income source second in importance, and their share has been increasing, albeit for different reasons. In Bulgaria this increase was primarily caused by the increase in the relative value of pensions (with regard to wages), whereas in the other three countries the increase was caused mostly by the increase in the number of pensioners (see Table 3), with a gradually decreasing relative value of pensions (i.e. pension/ wage ratio).

Other social protection benefits will be analysed in greater detail in section 5. Interfamily transfers have been increasing their share in household income in all countries except Slovenia. Obviously, this income source – as a transfer in kind or cash transfer (with remittances from abroad) – is important, but to a varying degree and to different households. In Bulgaria it is an income source which is more important for poorer households, whereas for Hungary and Romania the richer households benefit more from this transfer.

Since wages and pensions constitute the two largest income sources for households, they also to a large degree determine the growth of household income, depicted in Table 2.

Table 2:   The growth of household income

	Year	Median household equivalent income
Bulgaria	1993	100.0
	1997	82.9
	2000	93.0
	2002	101.9
Hungary	1993	100.0
	1998	79.0
	2002	110.0
Romania	1995	100.0
	1997	84.4
	2001	79.5
	2004	104.7
Slovenia	1993	100.0
	1997-99	124.0
	2001-03	136.0

Notes: Romania: data refer to average gross household equivalent income. Bulgaria: data refer to average equivalent disposable household income. For Slovenia and Hungary data refer to median equivalent disposable household income.

Source: Country studies.

As seen from Table 2, growth in household income was quite varied among the four countries. In Bulgaria, household income reached the level of the early 1990s only in 2002. In Hungary, household income followed a path very similar to pensions and wages, decreasing in the 1993-1997 period, followed by a continuous gradual increase. Data for Romania indicate a gradual decrease in household income in the 1995-2000 period, followed by a steady increase. In Slovenia, household income was on the rise since 1993, again showing that the "transformation depression" was over by 1992.

3   The socioeconomic structure of households

The changes in the socioeconomic structure of households clearly reflect changes which were described in Chapter 1: changes in activity rates, increases in the number of pensioners and a worsening demographic situation. Population ageing results in a decreasing share of younger age groups. This is visible in Table 3 through the decreasing share of dependants, i.e. persons without own income sources; these are mostly the young age groups. In the early 2000s, the share of employees in Bulgaria (2002) and Romania (2004) is still lower than in 1992 and 1995, respectively. As Romania has posted high output growth since 2001, this gives further credence to the description of Romanian growth as "jobless growth". In 2002, the share of employees in Hungary is higher than it was in 2003, whereas in Slovenia it was relatively stable during this period, and at a considerably higher level than in the other three countries.

Table 3:   The changing socioeconomic structure of households

	Bulgaria		Hungary		Romania		Slovenia	
	1992	2002	1993	2002	1995	2004	1993	2002
Employees	33.3	30.3	27.2	30.1	28.6	26.0	36.0	36.4
Non-agricultural self-employment	2.0	2.1	2.2	3.7	1.7	3.3	2.3	3.4
Active in agriculture	0.7	0.9	3.7	2.6	10.0	9.3	2.5	1.0
Unemployed	4.7	13.4	6.9	3.3	5.5	5.4	5.2	5.9
Pensioners	31.8	31.1	26.4	28.9	20.8	23.9	21.9	23.6
Dependants	27.6	22.3	29.7	27.3	35.5	32.1	31.12	29.3
Other	0.0	0.0	3.9	4.3	0.0	0.0	0.9	0.4
Total	100.0	100.0	100.0	100.0	100.0	100.0	100.0	100.0

Source: Country studies.

Notes: Hungary: Persons on paid childcare are included among "Other"; persons with occasional income are included among "Employees". Bulgaria: Active in agriculture are persons self-employed in agriculture. This share is very low due to a very high proportion of persons involved in agricultural activity in addition to their main occupation. Slovenia: Persons with occasional income are included among "Employees".

Table 3 provides a useful starting point for a comparison between the unemployment rate, as computed by the HBS data,[4] i.e. data presented in Table 3, and the unemployment rate based on the LFS; these comparative figures are presented in Table 4.

Table 4:   HBS and LFS unemployment rates

	Bulgaria		Hungary		Romania		Slovenia	
	1992	2002	1993	2002	1995	2004	1993	2002
Unemployment rate HBS	11.5	28.7	17.3	8.3	12.0	12.3	11.3	12.6
Unemployment rate ILO	-	18.1	11.3	5.8	-	8.0	9.1	5.9

Source: Country studies. For LFS unemployment rate in Bulgaria: Eurostat Yearbook 2006-07.

As seen from Table 4, the unemployment rate based on the household budget surveys is considerably higher than the unemployment rate based on the LFS. The fact that the HBS rate is higher than the LFS rate is not surprising, as the status of unemployed in household budget surveys is based on self-declaration by the respondent. Obviously, in Bulgaria, Romania and Slovenia there are many discouraged unemployed persons, who do not actively seek employment, quite possibly because of a small chance of finding a job. This gives an indication that restructuring is not over, and that there is a poor matching between the skills of the unemployed and the jobs offered. Only in Hungary do household survey data show a large drop in the share of unemployed between the early 1990s and 2000s, although we have to take into account other developments, i.e. substitution of early retirement and disability pensions, which have increased substantially in the 1990s.

The share of young dependants (below age 18) has decreased in all four countries, which is a visible outcome of the worsening demographic situation. In contrast, the share of dependants (persons without own resources) aged 18 and above has increased, particularly in Hungary, Romania and Slovenia – and this is due to the very large increase in enrolment for tertiary

---

4   The HBS unemployment rate is computed as the ratio between (a) unemployed and (b) employees, non-agricultural self-employment, active in agriculture and unemployed.

education. As seen from Table 5, the share of elderly dependants (aged 60 and above) has decreased in Bulgaria, Hungary and Slovenia, doubtlessly due to the improved coverage of pensions. This improved coverage is caused not only by the greater inclusiveness of the social security system (i.e. more active persons are now included in the system) but also by the extension of pension benefits (as an individual right) to groups of persons which were previously not included.

Table 5:   The share of dependants by age groups (as percentage of all persons)

	Year	Less than 18	18 to 29	30 to 59	60+	All
Bulgaria	1992	21.4	2.4	0.1	3.7	27.6
	2002	18.4	2.4	0.1	1.4	22.3
Hungary	1993	24.9	2.7	1.3	0.8	29.7
	2002	21.0	5.1	0.9	0.3	27.3
Romania	1995	24.7	5.4	2.6	0.8	33.5
	2004	21.2	6.0	4.2	0.8	32.1
Slovenia	1993	23.3	3.8	2.2	1.7	31.1
	2002	19.1	7.4	1.6	1.1	29.3

Source: Country studies.

4   Income sources and the socioeconomic structure of households

Figures 5 to 8 provide a more detailed picture of the three most important income sources (wages and salaries, pensions and income from agriculture) and their share in household income, showing these shares for each income decile. A corresponding figure is added, showing the shares of employees, pensioners and self-employed in agriculture (as percentage of all household members), by income deciles.

Figure 5a: Share of wages and salaries, income from agriculture and pensions, by income deciles, Bulgaria, 2002

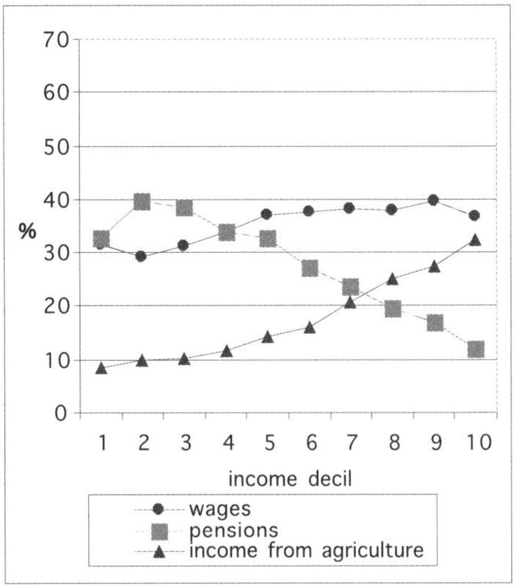

Figure 5b: Share of employees, pensioners and active in agriculture, by income deciles, Bulgaria, 2002

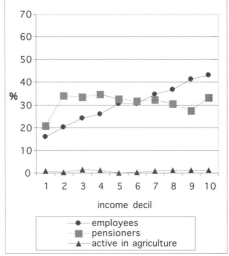

Source: Country studies.

Source: Country studies.

Figure 6a: Share of wages and salaries, income from agriculture and pensions, by income deciles, Hungary, 2002

Figure 6b: Share of employees, pensioners and active in agriculture, by income deciles, Hungary, 2002

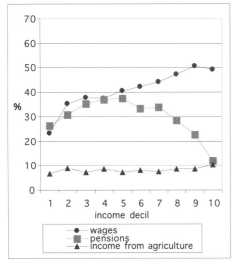

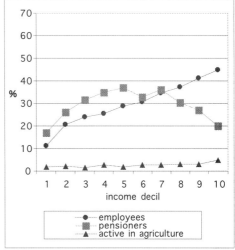

Note: In Figure 6a wages and salaries do not contain income from occasional work, while in Table 1 it was included.

Source: Country studies.

Note: In Figure 6b persons with occasional income are not added to employees, while in Table 3 category employees contains also persons with occasional income.

Source: Country studies.

Figure 7a: Share of wages and salaries, income from agriculture and pensions, by income deciles, Romania, 2004

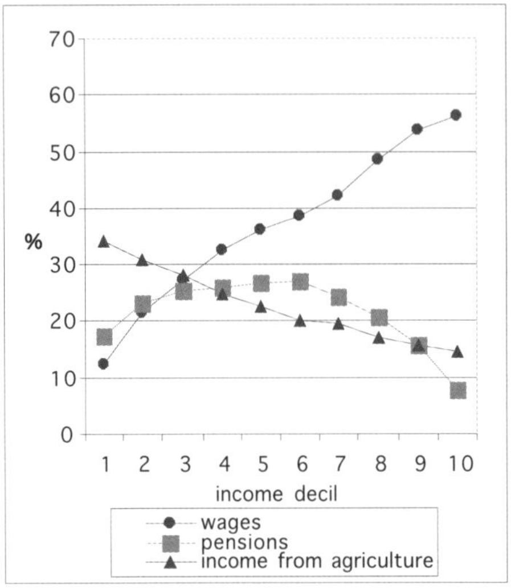

Figure 7b: Share of employees, pensioners and active in agriculture, by income deciles, Romania, 2004

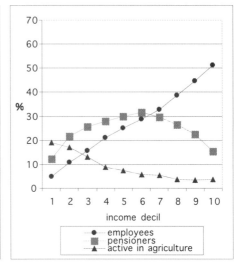

Source: Country studies.

Source: Country studies.

Figure 8a: Share of wages and salaries, income from agriculture and pensions, by income deciles, Slovenia, 2001-2003

Figure 8b: Share of employees, pensioners and active in agriculture, by income deciles, Slovenia, 2001-2003

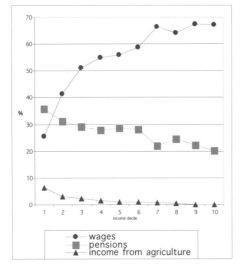

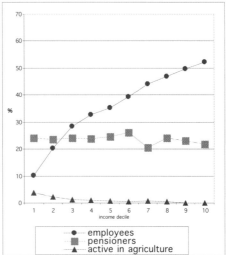

Note: In Figure 6a wages and salaries do not contain income from occasional work, while in Table 1 it was included.
Source: Country studies.

Note: In Figure 6b persons with occasional income are not added to employees, while in Table 3 category employees contains also persons with occasional income.
Source: Country studies.

The share of wages and salaries in household income of low-income households is small, and steadily increases with increasing household income. Mirroring this, the share of employees also monotonically increases by income deciles. They represent more than half of all household members in the top income decile in Hungary, Romania and Slovenia. In Bulgaria the increasing share of labour income (in household income), by income deciles, is much less pronounced than in the other three countries. Wages in Bulgaria represent a rather important income source even in the bottom income decile, which indicates a higher share of working poor.

In Hungary and Romania, the share of pensions in household income is rather low at both ends of the income distribution, i.e. in the bottom and top income deciles. A similar inverted U-shaped curve is also characteristic for the share of pensioners (as percentage of all household members) for these two countries. Obviously, other socioeconomic groups are taking the "bottom seats": in Hungary these are unemployed, persons on paid child-care and young dependants, whereas in Romania they are the unemployed and active in agriculture. In Bulgaria, the share of pensions in household income is continuously decreasing from the second decile, whereas the share of pensioners (apart from the bottom decile) is in the 25-35% range. A quite plausible explanation for this phenomenon is the specific nature of agriculture in Bulgaria, where most rural households engage in agriculture as a secondary activity (World Bank, 2002: 34), so that a large number of pensioners and workers are also engaged in agriculture. In Slovenia, the share of pensions in household income is decreasing by income deciles, whereas the corresponding share of pensioners (as percentage of all household members) is very stable.

In spite of the very low share of persons active in agriculture, the share of income from agriculture is quite high in Bulgaria. As already observed, this is due to the very large extent of agriculture as a secondary activity. Also, some analyses show that own consumption of food in Bulgaria represents a high share of total food consumption and that even in non-poor households own consumption of food is common (World Bank, 2002: 99). In Romania, the high share of persons active in agriculture in the lower income deciles shows the large extent of subsistence farming and the agricultural sector as an absorber of labour, where alternative sources of employment are scarce. Hungary exhibits a different pattern: in spite of the – overall – low share of persons active in agriculture, their share in the top income decile is quite high, indicating market-oriented agricultural activities.[5] In Slovenia the share

71

---

5   As observed from Tables HU3 and HU5 (in the Annex to the chapter on Hungary), in 2002 persons active in agriculture, situated in households in the tenth decile, accounted for 16.2% of all active persons in agriculture, and for 23.7% of total agricultural income.

of persons active in agriculture is very small, though they are somewhat more concentrated in the lower income deciles, due to the prevalence of subsistence farming, with a very small number of large, market-oriented agricultural estates.

5   Coverage of social benefits

Cash social benefits accounted for some 27% of household income in Bulgaria (in 2002), 33% in Hungary (2002), 23% in Romania (2004) and 31% in Slovenia (2002). The social protection systems in these countries are mostly based on the principle of social insurance, though some benefits are also disbursed on the basis of need, and some are universal, in that the whole relevant population receives the benefit in question. In all four countries these systems were under severe strain in the early years of transition, with a large increase in beneficiaries (pensioners, unemployed persons) and a strongly eroded contribution base, caused by a decreasing number of contributors and growth of the informal sector. The need to adapt was immediate, and it is instructive to observe the "coping strategy" adopted by the pension systems, which resorted to more or less *ad hoc* measures to ensure the financial viability of the system.

For example, Margan (2001: 7) reports, that from 1990 to 1999 pensions in Romania increased only occasionally, and not fully in line with price increases. Tinios and Markova (2001) report that indexation of pensions in Bulgaria in the 1990s was on an *ad hoc* basis, and this practice stopped only in 1998. Augustinovics et al. (2002: 30) report for Hungary that in the early and mid-1990s the very unfavourable calculation of the pension base resulted in low entry pensions. Also, from 1996 onward pensions were increased according to the nominal wage index of the *previous year*; this occurred amidst high inflation, which was about 20%. These measures resulted in a decrease in pension expenditures. In Slovenia, pension indexation was simply discontinued from November 1990 to May 1991.

These emergency measures decreased the relative value of pensions fairly rapidly, so that the pension/wage ratio stabilized only when these measures were discontinued. This is the case of Romania, where the pension/wage ratio has somewhat stabilized since 1999, with a recalculation of pensions being performed in 2001 and 2004. In Bulgaria, the pension/wage ratio bottomed out in 1997 and started to increase when the practice of *ad hoc* indexation was abolished. In Hungary, similarly, the pension/wage ratio reached its lowest level in 1997, when the indexation rule, in a period of rather high inflation, significantly reduced the value of real pensions.

The social protection systems in all the four countries returned "back to normal" in the early 2000s, meaning that the period of non-transparent "fixes" and *ad hoc* measures is a matter of the past. However, the question of coverage of the active population still remains pertinent, i.e. (a) how many active persons are actually insured and (b) how much contribution do they pay. For the former, coverage denotes the number of contributors, as percentage of the working-age population or as percentage of the labour force (Pallacios and Pallares-Miralles, 2000). For the latter, coverage is measured by the covered wage bill, which shows the amount of wages upon which social contributions have been levied. A low value of the covered wage bill typically implies a large informal sector, with many active workers evading payment of contributions. A study of five Central and East-European countries (Fultz and Stanovnik, 2004) has shown that contribution compliance is quite varied, as seen from Table 6.

Table 6: The covered wage bill and actual wage bill, as percentage of GDP, 2002

	Covered wage bill	Actual wage bill
Bulgaria	20.6	34.1
Hungary	27.5	34.2
Romania	16.4	36.4
Slovenia	35.1	46.6

Notes: The covered wage bill for Bulgaria was computed assuming an average contribution rate of 30%.

Source: For covered wage bill: Máté (2004) for Hungary, Vezjak and Stanovnik (2004) for Slovenia, Toma (2004) for Romania; for Bulgaria, data provided by Silviya Nikolova. For actual wages: data from country studies.

Of course, the gap between the covered wage bill and actual wage bill is not wholly due to contribution evasion: certain types of labour income are not subject to tax, and there are contribution ceilings in some countries. However, low values of the covered wage bill do signify a weak ability to collect social contributions; consequently, it also results in a weak social protection system. Clearly, the covered wage bill is rather low in Bulgaria and Romania, indicating that contributions are not levied on a large part of wages; this also translates in low coverage of the active population and low (future) pensions.

The country studies do not analyse this type of coverage, which concerns active insured persons and their payments into the social protection system, as these questions are beyond the scope of household budget surveys. However, a different indicator of coverage can be constructed, showing not the contributing side but the "receiving", i.e. benefit side. Here, coverage denotes the share of the relevant population receiving a given social benefit. We define these shares as "benefit coverage".

We present here the coverage of unemployment benefits and child benefits. The coverage of pensions is presented in the country studies; actually, the improved coverage of pensions can also be seen from Table 5, which shows that the share of elderly dependants (aged 60 and above without own pension rights) has decreased in the 1990s in Bulgaria, Hungary and Slovenia, whereas in Romania this share has remained low and stable. Here we do not deal with the adequacy of this coverage, i.e. its role in poverty alleviation and improvement of the income position of the beneficiary households. Table 7 provides a comparison of the coverage of unemployment benefits for the four countries.

Table 7:   The coverage of unemployment benefits

	Bulgaria		Hungary		Romania		Slovenia	
	1992	2002	1993	2002	1995	2004	1993	2002
Households with unemployed member (as % of all households)	3.8	10.5	16.2	7.7	13.3	12.9	14.1	14.5
% of households with unemployed member receiving unemployment benefit	33.3	14.0	80.8	78.4	60.7	24.8	52.0	30.2

Source: Country studies.

This table shows that unemployment is a persistent economic and social phenomenon. It seems that various macroeconomic measures and policies have but a meager impact on its reduction; only Hungary has scored a visible success, with a large decrease in the number of households with unemployed member(s). Thus, in 1993 every sixth household in Hungary (16.2%) had at least one unemployed member, whereas the corresponding figure for 2002 is only every fourteenth household (7.7 %). However, this seemingly positive assessment of decreasing unemployment has to be considered together with other developments, i.e. substitution of early retirement and disability pensions, which have increased substantially in the 1990s. Hungary has a high and stable coverage, in the 80% range. The coverage (i.e. unemployed receiving an unemployment benefit) in the other three countries has decreased considerably in this time period, doubtlessly as a result of deliberate policy: entitlement rules were severed and duration of entitlement was shortened.[6] So, not only did the number of unemployed receiving unemployment benefits decrease, but also the relative value of this benefit was lower. The replacement rate (i.e. average unemployment benefit as percentage of average wage) decreased substantially in all countries. In Bulgaria, the replacement rate dropped from over 60% in 1991 to about 33% in 2004. In Hungary the replacement rate decreased from 54% to 41% between 1993 and 2002, whereas in Slovenia the replacement rate dropped from 47% to 39% (between 1994 and 2002). Romania also experienced a decrease in the replacement rate. As will be seen in section 7, these social policy measures resulted in a deteriorating income position of the unemployed.

In contrast to unemployment benefits, characterized by a low coverage in Bulgaria, Romania and Slovenia, the coverage of family benefits in all the four countries is relatively high. In Hungary, coverage is absolute, and every household with a child receives a family benefit; in Romania the coverage is some 96% and in Slovenia some 88%; the large increase in Slovenia was caused by a deliberate policy change in the mid-1990s, with a clear intention for greater inclusion of all children; however, the final move to complete coverage and universality of this benefit was not achieved. Unlike Slovenia, where legislative action in 1994 and 1996 greatly expanded coverage, in Bulgaria legislation enacted in 2002 introduced means-testing for child benefits, and this in effect reduced coverage from 95% in 1992 to 71.9% in 2002, as the child benefit was an almost universal benefit under the previous system. In Romania the system of family benefits changed several times between 1995 and 2004. In 1997 the supplementary allowance for families with two children or more was established, in addition to the universal child allowance introduced in 1993 (Ivan Ungureanu, 2003). Hungary also experienced changes in legislation: in 1995 the rules for granting child allowances were altered and families above a given income ceiling became excluded from this type of benefit. The legislation changed again in 2000 when the income ceiling was abolished and coverage became 100%, very similar to the situation before 1995.

---

6   However, one must also bear in mind that the unemployment status in the household budget surveys is based on self-declaration.

Table 8:   The coverage of family benefits

	Bulgaria		Hungary		Romania		Slovenia	
	1992	2002	1993	2002	1995	2004	1993	2002
Households with children (as % of all households)	29.9	24.1	32.0	26.7	36.5	31.6	38.6	28.4
% of households with children receiving family benefits	95.4	71.9	99.0	100.0	87.3	95.6	19.8	88.0

Source: Country studies.

6   Income inequality

During the early years of transition, i.e. the early 1990s, most Central and East European countries experienced a large increase in income inequality. This was the result of the greater role of the private sector, resulting in a "decompression" and deregulation of wages and, concomitantly, a rising premium for education, particularly for tertiary education. Table 9 provides an aggregate measure of this premium, showing the relative equivalized income by education levels; the premium for tertiary education appears to be high in Romania and Hungary, the two countries with a relatively low share of persons with attained tertiary education. Table 9 also shows that, in the 10-year period from the early 1990s to the early 2000s, the education premium (for tertiary education) has increased in Bulgaria, Hungary and Romania, but remained fairly stable in Slovenia. This is not surprising, as data for Slovenia (shown in the country chapter) show that the education premium (for tertiary education) increased substantially in the very first years of transition, remaining stable after 1993.[7]

The share of persons with university education within each income decile is shown in Table 10; persons with university degrees are strongly concentrated in the upper income deciles in Hungary, Romania and Slovenia, and to a somewhat lesser extent in Bulgaria. If anything, the absolute difference between the shares of persons holding university degrees in the top income decile and the bottom income decile has increased during the 1990s.

---

7   For Slovenia, relative equivalized income for persons with attained primary education increased from 0.70 in 1993 to 0.76 in 2002. This increase was quite possibly the result of legislation on the minimum wage, enacted in the mid-1990s.

Table 9:   Relative equivalized income by education levels of labour-active persons aged between 25 and 64 years

	Bulgaria		Hungary		Romania		Slovenia	
	1992	2002	1993	2002	1995	2004	1993	2002
Primary	0.94	0.61	0.86	0.78	0.82	0.71	0.70	0.76
Vocational	1.03	0.91	0.94	0.90	0.92	0.87	0.90	0.85
Secondary	0.97	0.98	1.12	1.10	1.12	1.07	1.11	1.02
Tertiary	1.04	1.20	1.37	1.44	1.68	1.81	1.39	1.37
All	1.00	1.00	1.00	1.00	1.00	1.00	1.00	1.00

Note: HU: all persons aged between 25 and 64 years.
Source: Country studies.

Table 10:   Persons with attained tertiary education level as percentage of working-age population, by income deciles

	Decile										
	1	2	3	4	5	6	7	8	9	10	All
	early 1990s										
BG (1992)	12.9	11.9	15.2	14.7	15.7	17.5	17.0	18.6	18.8	19.1	16.5
HU (1993)	1.9	3.7	2.7	3.1	5.4	6.3	7.7	13.7	21.2	31.5	10.7
RO (1995)	1.0	1.0	1.0	2.0	3.0	4.0	7.0	10.0	16.0	30.0	8.0
SI (1993)	2.1	2.1	3.6	7.9	8.9	7.0	12.9	24.9	31.7	46.9	17.7
	early 2000s										
BG (2002)	5.3	8.2	11.1	16.4	16.7	18.5	24.5	23.5	29.4	30.9	18.8
HU (2002)	2.6	2.6	4.3	5.1	6.8	10.2	14.0	17.1	27.1	41.6	13.6
RO (2004)	1.0	1.0	1.0	3.0	3.0	6.0	7.0	13.0	20.0	44.0	10.0
SI (2001-03)	7.1	5.8	2.8	5.0	6.9	9.9	17.0	22.8	37.9	61.3	20.8

Notes: BG, HU and RO: all persons aged between 25 and 64 years; SI: labour-active persons aged between 25 and 64 years.
Source: Country studies.

Of course, increased levels of formal education do not necessarily imply a commensurate increase in human capital, as much depends on the quality of education and actual outcomes, i.e. how better education translates into improved productivity. For example, some studies indicate that the education quality in Bulgaria has sharply deteriorated between 1995 and 1999 (World Bank, 2003).

Is there a definite answer to the question on what has happened to income inequality during the 1990s in these four countries? Here, it is important to assess the dynamics of change within each country, as cross-country comparisons are on more slippery grounds. Some differences in definitions persist, as household income in Bulgaria, Hungary and Romania includes income in kind (mostly agricultural products), whereas in Slovenia it includes only current monetary income. Furthermore, the qualities of the household surveys differ, since underreporting of income varies between countries. In some countries the survey design underwent quite important changes, so that even comparisons within a given country are not problem-free. Bearing in mind these caveats, Table 11 presents the values of the Gini coefficient of inequality of household income.[8]

Table 11: Gini coefficients of inequality of household income

	Year	Gini coefficient
Bulgaria	1992	0.26
	1997	0.29
	2002	0.27
Hungary	1993	0.22
	1997	0.23
	2002	0.24
Romania	1995	0.31
	1997	0.29
	2001	0.30
	2004	0.31
Slovenia	1993	0.27
	1997-99	0.25
	2001-03	0.24

Source: Country studies.

The dynamics of income inequality are not the same in all four countries. In Bulgaria and Hungary, income inequality has somewhat increased in the 10-year period, though this increase is not spectacular. The high value of 0.29 for Bulgaria in 1997 is aberrational, as 1997 was a "crisis" year, marked by very high inflation and negative growth of output. Inequality in Romania has remained fairly high, but stable, since 1995. Slovenia is an "outlier", in that inequality has actually been decreasing since 1993; here, most of the "action" has occurred in the very first years of transition (late 1980s and

8   As mentioned in the introduction to this chapter, definitional issues are relegated to the technical annex. Here, we only note that the Gini coefficient is computed using equivalent disposable household income.

first years of 1990s), when inequality has been increasing. In general, the overall changes in the Ginis in each of the four countries appear to be small, suggesting broad stability. However, differences among the countries are rather large. Inequality is high in Romania, and rather low in Hungary and Slovenia, with Bulgaria occupying an intermediate position. In other words, the two countries with a relatively high GDP p.c. – Hungary and Slovenia – also have fairly low values of the Gini.

The Gini coefficient of income inequality was decomposed using the Rao decomposition of income inequality (Rao, 1969), i.e. the relation: $G = \sum s_k C_k$, where G refers to the Gini coefficient of total income inequality, s_k refers to the share of income source k in total household income and C_k refers to the concentration coefficient of income source k. This decomposition provides an analytical tool for the analysis of "contributions" of income sources ("components") to the overall income inequality.[9] Broadly, the interpretation of the decomposition is as follows: if a concentration coefficient of an income source k is less than the value of the Gini coefficient, a proportionate increase in this income source would result in a decrease in the overall Gini. The greater the share of this income source in total household income, the greater would be the decrease in the Gini coefficient. Conversely, for concentration coefficients, which are greater than the value of the Gini coefficient, a proportionate increase in this income source would result in an increase in the overall Gini. The greater the share of this income source in total household income, the greater would be the increase in the Gini.

The concentration coefficients for the four countries at two points in time are presented in Table 12. Clearly, the values of the concentration coefficients exhibit some common features:

(a)   The values of the concentration coefficients for wages are higher than the values of the Gini coefficient of income inequality, meaning that wages are distributed more unequally than total income, and that a proportionate increase in wages would result in an increase in the overall Gini coefficient.

(b)   With the exception of Bulgaria, the highest concentration coefficients are for income from capital, suggesting a very strong concentration of this income source among households in the upper income deciles.

(c)   The values of the concentration coefficients for (1) unemployment benefits, (2) family benefits and (3) other social benefits are mostly negative, suggesting that these benefits are mostly targeted toward the

---

9   See Technical Annex.

poor – and that proportionate increases in these benefits would result in a decrease in overall income inequality. Low-income households receive (in absolute terms) more of these benefits than high-income households. For these benefits, large changes in the values of the concentration coefficients can be explained by deliberate shifts in social policy. Thus, in Bulgaria the switch from a small positive value of the concentration coefficient for family benefits in 1992 to a negative value in 2002 is the result of new legislation introduced in 2002, introducing means-testing for this benefit. The large increase – from -0.385 in 1993 to -0.160 in 2001-03 – for the concentration coefficient for family benefits in Slovenia was caused by a policy shift, i.e. a move toward universality.[10]

The concentration coefficient for income from non-agricultural self-employment in Hungary is higher than the Gini coefficient of income inequality for total household income, implying that the share of this income source in household income of the high-income households is greater than its share in household income of the low-income households. The low values of the concentration coefficient for Romania and Bulgaria imply that most self-employed in these two countries are engaged in low-productive activities. A similar explanation can also be given for Slovenia, where the concentration coefficient of income from non-agricultural employment decreased considerably between 1993 and 2001-2003. In Hungary, Romania and Slovenia the share of non-agricultural self-employment increased between the early 1990s and early 2000s; it seems that in Romania and Slovenia for many of these new self-employed this represented a "coping" strategy.

The diverse values of the concentration coefficient for income from agriculture are the result of very different national experiences. In Bulgaria, agriculture is mostly not a primary activity, but a secondary one; also, it is more the domain of the rich. Hungary exhibits high values of the concentration coefficient, implying a strong entrepreneur-oriented agriculture. In contrast, the low (and even negative!) value for Slovenia is doubtlessly caused by the large share of subsistence agriculture, in spite of the fact that the share of agricultural population in Slovenia is rather low. For Romania, the decreasing value can be explained by the "coping" strategy adopted, with a relatively high share of agricultural population.

---

10   This means that almost all children receive this benefit, though the amount disbursed depends on actual household income, so that poorer households still receive larger amounts.

Table 12: Concentration coefficients in early 1990s and early 2000s

Concentration coefficients	Bulgaria	Hungary	Romania	Slovenia
	early 1990s			
	1992	1993	1995	1993
Wages and salaries	0.359	0.352	0.403	0.299
Income from occasional work	-	0.086	-	0.466
Income form self-employment (non-agriculture)	0.155	0.367	0.494	0.640
Income from agriculture	0.432	0.258	0.209	-0.030
Income from capital	0.048	0.753	0.650	0.702
Pensions	-0.069	0.030	0.165	0.110
Unemployment benefits	-0.061	-0.278	-0.199	-0.206
Family benefits	0.030	-0.037	-0.128	-0.385
Other social benefits	0.115	-0.092	0.037	-0.118
Interfamily transfers	0.103	0.302	0.577	0.520
Other income	0.248	0.487	-	0.645
All	**0.260**	**0.217**	**0.309**	**0.272**
	early 2000s			
	2002	2002	2004	2001-03
Wages and salaries	0.349	0.318	0.460	0.314
Income from occasional work	-	-0.023	-	0.222
Income form self-employment (non-agriculture)	0.178	0.461	0.232	0.251
Income from agriculture	0.469	0.286	0.175	-0.340
Income from capital	0.203	0.797	0.859	0.520
Pensions	0.047	0.118	0.187	0.162
Unemployment benefits	-0.014	-0.489	-0.005	-0.216
Family benefits	-0.067	-0.263	-0.149	-0.160
Other social benefits	0.053	-0.101	-0.219	-0.175
Interfamily transfers	0.155	0.292	0.442	0.041
Other income	0.268	0.367	-	0.335
All	**0.271**	**0.237**	**0.311**	**0.237**

81

Source: Country studies.

The concentration coefficients for pensions are positive in value,[11] but generally low. Though pensions are a very heterogeneous income source, in these four countries social insurance pensions represent the largest share of all pensions disbursed. In such systems, the main function of pensions is income replacement, not poverty relief. In other words, pensions ought not

---

11   With the exception of Bulgaria in 1992.

to be "too" concentrated among poorer households, as this would imply a very weak role of the income replacement function. Of course, pensions from the public pension system contain various solidarity elements, so that the dispersion of public pensions is typically much smaller than the dispersion of wages. So, one would expect concentration coefficients for pensions to be lower than those for wages, but not "too" low. In social insurance systems, very low positive values (or even negative values) of these concentration coefficients can occur in case of pension "compression", caused by – say – grossly inadequate and selective indexation of pensions. Governments in these four countries did actually resort to such measures,[12] justifying them by the deteriorating financial position of social insurance institutions and worsening of the pension system parameters. In most countries, the slide in the replacement rate (i.e. pension/wage ratio) continued even after the period of very inadequate indexation. We must however note that, though a decrease in the pension/wage ratio signifies a deteriorating income position of pensioners *vis-à-vis* employees, this does not necessarily translate into a worsening position of pensioners at the household level. Other socioeconomic groups seem to have fared worse than the pensioner population, so that they increased the share in the bottom deciles, i.e. they have replaced pensioners at the bottom of the income distribution. Who are these groups? In Bulgaria, Romania and Slovenia the share of unemployed (as percentage of all persons) in the bottom decile has increased markedly, in Hungary, Bulgaria, Romania and Slovenia the position of dependants (mostly children) seems to have deteriorated, with an increasing share in the bottom decile and decreasing share in the top decile. In sum, though pensioners have been "losing" in comparison to the wage-earners, some socioeconomic groups seem to have been losing even more.

7   Risk of Poverty

In the country studies poverty is defined in relative terms, i.e. as the share of persons whose equivalized household income is below a given percentage of the median household equivalent income. This is frequently referred to as the head-count ratio or poverty incidence, and the given percentage of the median household equivalent income is referred to as the poverty line or poverty threshold. The head count ratio, as an indicator of poverty,

---

12   These measures were described in section 5.

fails to take account of the depth of income poverty, i.e. the extent to which income of the poor falls below the poverty line. However, the use of different poverty thresholds (40%, 50% and 60%) does provide for a measure of the depth of income poverty. Table 13 presents the poverty incidence for various socioeconomic groups, with the poverty threshold being set at 60% of the median equivalent household income.[13]

Table 13: Risk of income poverty, in per cent (poverty line set at 60% of median household equivalent income)

Country	Year	All persons	Pension- ers	Children	Unem- ployed	Persons aged 60+
Bulgaria	1992	12.6	18.4	10.5	27.6	19.6
	1997	14.8	16.7	17.5	24.1	17.4
	2002	13.2	10.1	16.9	29.2	9.8
Hungary	1993	6.5	4.4	8.0	19.0	4.0
	1997	10.3	4.7	15.0	33.1	2.4
	2002	10.0	5.5	16.8	35.4	4.1
Romania	1995	19.9	14.4	26.9	34.2	17.2
	2001	20.2	12.3	29.3	32.4	14.7
	2004	20.6	13.3	29.9	37.9	14.3
Slovenia	1993	13.0	15.7	12.5	26.6	21.3
	1997-99	14.0	12.5	16.3	39.2	16.4
	2001-03	11.6	12.2	11.5	36.8	15.4

Source: Country studies.

As seen from Table 13, during the observed time period there have been relatively small changes in poverty incidence for the total population in Bulgaria, Romania and Slovenia. In Bulgaria, poverty incidence somewhat increased between 1992 and 2002, and the same applies for Romania, with a small increase between 1995 and 2004; in comparison with the other three countries, the poverty incidence in Romania is quite high. These poverty rankings are similar to the overall income inequality rankings, where we have observed that Romania stands out in terms of income inequality, with

13   The poverty incidence for other population subgroups was analysed in the country chapters. The country chapter for Romania presents separate calculations for the poverty incidence of the rural population, and the country chapters for Bulgaria, Hungary and Romania discuss the poverty incidence for the Roma population. The poverty incidence and material deprivation of the Roma are dealt with in greater detail in World Bank studies: World Bank (2001) for Hungary, World Bank (2002) for Bulgaria and World Bank (2003) for Romania.

Hungary and Slovenia experiencing rather low income inequality, measured with the Gini coefficient. From Table 13 we also observe that there has been an increase in poverty incidence in the first sub-period, followed by a decrease in the second sub-period – in all countries except Romania. In Bulgaria and Hungary, the large increases in the first sub-period can be explained by macroeconomic upheavals. Thus, Bulgaria experienced a severe financial and fiscal crisis in 1996-1997, whereas the increase in Hungary was caused by the Bokros austerity package in 1995-1997. What the crisis in Bulgaria and austerity package in Hungary have in common is that social expenditures were severely curtailed, strongly affecting the incomes of the most vulnerable population subgroups. The poverty trends, as shown in Table 13, are in broad agreement with the poverty trends for these countries derived from other studies.[14]

In the early 2000s, the risk of income poverty for pensioners was lower than that of the whole population, with the exception of Slovenia, where it was slightly higher. In Hungary and Romania, the poverty incidence for children is much higher than for the total population, without showing any signs of improvement. In Bulgaria the poverty incidence for children is also above average. In all four countries the poverty incidence for the unemployed is very high, with the poverty risk varying from nearly two to more than three times the poverty risk of the total population.

Tables 14 and 15 take a closer look at two potentially vulnerable groups – elderly women and children. Here, we observe whether there are certain characteristics which have an impact on the poverty rates for these two subgroups. Thus, as seen from Table 14, elderly unmarried women have a relatively high poverty risk; in all four countries, this elderly subgroup has the highest poverty rate, compared to the other three subgroups (married women, married men, unmarried men). Most of these women live in single-person households, with small pensions of their own right or a survivors' pension. The very low relative poverty risk for unmarried women in Hungary is a consequence of the fact that the poverty rates for pensioners and persons aged 60 and above is much lower than the overall poverty rate. This is due to satisfactory pensions and to the fact that there are very few elderly dependants, i.e. elderly persons without own sources of income.

On the other hand, Table 15 shows a very disquieting trend, namely that during the observed time period, the poverty risk for children has increased,

---

14   For Hungary, we refer to World Bank (2001), for Bulgaria – World Bank (2002) and for Romania – World Bank (2003).

regardless of whether they live in two-parent or single-parent households. Of course, the poverty risk for children living in single parent households is much higher than that of children living in two-parent households.

Table 14:   Relative poverty risk of women aged 60 or above in the early 1990s and 2000s (poverty line=60% of median household equivalent income, all persons=100)

	Bulgaria	Hungary	Romania	Slovenia
	early 1990s			
	1992	1993	1995	1993
Married women	117.5	40.0	70.4	160.0
Unmarried women	319.8	92.3	125.6	180.8
	early 2000s			
	2002	2002	2004	2001-03
Married women	55.3	29.0	53.4	129.3
Unmarried women	136.4	51.0	101.9	147.4

Notes: Relative poverty risk computed by dividing the group-specific poverty rate by the overall poverty rate, multiplied by 100.

Source: Country studies.

Table 15:   Relative poverty risk of children in the early 1990s and 2000s (poverty line=60% of median household equivalent income, all persons=100)

	Bulgaria	Hungary	Romania	Slovenia
	early 1990s			
	1992	1993	1997	1993
Children in two parent household	80.2	106.2	115.6	89.2
Children in single parent household	104.8	183.1	155.8	158.5
	early 2000s			
	2002	2002	2004	2001-03
Children in two parent household	114.4	145.0	140.8	90.5
Children in single parent household	210.6	244.0	208.7	195.7

Notes: Relative poverty risk computed by dividing the group-specific poverty rate by the overall poverty rate, multiplied by 100.

Source: Country studies.

8 Concluding remarks

Large political and institutional changes, which occurred in Bulgaria, Hungary, Romania and Slovenia since the early 1990s, culminated in the EU accession for Hungary and Slovenia on May 1, 2004 and for Bulgaria and Romania on January 1, 2007. However, these rapid political changes and the modernization drive have yet to produce significant changes and improvements in the socioeconomic structure at the household level. Though each of the four countries has its distinct and unique features, one could form two clusters. One is comprised of the two higher-income countries – Slovenia and Hungary, and the other of the two lower income countries – Bulgaria and Romania. The latter two countries are still characterized by a high share of agriculture; whereas in Bulgaria, agriculture mostly serves as a source of additional household income, in Romania the high share of agriculture is mostly the result of the "coping" strategy adopted by households, so that subsistence agriculture prevails. Furthermore, the importance of the informal economy is much larger in Romania and Bulgaria than in Hungary and Slovenia, as manifested by the low share of wages in GDP and by data showing a relatively low contribution compliance. Also, income inequality and poverty seem to be quite high in Romania, as compared to Hungary and Slovenia, with Bulgaria in an intermediate position.

On the other hand, there are characteristics which are not "cluster-specific". Unemployment rates, derived from household budget survey (HBS), are higher than the ILO (LFS) unemployment rates – quite possibly because the HBS rate is based on self-assessment and thus includes discouraged seekers of employment. Romania and Slovenia have quite high HBS unemployment rates, whereas the unemployment rate in Bulgaria is extremely high. It seems that large mismatches in the labour market still persist, and that there are continuous challenges for economic and social policy, with the aim of increasing employment and improving the human capital of the labour force.

All of the four countries also face serious demographic challenges, caused by low birth rates and rapid population ageing. These negative trends already have a very strong impact on the socioeconomic structure of households. In a relatively short time period (10 years), the number of younger dependants (less than 18 years old) decreased by at least 10% in all four countries. The number of dependants of age 18 and above increased; this is mostly due to the rapid spread of tertiary education. However, in

Bulgaria, their share decreased, doubtlessly also caused by large emigration of the relevant age groups.

The other large non-active population group – pensioners – has been steadily marching on, considerably increasing their population share in Hungary, Romania and Slovenia, whereas in Bulgaria their share was already quite high already in the early 1990s. Thus, in Romania and Slovenia almost every fourth household member is a pensioner, the share being even higher in Hungary (almost 3 out of 10) and Bulgaria (more than 3 out of 10). The share of pensions in household income has increased in a relatively short period of time. These negative demographic developments will clearly pose great strains on the social protection systems, challenges amplified by the need to pursue further structural reforms and economic modernization.

9   References

Augusztinovics, M./Gál, R./Matits, Á./Máté, L./Simonovits, A./Stahl, J. (2002) 'The Hungarian Pension System before and after the 1998 Reform', in: Fultz, E. (ed.), *Pension Reform in Central and Eastern Europe, Volume 1: Restructuring with Privatization: Case Studies of Hungary and Poland.* Budapest: ILO-CEET.

Deleeck, H./Van den Bosch, K./De Lathouwer, L. (1992) *Poverty and the Adequacy of Social Security in the EC.* Aldershot: Avebury.

Förster, M. (1994) Measurement of Poverty and Low Incomes in a Perspective of International Comparisons, *OECD Labour Market and Social Policy Occasional Paper no.14.* Paris.

Ivan Ungureanu, C. (2003) "Romania: Mother's Employment and Children Poverty", MONEE Country Analytical Report, UNICEF Innocenti Research Centre, Florence.

Margan, G. (2001) "Romanian Pension System and Reform", paper presented to the World Bank Conference "Learning from the Partners", 5-7 April, Vienna.

Máté, L. (2004) 'The Collection of Pension Contributions in Hungary', in: Fultz, E./Stanovnik, T. (eds), *Collection of Pension Contributions: Trends, Issues, and Problems in Central and Eastern Europe.* Budapest: ILO.

Milanović, B. (1998) *Income, Inequality and Poverty during the Transition from Planned to Market Economy.* Washington, D.C.: World Bank.

Mitchell, D. (1991) *Income Transfers in Ten Welfare States.* Aldershot: Avebury.

Palacios, R./Pallares-Miralles, M. (2000) International Patterns of Pension Provision, *Social Protection Discussion Paper Series, no. 9.* Washington, D.C.: The World Bank.

Stanovnik, T./Stropnik, N./Prinz, C. (eds) (2000) *Economic Well-being of the Elderly: a Comparison Across Five European countries.* Aldershot: Ashgate.

Tinios, P./Markova, E. (2001) "The Bulgarian Pension System and Reform: a Perspective from Greece", paper presented to the World Bank Conference "Learning from the Partners", 5-7 April, Vienna.

Toma, C. (2004) 'The Collection of Pension Contributions in Romania', in: Fultz, E./Stanovnik, T. (eds), *Collection of Pension Contributions: Trends, Issues, and Problems in Central and Eastern Europe.* Budapest: ILO.

Vezjak, K./Stanovnik, T. (2004) 'The Collection of Pension Contributions in Hungary', in Fultz, E./Stanovnik, T. (eds), *Collection of Pension Contributions: Trends, Issues, and Problems in Central and Eastern Europe.* Budapest: ILO.

World Bank (2001) *Hungary: Long-Term Poverty, Social Protection, and the Labour Market.* Washington, D.C.

World Bank (2002) *Bulgaria: Poverty Assessment.* Washington, D.C.

World Bank (2003) *Bulgaria: Public Expenditure Issues and Directions for Reform.* Washington, D.C.

World Bank (2003) *Romania: Poverty Assessment.* Washington, D.C.

Chapter 3

The Transition Process and Changes in Income, Income Inequality and Poverty: The Case of Bulgaria

Silviya Nikolova

Introduction

From 1992 to 2002, Bulgaria went through a difficult transition from a planned to a market economy, accompanied by years of economic instability. The prolonged transformational recession of the first half of the 1990s was followed in 1996-1997 by a severe financial crisis combining a collapse of the exchange rate, a run on the banking system and a fiscal crisis. The economy plunged into a new deep recession while inflation surged to near-hyperinflation levels. These processes have led to an increase in poverty and inequality among the Bulgarian population.

The 1996-1997 crisis resulted in a change of government in April 1997. The new administration tried, in cooperation with the IMF and other international organizations, to carry out essential reforms and lead the country out of the crisis. The Bulgarian *Lev* was pegged to the *Deutsche Mark* under a currency board arrangement and the central bank abandoned the conduct of an independent monetary policy. The reforms were instrumental in restoring macroeconomic and financial stability and the Bulgarian economy has been recovering since 1998. Absolute poverty rates started to decline with the gradual recovery in consumption levels.[1]

This chapter looks at trends in income inequality and poverty in Bulgaria during its turbulent period of transition. Our assessment is based on

---

1   World Bank (2002).

the analysis of the changes in the structure of household income, the changes in the socioeconomic structure of households and changes in income inequality and the risk of poverty. The main data sources for this analysis are the household budget surveys (HBS) conducted regularly by the National Statistical Institute (NSI), later referred to as "NSI HBS database".

1   Changes in wages and social protection expenditures

For the purpose of our study we performed a detailed statistical analysis of Bulgarian household budget survey data. Our results indicate that income inequality and poverty are strongly related to income from employment. The growing differentiation in income from employment is one of the main factors for the increasing gap between the poorest and the richest part of the population. As can be seen in Table 1, the share of wages in GDP in Bulgaria dropped from 53.0% in 1992 to 35.4% in 2004.[2]

Table 1:   Wages as per cent of GDP, 1992-2004

	'92	'93	'94	'95	'96	'97	'98	'99	'00	'01	'02	'03	'04
Share of wages in GDP	53.0	52.2	45.4	41.2	38.6	34.5	39.3	41.4	34.6	34.9	34.1	34.8	35.4

Source: NSI database.

Expenditures on pensions, measured as percentage of GDP, experienced a large decrease during the 1995-1997 period, and have since then been increasing, though they have still not reached the 1992 level (Table 2). This decrease was partly mitigated by some other social protection benefits, whose main goal was to improve the income situation of the poorest households in the country. However, welfare benefits were not indexed against inflation, so that (as can be seen in Table 2) aggregate social protection expenditures as percentage of GDP dropped in the years with high inflation rates – 1996 and 1997. Following the recovery of the Bulgarian economy, these expenditures (measured as percentage of GDP) increased back to the 1992 level. For the period 1992-1996, family benefits decreased considerably, from 2.5% to 0.9%

---

2   Note that a change in national accounts methodology was also introduced in 1994 so the data for later years are not directly comparable to those before 1994.

of GDP, and in the following years stabilized around this level. Partly as a consequence of inadequate family allowances, child poverty increased in this period. Unemployment benefits amounted to 0.8% of GDP in 1999 and 2000. Later, the entitlement rules were severed, which caused their further erosion, so that in 2003 and 2004 they amounted to only 0.3% of GDP. Low-income support benefits, as percent of GDP, slightly increased after 1999.

Table 2: Social protection expenditures, family benefits, low-income support benefits and other social benefits as per cent of GDP, 1992-2004

	Social protection expendi-tures as % of GDP	Pensions as % of GDP	Family benefits as % of GDP	Unem-ployment benefits as % of GDP	Low-income support benefits as % of GDP	All other social benefits as % of GDP
1992	14.1	9.9	2.5	0.6	0.5	0.7
1993	15.3	10.9	2.1	0.8	0.5	0.7
1994	12.9	9.7	1.7	0.6	0.4	0.6
1995	10.6	6.8	1.3	0.5	0.2	0.5
1996	9.0	6.9	0.9	0.4	0.2	0.4
1997	9.5	6.1	0.9	0.4	0.4	0.9
1998	11.3	7.9	0.9	0.4	0.2	0.8
1999	12.3	8.0	0.9	0.8	0.4	0.8
2000	14.1	9.4	0.9	0.8	0.6	0.9
2001	13.6	9.0	0.9	0.7	0.4	3.1
2002	13.4	9.0	0.8	0.7	0.7	3.1
2003	13.9	9.1	0.8	0.3	0.7	3.9
2004	13.8	9.2	0.9	0.3	0.6	3.0

Source: NSI data.

The decreasing share of wages in GDP was accompanied by a sharp and long-lasting decline in the values of average real wages and pensions (Figure 1). The lowest level was reached in 1997, when the average real wage amounted to 49.5% of its 1991 level and the average real pension amounted to 31.1% of its 1991 level. After 1998, average real wages and pensions increased slowly, though in 2004 they still remained far below their 1991 level. While the changes of real wages and pensions are broadly similar, pensions did experience a larger drop and recovered more slowly than wages.

Figure 1:   Growth of average real wages and pensions (1991=100), 1991-2004

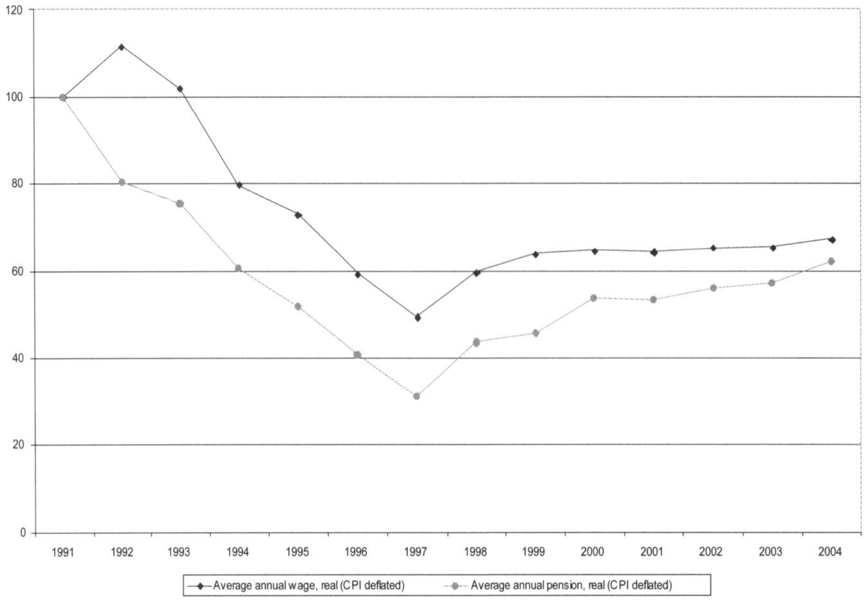

Source: NSI data.

The Bulgarian pension system was reformed, and a three-pillar system introduced in 1999-2000. The bulk of pensions are still being paid out of the general government budget where they account for the most significant part of social expenditures. Old-age pensions for normal retirement, military pensions and those for general invalidity and occupational injury are related to previous work experience and account for the greatest share in pension expenditures (Table 3). Until 1999, there was a steady growth in old-age pensions for normal retirement.[3] This rise partially reflects the ageing of the Bulgarian population. However, since 1999 the standard retirement age has been increased in several steps, and is to reach 60 years for women and 63 for men in 2009. In addition, there has been an increase in the share of pensions for general invalidity, too. The increase in the number of invalidity and social pensions can be linked to the Bulgarian labour market dynamics during the 1990s. As many people remained out of the labour market, some used the invalidity pension as a coping strategy for escaping unemployment,

---

3   In Bulgaria, early retirement is possible for employees working under hard and unhealthy conditions (labour categories I and II). However, the pensions they receive are old-age pensions which are lower than pensions for normal retirement.

whereas some remained unemployed and started receiving a pension only when they met the requirements for entitlement to a social pension.

Table 3: Recipients of pensions by pension type (thousands)

Year	Total	Old-age pension for normal retirement	General invalidity and occupational injury pensions	Military pensions	Military disablement pensions	Pensions awarded for special merit	Civilian disablement pensions	Farmers' pensions	Pensions of craftsmen, tradesmen and self-employed persons	Social pensions
1988	2326	1512	304		19	52	1	374	17	47
1989	2308	1548	289		17	49	1	338	18	48
1990	2372	1638	287		17	47	1	313	19	51
1991	2426	1769	281	51	16	2	1	286	19	52
1992	2495	1816	278	53	15	2	1	258	20	54
1993	2490	1839	276	54	15	2	1	231	19	54
1994	2472	1839	281	54	14	2	1	206	19	56
1995	2457	1843	281	54	14	3	1	182	19	60
1996	2427	1836	274	61	13	3	1	158	19	62
1997	2438	1867	265	69	13	3	1	138	19	63
1998	2434	1885	259	73	12	4	1	118	18	64
1999	2427	1897	251	79	12	4	1	101	18	64
2000	2504	1899	253	86	12	4	1	86	17	146
2001	2606	1880	279	89	12	4	1	73	17	251
2002	2646	1833	314	91	11	4	1	61	16	315
2003	2694	1781	361	93	11	4	1	50	15	378
2004	2741	1719	417	97	10	4	1	42	14	437
2005	2770	1672	455	96	10	4	1	34	13	485

Source: National Social Security Institute (2007).

As elderly unemployed have small chances for finding a new job,[4] seeking a pension for general invalidity was regarded as a possible survival strategy.

Social pensions are granted to people who do not meet the work experience requirements but do meet the retirement age requirement. Many of these people are the "losers" of the transition process, as they could not find a new job after they became unemployed. Since 2000, their number has been growing fast – after changes in the entitlement rules for this type of pension were introduced with the reform of the pension system in 2000, in particular allowing for earlier retirement.

Bulgaria's transition to a market economy brought about a collapse of the agricultural sector, as agricultural cooperatives were dismantled, but the process of land privatization was very sluggish. Some farmers went searching for a job in other economic sectors and many remained unemployed. These changes resulted in a reduction in the share of farmer pensions, their value being eroded to the level of social pensions. However, at that time farmer pensions were granted mainly to members of co-operatives and were paid on the basis of the co-operative work experience. With the land privatisation and the dismantling of co-operatives, the number of people applying for this type of pension dropped.

1.1 Pension-to-wage ratio

The ratio between average gross pension and average gross wage increased between 1992 and 1994. After 1994, the ratio decreased and reached its lowest level in 1997, when the average pension was only 29.3% of the average wage. This outcome is another confirmation of the worsening relative income position of pensioners during the transition. The pension-to-wage ratio started to increase slowly after 1998 and reached 43.4% in 2005. Another indicator, the ratio between the average old-age pension and the average gross wage did not differ significantly from the pension-to-wage ratio (see Figure 2).

---

4   About 60% of the unemployed in this group are long-term unemployed and have difficulties in re-entering the labour market (Tsanov, 2002).

Figure 2:   Changes in the pension/wage ratio, old-age pension/wage ratio, social pension/wage ratio and military pension/wage ratio in Bulgaria, 1992-2005

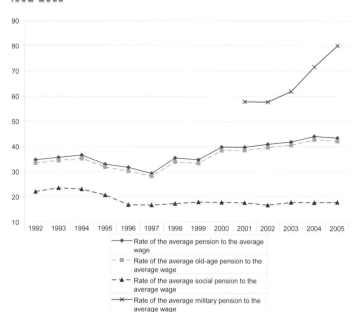

Source: National Social Security Institute (2007).

2   Changes in the structure of household income

Real net equivalent income has been recovering slowly after reaching its lowest level in 1997. However, its recovery still lagged behind that of real GDP, so that in 2002 real net equivalent income was still 40% lower than in 1993. Table 4 suggests that during the post-1997 recovery, incomes were much slower to recover than aggregate output of the economy. This is consistent with the shrinking share of wages in GDP as presented in Table 1, reflecting both the ongoing restructuring of relative prices in the economy but also the income policy in this period. The most important economic effect of the 1996-1997 crisis was the visible decrease in the living standard of the population.[5] After the introduction of the currency board, the Bulgarian economic policy was under very strong influence of the IMF. While gross profits increased, Bulgarian authorities were not allowed to raise wages in order to retain stable growth.

---

5   See Tsanov (2002).

Table 4:   Real net equivalent income and real GDP per capita

	1993	1994	1995	1996	1997	1998	1999	2000	2001	2002
Real GDP per capita	100	100.3	104.7	93.8	80.2	83.4	85.4	90.0	93.6	98.2
Real net equivalent income	100	84.9	77.2	53.1	45.5	57.3	58.3	54.8	51.3	60.4

Source: For GDP: Authors' computations based on NSI data. For real net income: Authors' computations
         based on NSI HBS database.

2.1   Income structure of households

The income structure of households depends on the activity status of their members. The period of transition in Bulgaria was accompanied by a sharp rise in unemployment; according to the National Employment Agency at the Ministry of Labour and Social Policy, the number of registered unemployed increased from 576.9 thousand in 1992 to 682.8 thousand in 2000. It has subsequently dropped to 450.6 thousand in 2004. While unemployment decreased, the number of active (employed and unemployed) persons dropped from 3643 thousand in 1994 to 3332 thousand in 2002.

Table 5 shows the structure of household income of Bulgarian households.

Throughout the 1992-2002 period, wages and salaries, income from agriculture and pensions were the most important income source.[6] Although the share of *wages and salaries* between 1992 and 1997 dropped by more than 7 percentage points (from 41.7% in 1992 to 34.5% in 1997), it still remained the largest source of household income. In 2002 it increased again, reaching 36.4% of household disposable income. The downward trend from 1992 to 1997 was mostly caused by decreases in the number of employees and the drop in the average real wage. With the post-1997 recovery these negative trends were gradually reversed, resulting in the recovery of the share of income from wages and salaries. Interestingly, the share of wages and salaries in the low-income households increased between 1992 and 2002, indicating growth in the number of working poor; in 2003 21%[7] of the poor in Bulgaria were working poor (European Foundation for the Improvement of Living and Working Conditions, 2004).

6   The World Bank (2002) reports similar results for 2001.
7   Workers living in a household where at least one member works and where the overall
     income of the household (including social transfers and after taxation) remains below
     the poverty line (60% of median equivalized income).

Income from agriculture includes income from sales of agricultural production and in-kind income from household plots. However, the in-kind part of the income from agriculture is more than 80% during the entire period. As can be seen from Table 5, this income source was second in importance for Bulgarian households in 1992 and 1997, but in 2002 dropped to third position. This suggests a gradual change in the structure of household disposable income after 1998, with a declining relative importance of income from agriculture. The decreasing share of income from agriculture is confirmed by macro data – the share of agriculture in GDP dropped slightly from 11.5% of GDP in 1992 to 10.7% in 2002.

The share of *pensions* in total household disposable income remained fairly stable, around 20%, between 1992 and 1997 and increased to 23.6% in 2002. Despite being the main income source for households in the first decile, the share of pensions (in household disposable income) decreased for the lowest two deciles and rose for the better-off households. A possible cause for this trend is that among social security disbursements, pensions were relatively better protected against inflation and special measures were taken in this direction after 1997. In accordance with the Mandatory Social Security Code (changed in 2001), pensions are indexed every year from 1st of June, pending a decision of the Supervisory Board of the National Social Security Institute. This indexation is performed on the basis of the overall increase in disposable income in the country and the consumer price inflation during the previous calendar year.[8] The level of the minimal pension has been increased and since 2005 the upper ceiling for pensions has also been raised. Another measure undertaken in this period was the lifting (in 1997) of the ban on employing pensioners; due to this ban, until 1997 pensioners worked mainly in the informal sector of the economy.

The share of income from non-agricultural *self-employment* grew slightly during the period between 1992 and 2002 but still remained very low, because of the low share of self-employed in Bulgaria and also because of high underreporting of this income source. *Property income* increased its share in total household income from 0.2% in 1992 to 0.8% in 2002. This tendency was mainly the result of the completion of the privatization process. However, despite this growing trend, this income source was still of minor importance for households in Bulgaria.

97

---

8   The indexation is based on the increase in the disposable income and in the consumer price index in proportion 25:75; since 01.01.2007, this proportion has been changed to 50:50.

The share of *unemployment benefits* in general did not follow the growing trend of unemployment in the country and even decreased between 1992 and 1997. However, in 2002 the share of unemployment benefits increased and amounted to 0.8% of household disposable income. The increase was particularly pronounced for households in the lowest income decile.

The share of *family allowances* in total household disposable income declined during the whole period, partly due to the diminishing number of children and partly also due to the decreasing real value of family allowances. The importance of *other social benefits* rose for households in the lowest income deciles.

The share of *interfamily transfers* (which include remittances from abroad) increased from 2.6% of total household disposable income in 1992 to 4.4% in 2002. This income source was of greater importance for the low-income households during the whole period. *Other income* includes income received from companies, home-made objects and income declared by the households as "other". In relation to the latter, they show to some extent the households' participation in the informal economy. Their share increased from 6.0% in 1992 to 8.7% in 1997 and then decreased to 6.7% in 2002.

The main income sources for the poorest households in Bulgaria were pensions and wages and salaries. As seen from Table 4, pensioners were also the largest socioeconomic category among low-income households. However, the share of pensions in household disposable income in the first decile decreased from 56.9% in 1992 to 32.6% in 2002, whereas the share of wages and salaries increased from 18.4% in 1992 to 31.4% in 2002, indicating growth of the group of working poor. The poorest households in Bulgaria also relied on income from agriculture, interfamily transfers and other income sources, including home-made goods, payments from firms and incomes declared as other, which shows their involvement in the informal economy. The share of other social benefits and unemployment benefits also increased in the period between 1992 and 2002.

The incomes of the wealthiest households in Bulgaria consisted mainly of wages and salaries, income from agriculture and, to a lesser extent, pensions. The fall in the shares of wages and salaries and income from agriculture between 1992 and 2002 was matched by a rise in the importance of pensions, income from self-employment, interfamily transfers and other income. Compared to the income structure of the whole population, the wealthiest households relied heavily on income from agriculture. However, income from agriculture is in direct relation to the expenditures made on the household plot. The higher total income of the wealthiest households allows them to make larger investments in their household plot. In contrast, the lack of resources limits the possibility for the poorer households to invest in agriculture and thus to increase their total income (Atanasov et al., 1998). As will be seen in section 4.3, high differentiation in income from agriculture was one of the main determinants of the overall income inequality in Bulgaria.

Table 5:   Structure of household income

	First decile			All			Tenth decile		
	1992	1997	2002	1992	1997	2002	1992	1997	2002
Wages and salaries	18.4	21.1	31.4	41.7	34.5	36.4	39.9	31.7	36.7
Income from non-agricultural self-employment	2.3	3.4	3.0	2.0	2.8	3.6	1.5	2.5	4.0
Income from agriculture	5.9	5.4	8.5	23.7	28.1	21.4	39.1	47.3	32.5
Property income	0.1	0.3	0.3	0.2	0.5	0.8	0.1	0.5	0.7
Pensions	56.9	48.2	32.6	20.0	19.7	23.6	9.5	9.7	12.1
Unemployment benefits	1.4	1.3	3.1	0.5	0.4	0.8	0.2	0.1	0.4
Family allowances	3.7	2.5	2.3	2.5	1.3	0.8	0.8	0.3	0.2
Other social benefits	1.1	3.8	5.1	0.8	1.1	1.5	0.5	0.5	1.6
Interfamily transfers	4.2	5.4	5.6	2.6	3.0	4.4	2.2	2.2	3.9
Other	6.1	8.4	8.1	6.0	8.7	6.7	6.2	5.3	8.0
Total	100	100	100	100	100	100	100	100	100

Source: Author's computations based on NSI HBS database.

If we take a brief look at the distribution of income sources across the income deciles (Annex, Table BG1), we can see that:

- The share of wages accruing to households both in the top and bottom decile increased throughout the period.
- Wages and salaries and income from agriculture were concentrated mainly in households in the upper income deciles during the whole 1992-2002 period.
- Pensions were more evenly distributed across the income deciles; however, in 2002 their income share in households situated in the lowest two deciles decreased.
- While property income was mostly concentrated among households in the middle and upper deciles in 1992, in 2002 it was concentrated mainly in the highest four deciles.

- In the beginning of the period, unemployment benefits were concentrated mainly among the lower and middle income households. However, their targeting worsened in 2002, with 15.5% of unemployment benefits received by households in the first decile, 11% by households in the fourth decile and 11.5% by households in the tenth decile.

2.2   The coverage of social benefits

This section provides data on the percentage of households receiving different types of social benefits. Its aim is to show to what extent Bulgarian households depend on the social protection system and how this has changed during the period of transition. We turn our analysis to the coverage of pensions, unemployment benefits, child allowances and other social transfers.

As can be seen from Table 6, *pensions* have almost 100% coverage, meaning that almost all households with a pensioner receive income from pensions.

Table 6:   Coverage of pensions

	A	B
1992	61.1	99.3
1997	62.8	99.7
2002	59.9	99.8

Notes: A: Households with pensioner(s), as percentage of all households.
B: Percentage of households with pensioners that receive pensions.
Source: Author's computations based on NSI HBS database.

Family allowances in Bulgaria include allowances for children up to the age of 18, allowances for children up to one year and a one-time grant at birth. Allowances for children up to the age of 18 account for the greatest share of these benefits. In 1992 these allowances were a nearly universal benefit received by more than 95% of households with children and were not linked to household income. The National Social Security Institute paid these benefits for children of the insured persons, whereas the municipal social assistance system was responsible for payment to uninsured persons. Only children of the self-employed were excluded, if their (insured) parents did not pay contributions. In 2002 a new Family Allowances Act was introduced, relating the payment of monthly family allowances to household income. This restrictive step was made in order to achieve a reduction in the number of recipients while at the same time increasing the level of benefits, thus aiming to improve the targeting of these benefits. In accordance with the Act, only households with average monthly income below a certain threshold, set by the government, are eligible. However, despite the drop in coverage, child allowances were virtually equally distributed across the income deciles (Table 7). A possible explanation for this could be the fact that child allowances are granted on the basis of the insurance income. At the same time many of the employed in the private sector are insured on lower insurance income and they receive the rest of their wage "under the table". As a result, child allowances are received not only by families in the lower income deciles but also by those in the upper part of the income distribution who are partly in the shadow economy. This indicates that the targeting of family allowances needs further improvement. Besides, the profits of the sole traders are not taken into account when assessing the eligibility for family allowances.

There are two explanations for the relatively low coverage of family benefits in the lower income deciles. First, these benefits are granted on the condition that the child attends school. The other reason is that, up to 2004, child allowances were transferred from the National Social Security Institute to the employer (for employed persons). In cases where the employer does not remit social security contributions to the National Social Security Institute, the latter simply does not transfer child allowances to the employer. This practice was abolished in 2004, when child allowances were disbursed directly to mothers by the territorial social security offices.

The main function of *unemployment benefits* is to provide the unemployed with replacement income for a certain period after a job loss, while motivating them to actively search for a new job. The coverage of unemployment benefits in Bulgaria decreased considerably in the 1997-2002 period. This was due to changes restricting the duration of eligibility and thus limiting the number of long-term unemployed eligible for unemployment benefits. At the same time, the real value of the average unemployment benefit dropped substantially, reaching 36% of its 1991 level (Figure 3). The significant drop occurred during the turbulent years of the Bulgarian transition, characterized by high inflation. After the beginning of the recovery of the economy, the real value of the average unemployment benefit remained fairly stable. A similar trend is observed also for the replacement rate (the share of the average unemployment benefit in the average wage); it was decreasing between 1992 and 1997, and stabilized at about 33% in the years after 1997.

Table 7:   Coverage of family benefits

Income deciles	1992		1997		2002	
	A	B	A	B	A	B
1	25.0	75.9	28.1	79.7	29.0	67.5
2	18.6	90.7	23.1	89.5	25.9	63.5
3	27.2	96.8	26.9	82.8	27.0	71.4
4	38.1	100.0	31.4	94.8	26.9	77.9
5	36.2	96.4	30.6	89.0	25.2	73.6
6	37.2	100.0	29.1	91.4	27.4	73.1
7	35.9	94.0	31.4	94.8	23.8	79.4
8	30.6	97.2	38.8	94.6	23.2	72.7
9	32.9	98.7	21.5	98.1	20.3	67.2
10	16.8	97.4	18.6	93.0	12.2	74.3
All	29.9	95.4	28.0	90.8	24.1	71.9

Notes: A: Households with child(ren), as percentage of all households in the income decile.
         B: Percentage of households with child(ren) receiving family benefits.

Source: Author's computations based on NSI HBS database.

Figure 3:   Average real value of the unemployment benefit and average unem-
            ployment benefit as % of the minimum and average wage, 1991-2004

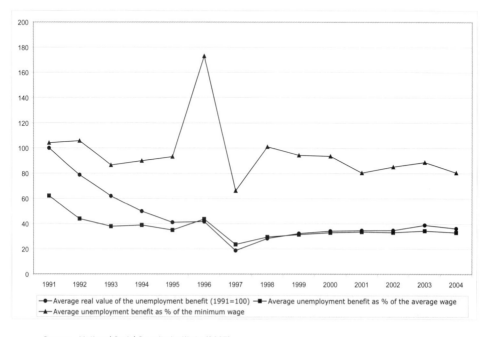

Source: National Social Security Institute (2007).

During the first years after the implementation of this social benefit for the unemployed, its average value was greater than the minimum wage and was not an incentive for searching for a new job. A similar situation was observed in 1996 when the average unemployment benefit was 173% of the minimum wage. After the changes in the entitlement rules and in the amount of the benefit, the average unemployment benefit decreased in relative terms and in 2004 represented 82% of the value of the minimum wage.

The share of households with unemployed member(s) receiving unemployment benefits more than halved in 2002 as compared to 1992, despite the rising unemployment rate (Table 8).

Table 8:   Coverage of unemployment benefits

Income deciles	1992		1997		2002	
	A	B	A	B	A	B
1	8.2	26.3	11.2	44.4	17.5	16.0
2	3.5	12.5	8.3	25.0	11.5	18.2
3	3.5	50.0	8.7	33.3	6.0	15.9
4	4.3	20.0	9.1	22.7	4.6	15.4
5	2.6	16.7	7.0	29.4	5.6	18.8
6	3.0	28.6	6.6	18.8	4.6	10.7
7	3.0	42.9	6.2	20.0	6.3	16.7
8	3.9	44.4	6.2	20.0	4.6	17.6
9	4.3	60.0	5.0	41.7	2.8	25.0
10	1.3	66.7	4.6	18.2	1.8	20.0
All	3.8	33.3	7.3	27.8	6.5	14.0

Notes: A: Households with unemployed member(s), as percentage of all households in income decile.
          B: Percentage of households with unemployed member(s) receiving unemployment benefit.
Source: Author's computations based on NSI HBS database.

The unemployment benefit system has been modified several times since the early 1990s. During most of the 1990s, this system was structured in a way that *de facto* did not motivate recipients to actively search for a job. The social safety net contributed to an increase in the number of unemployed persons in working age receiving social assistance benefits, and to an increase in the share of the long-term unemployed who were losing working habits, training and motivation for work. In order to reverse these trends, the entitlement rules were changed several times since 1997, resulting in a reduction in the duration of entitlement to unemployment benefit. At the same time, the government initiated programmes of public works and for other forms of temporary employment as well as programmes for vocational training of the unemployed. Unemployed who are eligible for assistance with monthly grants are included in programmes for employment and those who refuse participation in these programmes are excluded from assistance for a period of one year. The 2002 reform abolished the additional non-means-tested allowances for long-term unemployed which was equivalent to 60% of the minimum wage and was granted for three months to those still unemployed six months after the expiration of their unemployment benefit. Now, long-term unemployed are not eligible for unemployment benefits, nor are young people looking for their first job. Together they represent approximately half of the registered unemployed.

Our results on coverage are consistent with the data of the National Employment Agency, which show that in 1992, 39.9% of the officially registered unemployed were eligible for unemployment benefits while in 2002 this share dropped to 19.4% (Table 9).

Table 9:   Registered unemployed receiving unemployment benefits

Year	Registered unemployed	Registered unemployed receiving unemployment benefits (as percentage of all registered unemployed)
1992	499693	39.9
1993	600800	35.1
1994	537019	34.5
1995	434627	30.5
1996	422532	31.2
1997	536704	31.9
1998	466493	24.8
1999	527058	28.6
2000	693481	27.1
2001	669610	23.4
2002	655998	19.4

Source: National Employment Agency.

According to Tsanov et al. (2003) poverty among registered unemployed eligible for unemployment benefits is nearly four times lower than that among registered unemployed ineligible for unemployment benefits. The latter comprise mainly the long-term unemployed and first-time job seekers. Poverty among non-registered unemployed is also high but is approximately

1.5 times lower than that among registered unemployed not eligible for unemployment benefits. This suggests that most probably part of the non-registered unemployed have some informal employment.[9]

The share of households receiving social assistance benefits decreased from 6.4% in 1992 to 3.5% in 2002 (Table 10), as a result of the government policy of restricting rules for the eligibility for social assistance benefits. Most social assistance programmes were introduced in 1991 in a "social safety net" system. Financing comes from the state budget and includes financial support for households and individuals without other sources of income and who are below a certain poverty line, and provision of institutional care for elderly, disabled, orphans, etc. As Table 10 shows, the targeting of the social assistance benefits improved in the period observed and in 2002 these benefits were strongly concentrated in the lowest decile. However, the share of "other social benefits" which includes not only social assistance benefits but scholarships and other benefits too, and accruing to households in the tenth decile increased from 14% in 1992 to 23% in 2002. Although most scholarships[10] are not means-tested, this growth indicates a worsening in the overall targeting of "other social benefits".

Table 10:   Coverage of social assistance benefits (percentage of households receiving the benefit)

Income deciles	1992	1997	2002
1	9.5	9.9	8.4
2	4.7	7.4	2.1
3	6.9	8.7	2.8
4	6.9	10.7	3.8
5	5.2	6.6	3.8
6	6.5	2.5	3.1
7	6.5	7.0	3.8
8	6.5	2.9	2.4
9	4.7	5.8	2.8
10	6.9	3.7	1.7
All	6.4	6.5	3.5

Source: Author's computations based on NSI HBS database.

---

9   Tsanov et al. (2003).

10   There are two types of scholarships in Bulgaria: (1) scholarships linked to the educational attainment of the students and (2) scholarships for children living in poor families. The BHBS does not enable a distinction between them.

In practical terms, while the incidence of cash social transfers is higher among the poor and the average benefit received (with the exception of pensions) is higher for poor than non-poor households, cash social transfers account for a relatively small share of total household income. Accordingly, their effect on poverty reduction is rather small: only about a third of ex-ante poor households moved out of poverty as a result of social benefits.[11] This can be explained by a combination of factors: low incidence, low benefit levels and, to an extent, poor targeting. Thus, over a third of households were receiving various forms of social assistance, and 58% of those receiving child allowances were not poor before the receipt of the benefit (World Bank, 1999b).

3   Changes in the socioeconomic structure of households

Tables 11 and 12 show the structure of households according to the socio-economic status of household members, by income deciles. In 1992, *employees* accounted for 33.3% of all household members with their share dropping to 30.3% in 2002. According to the National Statistical Institute, the total number of employees was 3273 thousand in 1992 and 2978 thousand in 2002. Despite this downward trend, the share of employees in the two lowest deciles grew in 2002, which meant that the number of working poor – those with the lowest wages – increased during that period.

Between 1992 and 2002, there was almost no change in the share of *self-employed* persons. Within this period, the sharp economic crisis in 1997 did result in a drop in their share to 1.7%. In 1991 and 1997, the self-employed were fairly uniformly distributed across income deciles. In 2002, an increase in the share of self-employed in the upper income deciles and a lower share in the lower deciles were observed, indicating an improvement in their relative income position.

The share of *self-employed in agriculture* in Bulgaria remained very low and stable during the whole period, but their distribution across deciles changed. While in 1992 there were no self-employed in the lowest two

---

11   A household is classified as poor ex-ante if average household expenditure per capita net of all social transfers is less than the poverty line. The poverty line is set at two-thirds of the average per capita consumption in 1997 (World Bank, 1999b).

deciles and they were strongly concentrated in the highest deciles, in later years the percentage of self-employed in agriculture somewhat decreased in the higher deciles and increased in the lower income deciles. However, the definition of this category in the BHBS does not provide for a good estimate of the number of people actually engaged in agriculture. Namely, a very high proportion of persons are involved in agricultural activity in addition to their main occupation, and they are not counted as self-employed in agriculture. As seen from Table 5, income from agriculture is one of the main income sources for Bulgarian households. In other words, a large number of Bulgarian households continue to rely on household plots for income support. Most of these households are engaged in subsistence farming, perhaps selling a modest surplus on the market, which is complementary to other more important income sources. According to the World Bank (2002), participation in agriculture has an important positive effect on welfare. However, work on household plots is rarely the primary source of earnings for the household, or workers therein. In terms of the determinants of who has second and third jobs, access to land is only one important factor. A wide number of other contributing factors influencing the probability of being a wage worker in rural areas have been identified, ranging from ethnicity to the fact that wage employment in agriculture pays less than in other sectors of the economy (Sahn et al., 2002).

The proportion of *unemployed* household members rose from 4.7% in 1992 to 13.4% in 2002. Their share in the lower income deciles increased substantially, and in 2002 they became the largest socioeconomic group in the first decile.[12] According to data from the National Statistical Institute, the registered unemployment rate reached 16.3% in 2002.

The *pensioners'* share remained fairly stable during the period, with a small drop from 31.8% in 1992 to 31.1% in 2002. These results are confirmed by the National Social Security Institute data showing that there were 2443 thousand pensioners in 1992 and 2344 thousand in 2002.[13] Their share in the middle and upper part of the income distribution increased, particularly in

---

12   It must be noted that the Bulgarian HBS registers as unemployed those who have not worked through the survey period or have worked less than five days and consider themselves as unemployed. In this respect, those defined as unemployed include also the discouraged people who do not actively search for a new job, yet considering themselves not as inactive but as unemployed.

13   National Social Security Institute (2006).

the middle deciles. The change observed was a consequence of the measures taken by the Bulgarian authorities to improve the income position of pensioners and to partly protect pensions against inflation.

The situation of *dependants below the age of 18* is quite disturbing. There is a clear tendency of a decreasing share of children in Bulgaria. In 1992, they amounted to 21.4% of all household members but within a decade their share decreased by 3 percentage points, to 18.4%. The share of dependants up to 18 years in the upper income deciles declined; however, during the whole period they were the second-largest group of persons in the first decile. The current scheme of family allowances is poorly designed, so that these allowances do not have a real impact on children's welfare as the amounts are too low to reduce poverty.

The group of *dependants* aged 18 and above includes young people in education, elderly with no pension and inactive persons engaged in domestic work. Their share dropped from 6.2% in 1992 to 3.9% of all household members in 2002. As can be seen from Table 12, young people aged 18-29 accounted for the biggest share in this category. Dependants in the age group 30-59 include mostly women engaged in domestic work. However, as seen from Table 13, these numbers imply that the share of housewives in Bulgaria is rather low. The clue to this puzzle lies in the analysis of the income situation of Bulgarian households. Namely, after 1989 women engaged in domestic work had to move into the labour market and work in order to financially support their families. Women who became unemployed and could not find a new job declared themselves as long-term unemployed and discouraged. A comparison with the BLFS shows that while in 1993 103.8 thousand of the inactive women declared themselves as discouraged, in 2004 this number amounted already to 267.45 thousand. As for dependants above 60 years, this group includes persons with not enough years of service to qualify for a retirement pension and that are below the age for eligibility for an old-age social pension. That is why their share was very low.

The distribution of household members, by socio-economic status, presented in Table BG2 suggests the following :

- Employees are more concentrated in households in the higher income deciles.
- The concentration of self-employed in households in the highest deciles increased between 1992 and 2002, indicating improvement in their relative income position.
- In contrast, the concentration of self-employed in agriculture shifted from households in the upper to the lower deciles.
- Roughly one quarter of all unemployed lived in households situated in the first income decile.
- The pensioners' concentration shifted from households in the lowest to the middle income deciles.
- While in 1992 dependants below age 18 were situated mainly in households in the middle of the income distribution, in the following years they shifted to the lower deciles.

Table 11: **The socioeconomic structure of households: first decile, tenth decile, and all households**

	First decile			All			Tenth decile		
	1992	1997	2002	1992	1997	2002	1992	1997	2002
Employees	14.4	14.0	16.0	33.3	30.2	30.3	43.6	36.4	43.1
Self-employed	1.8	1.5	0.7	2.0	1.7	2.1	1.9	1.5	2.8
Self-employed in agriculture	0.0	0.6	0.8	0.7	0.9	0.9	2.6	1.6	1.3
Unemployed	12.0	20.0	33.1	4.7	10.7	13.4	2.4	8.6	6.0
Pensioners	42.9	30.4	20.8	31.8	31.3	31.1	31.0	35.4	33.3
Dependants aged less than 18	20.3	24.9	23.3	21.4	20.2	18.4	13.5	13.5	9.9
Dependants aged 18 and above	8.7	8.6	5.4	6.2	5.1	3.9	5.0	3.1	3.6
Total	100	100	100	100	100	100	100	100	100

Source: Author's computations based on NSI HBS database.

Table 12:   The socioeconomic structure of households, by income deciles

Decile	Employees	Self-employed	Self-employed in agriculture	Unem-ployed	Pension-ers	Depend-ants age < 18	Depend-ants age ≥ 18	All
				1992				
1	14.4	1.8	0.0	12.0	42.9	20.3	8.7	100
2	19.4	1.9	0.0	5.2	51.5	17.8	4.3	100
3	28.7	0.7	0.2	4.3	35.9	21.9	8.4	100
4	32.7	3.1	0.7	5.2	24.4	27.8	6.2	100
5	37.1	1.9	0.2	4.7	27.1	24.1	5.0	100
6	38.5	1.3	0.4	2.9	26.3	23.5	6.9	100
7	37.9	3.2	0.4	3.4	27.2	23.1	4.7	100
8	37.5	1.8	1.2	3.7	30.2	19.4	6.3	100
9	42.9	2.4	1.0	3.7	21.6	22.4	6.0	100
10	43.6	1.9	2.6	2.4	31.0	13.5	5.0	100
All	33.3	2.0	0.7	4.7	31.8	21.4	6.2	100
				1997				
1	14.0	1.5	0.6	20.0	30.4	24.9	8.6	100
2	17.6	0.6	0.9	12.3	43.8	19.3	5.6	100
3	26.2	1.6	0.9	11.3	34.9	19.2	6.0	100
4	26.9	1.2	0.3	10.0	33.8	22.3	5.6	100
5	34.2	1.8	1.0	10.4	25.6	22.2	4.8	100
6	36.2	0.9	0.4	9.2	28.7	20.2	4.4	100
7	34.0	2.6	1.5	8.8	28.1	20.2	4.8	100
8	38.5	2.6	0.6	7.5	22.4	25.0	3.4	100
9	38.2	2.3	0.9	9.2	30.0	15.1	4.3	100
10	36.4	1.5	1.6	8.6	35.4	13.5	3.1	100
All	30.2	1.7	0.9	10.7	31.3	20.2	5.1	100
				2002				
1	16.0	0.7	0.8	33.1	20.8	23.3	5.4	100
2	20.2	0.9	0.4	19.2	34.0	20.9	4.4	100
3	24.1	2.5	1.6	15.0	33.5	21.0	2.4	100
4	25.8	3.1	1.1	12.2	34.8	18.3	4.8	100
5	30.4	0.7	0.1	12.0	32.7	20.2	3.8	100
6	30.5	2.5	0.3	10.3	31.7	21.3	3.4	100
7	34.7	2.1	0.8	11.0	32.2	15.1	4.1	100
8	36.9	2.6	1.1	8.3	30.4	17.9	2.8	100
9	41.4	3.4	1.1	7.3	27.4	15.6	3.8	100
10	43.1	2.8	1.3	6.0	33.3	9.9	3.6	100
All	30.3	2.1	0.9	13.4	31.1	18.4	3.9	100

Source: Author's computations based on the NSI HBS database.

Table 13: The share of dependants, by age groups and gender
(as percentage of all persons)

	Less than 18	18 to 29	30 to 59	60 +	All
1992					
Men	10.9	1.4	0.0	0.0	12.3
Women	10.5	1.0	0.1	3.7	15.3
All	21.4	2.4	0.1	3.7	27.6
1997					
Men	10.3	1.5	0.0	0.0	11.8
Women	9.9	1.6	0.1	1.9	13.5
All	20.2	3.1	0.1	1.9	25.3
2002					
Men	9.1	1.2	0.0	0.0	10.3
Women	9.3	1.2	0.1	1.4	12.0
All	18.4	2.4	0.1	1.4	22.3

Source: Author's computations based on NSI HBS database.

4   Income inequality

4.1   Income inequality and human capital

Individual human capital endowment has a direct relation to income in-equality, as wage income and employment status depend strongly on the educational level attained. The problem of unemployment in Bulgaria is accentuated by a skills gap, i.e. low or inadequate human capital endow-ment. Many of the unemployed will not be able to find a job even if there are enough job vacancies because their educational attainments fall short of those required by employers. Young, low-educated persons, especially those from ethnic minorities, face the highest risks of unemployment. The level of education and, therefore, earning opportunities of the poor appear remark-ably lower than those for the population at large (World Bank, 1999b).

According to the World Bank (2002) more than 60% of individuals from non-poor households have secondary or higher education, while the same share for individuals from poor households is below 30%. In 2003, 78.2% of the persons living in households with an unemployed head without primary education[14] were found to be poor, while for those with primary education the percentage was 46.6 and the share of university graduates in this category was 8.2% (Tsanov et al., 2003).

As seen from Table 14, the attained educational level of household members aged 25-64 in Bulgaria improved between 1992 and 2002:

- The shares of persons (aged 25-64) with only primary and basic education decreased from 4.1% and 31.5%, respectively, in 1992 to 2.3% and 20.9%, respectively, in 2002. This trend was observed across all income deciles.

- The share of those with a secondary and tertiary level of education increased from 47.9% and 16.5%, respectively, in 1992 to 58.0.% and 18.8%, respectively, in 2002. The share of household members with secondary education increased in all deciles, while the share of persons aged 25-64 with attained tertiary educational level decreased in the lower three decile groups and increased in the higher decile groups.

- The concentration of persons with tertiary education in the highest three deciles increased by 2002 as compared to 1992.

Education and training appear to be the factors most strongly affecting the incidence of unemployment and poverty. A drop-out from school is not only a consequence of poverty,[15] but it also creates risks for the next generation to fall into the poverty trap. The most serious problems in this respect occur within the minority groups, particularly the Roma population. The share of persons above age 18 without completed secondary education varies across ethnic groups. Their share is 19% among Bulgarians, 47% among Turks and 80% among Roma. Even with formally equal access to education, the indirect factors, such as cultural traditions and specific opportunity costs, prove to be an obstacle for social equity (World Bank, 2002).

---

14   The Bulgarian system of education includes four educational levels – primary, basic, secondary and tertiary. "Primary education" refers to at most 4 years of schooling, "basic education" to 8 years of schooling and "secondary education" to 11 or 12 years of schooling.

15   The major part of the drop-outs in Bulgaria are children from extremely poor families (World bank, 2002).

Table 14: Attained educational level of household members aged 25-64 years, by income deciles, 1992 and 2002

Decile	1992				Decile	2002			
	Primary or less	Basic	Secondary	Tertiary	All		Primary or less	Basic	Secondary	Tertiary	All
1	11.3	34.7	41.1	12.9	100	1	9.6	33.5	51.6	5.3	100
2	6.3	31.0	50.8	11.9	100	2	4.0	29.6	58.2	8.2	100
3	3.3	28.9	52.7	15.2	100	3	2.1	21.8	65.0	11.1	100
4	3.4	30.9	51.0	14.7	100	4	2.5	21.6	59.5	16.4	100
5	3.8	29.0	51.5	15.7	100	5	1.3	18.5	63.5	16.7	100
6	3.1	27.3	52.0	17.5	100	6	1.3	20.7	59.6	18.5	100
7	2.9	31.3	48.8	17.0	100	7	0.7	18.3	56.5	24.5	100
8	2.8	35.8	42.8	18.6	100	8	0.9	14.9	60.6	23.5	100
9	3.1	30.7	47.4	18.8	100	9	0.5	14.0	56.2	29.4	100
10	4.9	35.9	40.1	19.1	100	10	0.5	17.7	50.9	30.9	100
All	4.1	31.5	47.9	16.5	100	All	2.3	20.9	58.0	18.8	100

Source: Author's computations based on NSI HBS database.

Table 15 presents the changes in the relative income position of the labour-active persons in Bulgaria. The differences between the returns to education increased over the transition period. While the relative equivalized income for persons with primary or less education dropped between 1992 and 2002, that of persons with secondary education remained fairly stable. Only the relative income position of persons with tertiary education improved during this period.

Table 15: Relative equivalized income by education levels of labour-active persons aged between 25 and 64 years

Education level	1992	1997	2002
Primary or less	0.94	0.84	0.61
Basic	1.03	0.98	0.91
Secondary	0.97	1.00	0.98
Tertiary	1.04	1.08	1.20
All	1.00	1.00	1.00

Source: BHS 1992, 1997, 2002.

4.2 Income inequality and income distribution

We use two measures of income inequality – the Gini coefficient and the top 20%/bottom 20% ratio. They are presented in Table 16, which also shows inequality measures based on household expenditures.

In 1992, the wealthiest 20% of Bulgarian households received on average 3.7 times the income received by the poorest 20%. This ratio increased to 4.3 in 1997 and dropped to 3.9 in 2002. The same trend is shown by the Gini coefficients, indicating the highest income inequality in 1997.

The inequality measures based on household consumption[16] show an increase in inequality in Bulgaria. During the whole period income inequality exceeded expenditure inequality, indicating that measures based on income overestimate the inequality in Bulgaria, due to income underreporting. The greatest difference was in 1997 when massive participation in the informal economy was one of the coping strategies for the Bulgarian households during the hyperinflation crisis.

16   Household consumption includes expenditures on food, beverages and non-food items. Repayment of loans and interest relief funds, savings, other transfers as well as expenses on household production activities are excluded.

Table 16: Distribution of net income across income quintiles and distribution of expenditures across expenditure quintiles

Incomes				Expenditures			
Quintile	1992	1997	2002	Quintile	1992	1997	2002
1	9.57	8.85	9.43	1	11.27	10.44	10.34
2	13.94	13.23	13.66	2	14.99	14.60	14.46
3	17.94	17.17	17.53	3	18.30	17.94	17.92
4	23.09	22.73	22.80	4	22.39	22.51	22.50
5	35.46	38.02	36.58	5	33.04	34.51	34.79
Top 20% / bottom 20%	3.70	4.30	3.88	Top 20% / bottom 20%	2.93	3.30	3.36
Gini coefficient	0.260	0.290	0.272	Gini coefficient	0.218	0.240	0.245

Source: Author's computations based on NSI HBS database.

4.3 *Decomposition of inequality by income components*

To examine the contribution of the different income sources to the overall inequality, the Rao (1969) decomposition will be used:

$$G = \sum s_k C_k$$

where G is the Gini coefficient

s_k is the share of income source k in total income

C_k the coefficient of concentration of income source k

The decomposition of income inequality in Bulgaria is presented in Table 17.

Pensions were in 1992 and 1997 an absolute income equalizer, which means that poor households received more of this income source – in absolute terms – than the rich ones. In 2002, their concentration coefficient became positive but remained very low, so that pensions became a relative income equalizer in this year, suggesting that for the poor households this income source represented a greater share of household income than for the rich households.

Unemployment benefits were an absolute income equalizer in 1997 and 2002, and a relative one in 1997.

Table 17:   Decomposition of income inequality

Income sources	1992	1997	2002
	Concentration coefficients		
Wages and salaries	0.3589	0.4081	0.3486
Income from non-agricultural self-employment	0.1549	0.1913	0.1783
Income from agriculture	0.4319	0.4607	0.4687
Property income	0.0481	0.1385	0.2028
Pensions	-0.0695	-0.0225	0.0475
Unemployment benefits	-0.0612	0.0078	-0.0136
Family allowances	0.0296	0.0236	-0.0665
Other social benefits	0.1155	-0.0694	0.0528
Interfamily transfers	0.1027	0.1163	0.1553
Other	0.2476	0.1761	0.2681
Total	0.2600	0.2902	0.2715
	Income shares		
Wages and salaries	0.4166	0.3453	0.3638
Income from non-agricultural self-employment	0.0201	0.0276	0.0362
Income from agriculture	0.2368	0.2808	0.2143
Property income	0.0023	0.0052	0.0077
Pensions	0.2001	0.1967	0.2361
Unemployment benefits	0.0048	0.0039	0.0079
Family allowances	0.0247	0.0126	0.0075
Other social benefits	0.0083	0.0110	0.0154
Interfamily transfers	0.0263	0.0298	0.0438
Other	0.0595	0.0867	0.0669
Total	1.0000	1.0000	1.0000

Source: Author's computations based on NSI HBS database.

In 2002, the changes in the Bulgarian legislation regarding *family allowances* achieved their purpose – this income source became an absolute income equalizer and was received to a greater extent by poorer households. The concentration coefficients for 1992 and 1997 were also much lower than the Gini, but positive, and thus in these years family allowances acted as a relative income equalizer.

Despite their low level, *other social benefits* contributed to the overall reduction in income inequality in the sense that inequality would have been greater without this income source. However, these social benefits were not targeted only towards the poor, and they were an absolute income equalizer only in 1997.

Interfamily transfers also can be seen as a relative income equalizer – although positive, their concentration coefficients were far below the value of the Gini coefficient and, as already seen, they have a greater importance for households in the lower deciles.

The concentration coefficient of income from self-employment increased in 1997 compared to 1992 and then decreased again in 2002.

Clearly, the main contributors to overall income inequality during the period 1992-2002 were wages and salaries and income from agriculture, and their concentration coefficients were very high and by far exceeded the values of the Gini coefficients of income inequality. It thus appears that one of the important characteristics of the poorest households is their inability to engage even in subsistence farming.

5   Risk of poverty

As already seen, the economic changes in Bulgaria during the 1990s resulted in an increase in income inequality and growth in unemployment. According to World Bank estimates, in 1997 over 36% of the population in Bulgaria or some 3 million people were living in poverty[17] (World Bank, 1999b).

This section will address the following question: how did transition affect income poverty of the vulnerable population groups – unemployed, pensioners, children, dependants below age 18 and those aged 60 and above? The incidence of poverty is measured by using three poverty lines – 40%, 50% and 60% of median household equivalent income.

As seen in Table 18, the risk of income poverty for the *total population* had slightly increased in 1997 as compared to 1992 followed by a decrease in 2002. However, for all poverty lines, the lowest poverty rates were recorded in 1992, which means that the risk of poverty for the Bulgarian population increased in the observed period of time.

The poverty incidence among *unemployed* persons was much higher than that for the total population. This is in line with other studies, which show that the unemployed are extremely poor even after accounting for the benefits received: according to Sahn et al. (2002), 41% of households that were recipients of unemployment benefits are considered to be poor, and

---

17   The poverty line is defined at two-thirds of the mean per capita consumption in 1997.

55% of rural households that were recipients of unemployment benefits were poor in 2001. That suggests that income support for unemployment has only a modest impact on poverty reduction. For the unemployed, the risk of living in poverty fell in 1997 compared to 1992 but then slightly increased in 2002, if we consider only the 40% and 50% poverty lines. This trend is influenced by policy measures for unemployment reduction discussed previously in section 2.2. In 2002, 29.2% of all unemployed in Bulgaria lived in households whose household equivalent income was lower than 60% of the median household equivalent income and 10.3% of all unemployed lived in "extreme" poverty, with household equivalent income lower than 40% of the median household equivalent income.

Table 18: Incidence of income poverty (in per cent)

Poverty line as % of median equivalent household income	1992	1997	2002
All persons			
40	2.1	4.4	3.3
50	6.3	8.4	6.6
60	12.6	14.8	13.2
Unemployed			
40	10.2	10.0	10.3
50	20.2	16.4	17.8
60	27.6	24.1	29.2
Pensioners			
40	1.5	2.4	1.1
50	7.4	7.4	3.5
60	18.4	16.7	10.1
Children aged 0-14			
40	2.5	7.7	4.1
50	6.4	12.0	7.9
60	10.5	17.5	16.9
Persons aged 60+			
40	1.8	2.4	0.8
50	8.5	7.6	3.1
60	19.6	17.4	9.8

Source: Author's computations based on NSI HBS database.

Unlike those for the total population and for the unemployed persons, poverty rates among *pensioners* in Bulgaria show different trends, depending on the poverty line used. Notably, in 2002 the share of poor pensioners was lower than that in 1992 for all three poverty lines. Besides, the poverty rate for pensioners was lower than the poverty rate for the total population. This means that by the end of this period, pensioners in Bulgaria were relatively better off than in 1992; this was the result of the government policy to raise pensions and improve pension protection against inflation. In 2002, only 1.1% of all pensioners lived in households with a household equivalent income less than 40% of the median equivalent household income and 10.1% lived in households with a household equivalent income less than 60% of the median household equivalent income.

Poverty among children (*dependants below age 18*) followed poverty trends for the total population for the lower two poverty lines (40% and 50% of the median household equivalent income), meaning that the incidence of poverty increased between 1992 and 1997, followed by a decrease between 1997 and 2002. However, for the upper poverty line (60% of the median household equivalent income), the incidence of child poverty increased steadily between 1992 and 2002. Overall, the incidence of poverty measured against the three poverty lines was greater in 2002 compared to its 1992 levels, clearly showing increasing poverty among children in Bulgaria. One of the reasons is the low level of family allowances and the lack of adequate inflation protection for these benefits. In 2002, 17.3% of all children lived in households with an equivalent income less than 60% of the median equivalent income and 4.3% lived in the poorest households – with a household equivalent income below 40% of the median household equivalent income (see Table 19).

How does child poverty differ for children living in single-parent and in two-parent households? The most disadvantaged children in Bulgaria are those in single-parent families (almost exclusively headed by single women) and, to some extent, children born out-of-wedlock and children with very young mothers. They have a higher relative risk of poverty and tend to suffer disproportionately from malnutrition and ineffective food balance, with long-term negative effects on their health, and have a higher risk of being placed in child-raising institutions.[18]

In 1992 and 2000, the risk of poverty among children aged 0-14 years living in two-parent households was slightly lower than that for all children.

---

18   Gantcheva and Kolev (2001).

In contrast, the risk of poverty among children aged 0-14 living in single-parent households was considerably higher than the poverty rates of all children and of children living in two-parent households. Single-parent families represented 8% of the regular beneficiaries of Social Assistance Centres in 1995, 7% being single mothers and 1% widows or divorced.

Large families (with three or more children) are also found to be at a high risk of poverty. According to Noncheva (1997), the number of children per family is the most important factor determining the risk of poverty. More than two thirds of the families with three and more children live below the poverty line,[19] which is the highest poverty rate among all groups. On the other hand, these families represent 21% of households living in extreme poverty[20] receiving regular social benefits but account for only 4.5% of all families. Families with three or more children are of Roma or Turkish origin mostly. In these cases, poverty-related risks consist not only of the low income level, but also of the lack of family planning and family counselling programmes, as well as of the low quality of child care provided (Noncheva, 1997).

Table 19: Incidence of income poverty among dependants and children (in per cent)

Poverty line as % of median equivalent household income	Dependants below age 18			Children 0-14 years living in single parent households		
	1992	1997	2002	1992	1997	2002
40	2.5	7.1	4.3	0.8	11.2	11.8
50	6.3	11.5	8.6	4.1	16.9	18.1
60	11.0	16.9	17.3	13.2	24.7	27.8
Poverty line as % of median equivalent household income	Dependants below age 18			Children 0-14 years living in two-parent households		
	1992	1997	2002	1992	1997	2002
40	3.5	9.6	6.9	0.3	7.0	2.9
50	9.4	13.5	11.0	6.7	11.0	6.2
60	14.8	20.9	17.6	10.1	16.1	15.1

Source: Author's computations based on NSI HBS database.

---

19   Two thirds of the average household's expenditures (Noncheva, 1997).
20   Relative poverty line set as 50% of the average household expenditures (Noncheva, 1997).

The relative income position of *dependants aged 18 and above* is shown in Table 19. After the fairly large increase in 1997, their risk of income poverty diminished in 2002 but remained higher than its 1992 level, for all poverty lines. The poverty incidence among dependants aged 18 and above was considerably higher than that for the total population.

Table 20: **Incidence of income poverty among married and non-married persons aged 60 and above (in per cent)**

Poverty line as % of median equivalent household income	Non-married men aged 60 years and above			Non-married women aged 60 years and above		
	1992	1997	2002	1992	1997	2002
40	1.2	2.9	1.4	5.7	4.8	2.0
50	7.1	7.7	4.8	26.5	15.4	7.0
60	23.8	15.4	9.5	40.3	31.4	18.0
Poverty line as % of median equivalent household income	Married men aged 60 years and above			Married women aged 60 years and above		
	1992	1997	2002	1992	1997	2002
40	0.6	1.3	0.1	1.2	1.6	0.2
50	3.9	4.4	1.0	4.4	4.5	1.6
60	1.4	12.4	5.4	14.8	11.5	7.3

Source: Author's computations based on NSI HBS database.

The risk of income poverty among married and non-married (including widows, never married, separated, divorced) women aged 60 years and above increased steadily between 1992 and 2002 (see Table 20). The poverty incidence among non-married women was much higher than among married women. For example, in 2002 7.3% of married women aged 60 years and above and 18.0% of non-married women aged 60 years and above lived in households with an equivalent income less than 60% of the median equivalent income.

Similar trends were observed for married and non-married men aged 60 years and above, yet the risk of poverty was lower than that for women. In 2002, 5.4% of married men aged 60 years and above and 9.5% of non-married men aged 60 years and above lived in households with an equivalent income less than 60% of the median equivalent income.

5.1 Poverty among the Roma ethnic minority in Bulgaria

The Bulgarian household budget survey does not allow for an analysis of poverty among the Roma minority. Thus, this section provides only a brief review of the literature dealing with Roma poverty in Bulgaria.

According to the 2001 Census, Roma account for 4.68% of the population of Bulgaria. However, they are one of the groups most vulnerable to poverty. During the central-planning system, many Roma were employed in agriculture and other publicly supported low-skilled jobs. With the collapse of the communist system and the land restitution these opportunities virtually vanished, contributing to high poverty levels among the Roma in the rural areas. The economic situation of Roma therefore deteriorated sharply during the transition. Employment among the Roma minority was dominated by occasional jobs without proper contracts (Ivanov and Zheliazkova, 2002), and their unemployment rates in the 1990s were far above the country's average. In 1998, for instance, unemployment among Roma was reputedly between 80% and 90%. Some of the unemployed Roma were engaged in different spheres of the shadow economy, but this was sporadic, payments were extremely low and irregular. Some of their activities were illegal (e.g. production and bottling of alcohol, trading with currency or stolen goods, drug-selling, etc). A significant number of Roma women were not registered as unemployed for different reasons such as lack of regular address registration, passing from one maternity to another, higher incidence of disabilities, irregular registration with the social services, etc.[21] A study of poverty jointly undertaken by the Bulgarian NSI and the Ministry of Labour and Social Affairs (Tsanov et al., 2003) found that more than 60% of Roma households lived in poverty.[22] This share was 6.7 times higher than that for the Bulgarians and 2.7 times higher than the poverty rate of the Turkish community. 76.3% of the Roma households with one child were found to live in poverty. Paradoxically, poverty levels decreased with the increasing number of children; this occurred only among the Roma minority. A possible explanation is that, if entitled to social assistance, families with more than two children received more social welfare benefits, including child allowances. In general, Roma were found not only to account for the largest share in the overall poor population but were also found to be the poorest in absolute terms.[23]

21   Ivanov and Zheliazkova (2002).
22   The poverty line defined as 60% of the median household equivalent expenditure.
23   Tsanov et al. (2003).

A World Bank poverty study also showed that as a result of the high unemployment rates among Roma, they suffered from higher poverty rates compared to the non-Roma population of the country. More than 84% of the Roma in Bulgaria were living in poverty in 1997[24] (World Bank, 1999a). The study shows that even when controlling for all other socio-demographic factors,[25] Roma households were still likely to consume only two-thirds of that of non-Roma households. A Roma individual was found to be 10 times more likely to be poor than an ethnic Bulgarian. Roma were also found by the World Bank (2002) to account for almost three quarters of the poverty depth index[26] in 2001. This study also showed that Roma are less educated – over 80% not reaching secondary school. Secondary enrolments for Roma remained in the single digits, at 6%, in comparison with a national level of 46%. The main factors keeping children out of school relate to economic circumstances, demand and motivation of parents and students, and specific issues facing ethnic minorities such as language, and social exclusion in the case of Roma.[27]

The access to basic services is part of the quality of life and could be directly linked to poverty. In this respect, according to the World Bank (1999a) four out of five Roma households were found to lack access to modern sanitation facilities, and only one household in four had access to public sewage. Only one Roma household in ten had access to a telephone. Less than one third of Roma households used upgraded cooking facilities, such as electric or gas stoves, in comparison to three quarters among the non-Roma households. Three out of four Roma households were still using coal or wood for cooking, and virtually all households used coal and wood for heating. Roma were more likely to fall through the cracks of the health system than other groups, because they lack necessary identification and registration papers. The lack of information and poor communication with providers also meant that many Roma were not signed up with primary care physicians (World Bank, 1999a). Roma are more susceptible to health problems stemming from overcrowding, lack of sanitation and substandard housing conditions in settlements. Reports of outbreaks of communicable diseases, including hepatitis, polio, diphtheria and tuberculosis in Roma neighbourhoods are not uncommon (World Bank, 2002).

---

24 The poverty line is defined as two-thirds mean per capita consumption in 1997.

25 Such as age, education and employment status of the household head, household size, residential area.

26 Measured as the difference between the poverty line and the average income of the poor.

27 World Bank (2002).

According to Ivanov and Zheliazkova (2002), the income sources of the Roma were indicative of the degree to which they were dependent on social assistance; 49% of the respondents in the survey reported social benefits as a source of income during the last six months, 39% mentioned old-age pensions, 34% child allowances and 32% were engaged in some temporary non-contracted job. Only 22% of the respondents mentioned work under a regular labour contract as a source of income during the last six months and 6% had a regular wage without a labour contract. Despite the high unemployment rates, unemployment benefits were mentioned only by 8.3% as an income source; most of the unemployed Roma were long-term unemployed and were not entitled to unemployment benefits anymore. Roma families' income did not suffice to cover the basic needs. The average income of Roma families with three and more children hardly reached 54% of the average income for the country in 2002. The study also reveals that 38% of the respondents were constantly starving, 27% lived in starvation 1-2 days every month and 10% starved 1-2 days during the year; 24% of the Roma claimed that they had never starved. The share of those starving was found to be substantially higher in the villages and small towns than in bigger cities and the capital. Most Roma families entitled to social benefits could only rely on child allowances (which are not generous) or (a selected few) on the pension of some of their older parents. Therefore social assistance, pensions and occasional job(s) without contract were found to be the main income sources for Roma in Bulgaria. When asked about the material status of their families, 49% defined it as poor, 30% as miserable, 20% determined it as average, and hardly 0.6% as rich. Most of the Roma living in poverty and misery were in rural areas or remote regions (Ivanov and Zheliazkova, 2002).

6   Concluding remarks

Wages and salaries, income from agriculture and pensions were the most important income sources for Bulgarian households. However, the share of incomes from employment dropped in the 1992-2002 period, due to the overall decrease in the number of employed persons in the economy and a decrease in real wages. Incomes from agriculture followed a similar path, while the importance of pensions as a source of income has increased. Despite their slight rise, the shares of income from self-employment and property have still remained at fairly low levels. The share of interfamily transfers in household income grew and their importance for the low-income deciles has increased.

The poorest households in Bulgaria – those in the first income decile – have mainly relied on pensions and wages and salaries. Despite an increasing share of social benefits (unemployment benefits, family benefits and other social benefits) in the income of the poorest households, this share still remains very low. The income of the wealthiest households has consisted mainly of wages and salaries, income from agriculture and pensions.

The socioeconomic structure of households changed substantially between 1992 and 2002. The share of employed household members decreased and the proportion of self-employed remained fairly unchanged, whereas the share of the unemployed rose considerably. There has been a slight drop in the share of pensioners accompanied by a reduction in the share of dependants.

Employees have been more concentrated in households situated in the upper income deciles. While the concentration of self-employed in households in the highest deciles has increased between 1992 and 2002, indicating improvement in their income position, the concentration of self-employed in agriculture has shifted from households in the upper to the lower deciles. The concentration of pensioners shifted from households in the lowest to the middle income deciles, indicating a relative improvement in their income position. The concentration of dependants below age 18 shifted from households in the middle to the lower deciles.

While in 1992 in Bulgaria the highest risk of falling into the category of the poorest was faced by pensioners and children, in 2002 unemployed and children were heavily exposed to the risk of living in poor households.

Inequality in Bulgaria reached its peak in 1997 and decreased in the following years, yet remaining higher than its 1992 level. Social transfers have somewhat contributed to a reduction in the overall income inequality in 1992 as well as in 2002.

The risk of poverty for the total population increased between 1992 and 1997 and subsequently in 2002 fell almost to its 1992 level. In 2002, 13.2% of the total population lived in households with an equivalent income less than 60% of the median household equivalent income and 3.3% in households with an equivalent income below 40% of the median household disposable income. The incidence of poverty among unemployed persons has been much higher than that among the population as a whole and among the other population groups. It is only among pensioners and persons aged 60 and above that the risk of living in poverty dropped in 2002 compared to 1992. The incidence of poverty among children has increased in this time period. Their risk of living in poverty has been much higher than the average, particularly for children living in single-parent households The relative income position of dependants above age 18 also worsened between 1992 and 2002.

The high unemployment rates among the Roma minority resulted in a high risk of living in poverty for individuals in this ethnic group. The incidence of poverty among Roma has been the highest among all ethnic communities in Bulgaria and Roma households are also the poorest in absolute terms. Poverty among poor Roma communities is multidimensional, encompassing substandard housing conditions, low education levels, and poor health status, all compounded by social exclusion and discrimination within society (World Bank, 2002).

126

7 References

Ackrill, Robert/Dobrinsky, Rumen/Markov Nikolay/Pudney, Steven (2002) 'Social Security, Poverty and Economic Transition: An Analysis for Bulgaria 1992–96', *Economics of Planning*, 35 (1): 19-46.

Atanasov, Atanas/Toneva, Zdravka/Todorova, Sasha (1998) 'The Economic Situation in 1992-1997 and Bulgarian Pensioners' Living Standard', *Statistics* 6/98, National Statistical Institute, Sofia (in Bulgarian)

European Foundation for the Improvement of Living and Working Conditions (2004) "Working Poor in the European Union", Seminar Report, Brussels, 1-2 July 2004 [Online]. Available at: http://www.eurofound.europa.eu/pubdocs/2004/127/en/1/ef04127en.pdf

Gantcheva, Roumiana/Kolev, Alexandre (2001) *Children in Bulgaria: Growing Impoverishment and Unequal Opportunities*; Innocenti Working Paper No. 84, UNICEF, Innocenti Research Centre, Italy

Górniak, Jaroslaw (2001a) 'Poverty in Transition: Lessons from Eastern Europe and Central Asia', in: Grinspun, A, (ed.), *Choices for the Poor. Lessons from National Poverty Strategies*. New York: UNDP.

Hassan, Fareed M.A./Peters, R. Kyle (1995) *Social Safety Net and the Poor during the Transition: The Case of Bulgaria*, World Bank Policy Research Working Paper Series No. 1450.

Ivanov, Andrey/Zheliazkova, Antonina (2002) *The Roma in Central and Eastern Europe: Avoiding the Dependency Trap*. Bratislava: UNDP, Regional Bureau for Europe and the Commonwealth of Independent States.

National Social Security Institute (2007) *Demography, Economy and Social Insurance 1986 – 2006.* Sofia

National Statistical Institute of Bulgaria, *Statistical Yearbook* (various editions), Sofia.

Noncheva, Theodora (1997) *Poverty in Bulgaria: Researches and Debates*, Center for The Study of Democracy, Sofia [Online].
Available at: http://www.warwick.ac.uk/russia/BGREP.DOC

Rao, V.M. (1969) 'Two decompositions of concentration ratio', *Journal of the Royal Statistical Society* 132: 418-425.

Sahn, D./Younger, S./Meyerhofer, C. (2002) *Rural Poverty in Bulgaria, Characteristics and Trends*, Cornell Working paper 132

Tsanov, V./Bogdanov, B./Stoyanova, K./Kotseva, M./Beleva, I./Mircheva, D./Tzvetkov, A. (2003) *Bulgaria: The Challenges of Poverty*. Sofia: National Statistical Institute.

Tsanov, Vassil (2002) *Economic Integration and Social Security in Bulgaria during Transition*; Project on Globalization, Inequality and Health, RUIG/UNRISD; Draft paper [Online]; Available at: http://www.ruig-gian.org/ressources/comeliau-socialsecurity_Bulgaria-Tsanov.pdf

Tsvetkova-Angelova, Jaklina (2001) *Trends and Indicators on Child and Family Well-being in Bulgaria*. UNICEF, Innocenti Research Centre, Italy

World Bank (1999a) *Consultations with the Poor. National Synthesis Report. Bulgaria*. Washington D.C.: The World Bank.

World Bank (1999b) *Bulgaria – Poverty During the Transition*, Report No. 18411, Washington, D.C.: The World Bank.

World Bank (2002) *Bulgaria – Poverty Assessment*, Report No. 24516-BUL, Washington, D.C.: World Bank.

Annex

Table BG1: Distribution of household income sources across income deciles, Bulgaria 1992, 1997 and 2000

	1992										
Decile	D1	D2	D3	D4	D5	D6	D7	D8	D9	D10	Total
Wages and salaries	1.8	2.8	5.0	7.3	9.0	11.6	12.3	13.0	17.1	20.1	100
Income from non-agricultural self-employment	4.6	3.7	3.6	6.6	9.3	10.5	13.8	14.9	17.6	15.3	100
Income from agriculture	1.0	2.0	3.6	5.2	6.2	6.6	9.6	14.0	17.1	34.7	100
Property income	1.5	3.2	13.0	13.1	17.1	9.4	15.9	8.5	8.1	10.1	100
Pensions	11.7	14.9	12.4	9.4	8.9	7.7	8.4	9.3	7.4	10.0	100
Unemployment benefits	11.7	13.1	9.6	12.9	9.1	15.4	7.1	7.6	6.1	7.3	100
Family allowances	6.1	5.8	9.6	13.4	12.2	12.8	12.0	9.8	11.3	7.1	100
Other social benefits	5.4	6.1	7.6	7.8	8.3	12.7	11.8	13.8	12.6	13.8	100
Interfamily transfers	6.5	7.6	9.7	7.9	11.0	8.5	10.1	10.1	11.4	17.3	100
Other	4.2	5.3	6.5	7.5	8.9	10.3	11.1	12.5	12.0	21.7	100
All	4.1	5.5	6.5	7.4	8.5	9.5	10.8	12.3	14.4	21.0	100
	1997										
Wages and salaries	2.3	3.4	5.1	6.5	8.8	10.5	12.0	14.7	15.4	21.1	100
Income from non-agricultural self-employment	4.5	2.3	4.6	6.6	8.0	6.9	11.9	16.1	18.4	20.7	100
Income from agriculture	0.7	1.7	2.2	3.7	5.2	7.1	8.9	12.0	19.6	38.8	100
Property income	2.5	4.3	10.1	2.9	11.3	10.2	16.2	12.7	9.4	20.4	100
Pensions	9.1	12.4	12.0	10.7	9.9	8.6	8.5	8.3	9.2	11.3	100
Unemployment benefits	12.5	7.9	4.2	11.4	9.6	12.4	11.1	11.2	12.6	7.1	100
Family allowances	7.5	6.6	8.9	11.2	12.4	11.0	12.0	14.5	10.0	5.8	100
Other social benefits	12.9	13.9	11.8	10.1	10.2	7.4	8.3	8.6	6.3	10.5	100
Interfamily transfers	6.7	6.4	8.5	11.1	7.4	9.2	9.9	11.1	13.1	16.7	100
Other	3.6	5.7	7.9	9.9	9.3	11.4	13.0	11.9	13.2	14.0	100
All	3.7	5.1	6.1	7.1	8.1	9.1	10.4	12.3	15.0	23.0	100

Decile	2002										
	D1	D2	D3	D4	D5	D6	D7	D8	D9	D10	Total
Wages and salaries	3.4	4.4	5.5	6.8	8.4	9.6	11.2	12.7	16.0	22.1	100
Income from non-agricultural self-employment	3.3	3.0	7.1	10.0	2.3	9.7	8.9	11.2	20.5	24.0	100
Income from agriculture	1.6	2.5	3.0	4.0	5.5	6.9	10.3	14.2	18.7	33.2	100
Property income	1.5	2.9	2.8	5.1	9.2	7.4	13.6	25.1	11.4	21.0	100
Pensions	5.5	9.2	10.4	10.4	11.5	10.7	10.5	10.1	10.5	11.2	100
Unemployment benefits	15.5	8.1	7.4	11.1	8.6	8.9	12.6	9.7	6.5	11.5	100
Family allowances	12.2	10.6	13.1	12.1	8.1	11.2	11.3	8.9	7.5	5.0	100
Other social benefits	13.0	10.4	6.6	7.9	6.2	8.9	8.4	10.0	6.1	22.6	100
Interfamily transfers	5.1	7.0	7.0	7.4	9.4	11.0	10.1	11.2	12.4	19.5	100
Other	4.8	6.0	6.3	7.4	7.7	9.0	9.8	11.2	11.7	26.1	100
All	4.0	5.5	6.4	7.3	8.3	9.3	10.6	12.2	14.7	21.9	100

Source: Author's computations based on NSI HBS database.

129

Table BG 2:   Distribution of household members (by socioeconomic status)
across income deciles, Bulgaria 1992, 1997 and 2002

				1992				
Decile	Em-ployees	Self-em-ployed	Self-employed in agriculture	Unem-ployed	Pen-sioners	Dependant age < 18	Dependant age > 18	All
1	4.3	8.8	0.0	25.5	13.5	9.5	14.1	12.9
2	5.8	9.6	0.0	10.9	16.2	8.3	6.9	11.5
3	8.6	3.7	2.2	9.0	11.3	10.3	13.6	10.1
4	9.8	15.4	10.9	10.9	7.7	13.0	10.1	9.8
5	11.1	9.6	2.2	9.9	8.5	11.3	8.1	9.3
6	11.6	6.6	6.5	6.2	8.3	11.0	11.2	9.3
7	11.4	16.2	6.5	7.1	8.6	10.8	7.7	9.0
8	11.3	8.8	17.4	7.8	9.5	9.1	10.3	9.4
9	12.9	11.8	15.2	7.8	6.8	10.5	9.8	9.2
10	13.1	9.6	39.1	5.0	9.8	6.3	8.1	9.5
All	100	100	100	100	100	100	100	100
				1997				
1	4.7	8.9	6.8	18.7	9.7	12.3	17.1	9.0
2	5.8	3.5	10.2	11.5	13.9	9.6	11.3	10.1
3	8.7	9.7	10.2	10.5	11.2	9.5	11.6	9.9
4	8.9	7.1	3.4	9.3	10.8	11.0	11.0	9.7
5	11.3	10.6	11.9	9.7	8.2	11.0	9.6	9.4
6	12.0	5.3	5.1	8.6	9.2	10.1	8.7	10.1
7	11.2	16.8	17.0	8.2	9.0	9.9	9.6	10.0
8	12.7	15.0	6.8	7.0	7.2	12.6	6.7	9.6
9	12.6	14.2	10.2	8.6	9.6	7.5	8.4	10.8
10	12.1	8.9	18.6	8.1	11.3	6.7	6.1	11.3
All	100	100	100	100	100	100	100	100
				2002				
1	5.3	3.1	9.4	24.6	6.7	12.7	14.1	11.5
2	6.7	5.0	4.7	14.3	11.0	11.4	11.3	11.2
3	7.9	11.2	18.8	11.1	10.8	11.5	6.2	10.5
4	8.5	14.3	12.5	9.1	11.2	10.0	12.4	9.8
5	10.0	3.1	1.6	9.0	10.5	11.0	10.0	9.7
6	10.0	11.8	3.1	7.7	10.2	11.6	8.9	9.5
7	11.4	9.9	9.4	8.2	10.4	8.2	10.7	9.4
8	12.2	12.4	12.5	6.2	9.8	9.7	7.2	9.6
9	13.7	16.2	12.5	5.4	8.8	8.5	10.0	9.6
10	14.2	13.0	15.6	4.4	10.7	5.4	9.3	9.3
All	100	100	100	100	100	100	100	100

Source: Author's computation based on NSI HBS database.

Chapter 4

Changes in Income, Income Inequality and Poverty: The Case of Hungary

György Molnár / Viktoria Galla

1 Changes in wages, pensions and social protection expenditures

The socioeconomic and income structure of Hungarian households experienced large changes in the early transition years. The most important shifts were in the size of the active and inactive population. Employment was decreasing dramatically until 1993, and then kept slowly declining until 1997 (Figure 1). The drop in total employment was 30% between 1989 and 1997. From 1997 employment rose somewhat, but it stagnates since 1999.

The decline of the real GDP – parallel with employment – began in 1990, the drastic decline lasted until 1992, reaching its lowest point in 1993. Between 1989 and 1993 the extent of the GDP shrinkage was 18% (Figure 1). While the decline in employment continued, a slow recovery of GDP began in 1993, accelerating after 1996.

In spite of the large decrease in GDP, around the years of the system change (between 1988 and 1994) the real value of gross wages and salaries had been more or less stagnating, but the net wages – due to the almost unchanged income tax brackets in a period of high inflation – declined almost at the same rate as the GDP (see Table 1). Due to the forward-looking pension indexation system, pensions more or less followed the movement of net wages. In the 1994 election year the real value of net wages was raised by 7%, the real value of pensions by 2%.

Figure 1: Real GDP and total employment, 1989=100

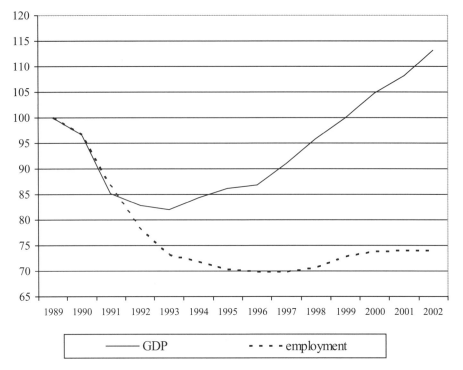

Source: GDP – Hungarian Statistical Yearbook 2002, HCSO, Budapest, 2003. Employment – Economic Survey of Europe, UN ECE, 2005, No. 2. Table A9.

In the first years of transition the government tried to maintain the level of some forms of social protection benefits to partly compensate the effects of growing unemployment and shrinking GDP (see Table 2). This type of governmental policy – which was categorized by Milanovic[1] as populist – went on till 1994. As the fall of the GDP was not accompanied by a similar decrease in real incomes, the budget deficit and the balance of payments reached a critical level. This led to the introduction of an austerity package in March 1995, known as the Bokros package.[2]

---

1   Milanovic (1998).
2   In 1995 Hungary's foreign deficit reached about $3 billion, giving the highest per capita debt in Europe. The economic situation became critical, so the government decided to implement an austerity package. It was brought in by the new Minister of Finance, Lajos Bokros, and came to be known as the Bokros package. Introducing new taxes, increasing import duties and cutting back government expenditures the budget deficit was diminished. The Hungarian currency was devalued by 9% in March and underwent further creeping monthly devaluation, aimed at reducing its value against the Deutsche Mark by up to 20% over a year. The inflation rate was over 28% in 1995 and 23% in the next year. As a result of the Bokros package the current account deficit fell from 5.6% of GDP in 1995 to 2.2% of GDP in 1997.

Table 1: Changes in average real wage, average real pension and share of wages in GDP, 1988-2003

	Index of average real gross wage (1992=100)	Share of wages in GDP	Index of average net wage (1992=100)	Index of average real pension (1992=100)
1988	100.7	33.1	111.7	115.9
1989	101.5	33.1	111.8	116.8
1990	100.1	33.8	107.4	113.8
1991	98.9	38.0	101.9	105.2
1992	100.0	39.6	100.0	100.0
1993	99.5	38.2	96.1	96.3
1994	102.7	36.1	103.0	98.5
1995	93.5	33.9	91.4	88.1
1996	91.1	33.7	86.3	80.6
1997	94.2	33.1	90.8	80.8
1998	97.5	33.0	90.8	85.9
1999	100.9	32.4	93.0	88.7
2000	104.4	32.0	94.6	89.9
2001	112.9	33.8	100.7	95.7
2002	126.9	34.2	114.9	105.3
2003	135.7	35.1	126.9	114.1

Source: Pension and wage: Hungarian Statistical Yearbook, different years. GDP: Eurostat: http://epp.euro-stat.ec.europa.eu/portal/page?_pageid=1073,46870091&_dad=portal&_schema=PORTAL&p_product_code=NAMA_GDP_C

The high inflation (28.2% in 1995) decreased the real value of the wages in 1995 and 1996. In 1995 the forward-looking pension indexation was replaced by backward-looking indexation, consequently pensions decreased more than net wages (see Figure 2). After two years of heavy decline, 1997 was a turning point in the wage trends, and between 2000 and 2003 the growth rate of wages was quite high. Real net wages reached their 1989 value in 2002, pensions only in 2004.

In Table 2 we can follow the growing share of social protection expenditures within the shrinking GDP between 1990 and 1994, followed by a sharp reduction between 1995 and 1997. Beside the inflation effect, in 1995 the government narrowed the rights to and accessibility of different forms of social protection benefits. The recovery of the social protection expenditures began only in 2001 and accelerated in 2002 and 2003.

Table 2:   Social protection expenditures as percentage of GDP

	Social protection expenditure as percentage of GDP	Unemployment cash benefits as percentage of GDP	Pensions as percentage of GDP	Cash social assistance as percentage of GDP	Family benefits as percentage of GDP
1990	26.7	0.1	9.7	0.5	4.0
1991	32.1	0.6	10.5	1.1	4.6
1992	34.4	1.0	10.9	1.3	4.1
1993	35.0	1.5	11.0	1.1	3.9
1994	34.7	1.5	11.4	1.8	3.3
1995	30.1	1.1	10.4	1.7	2.6
1996	27.3	0.9	9.7	1.6	2.1
1997	26.0	0.7	9.4	1.5	1.9
1998	26.7	0.7	9.8	1.2	1.8
1999	26.6	0.7	9.8	1.2	1.5
2000	25.5	0.6	9.3	1.1	1.7
2001	25.9	0.5	9.6	1.0	1.6
2002	28.0	0.4	10.1	1.1	1.7
2003	29.1	0.4	10.0	1.5	1.9

Source: Hungarian Statistical Yearbook, different years.

Social protection expenditures: pensions, unemployment benefits, sick-pay, child care and family allowances, regular and non-regular social assistance benefits, scholarships and other grants, subsidy on interest of housing loans, privately funded social benefits, health care, cultural, sport, recreation benefits, subsidy on public transport, depreciation of state-owned dwellings, other benefits in kind.

Pensions: old-age pensions, other benefits related to pension, early retirement pensions, and disability pensions.

Cash social assistance: regular and non-regular social assistance benefits, scholarships and other grants, subsidy on interest of housing loans, privately funded social benefits.

Family allowances: pregnancy-confinement benefit, child care allowance, child care fee, family allowance, pregnancy allowance, maternity grant, child-rearing support.

In the late 1980s open unemployment was still an unknown phenomenon, but in 1991 the process accelerated and thousands of people became unemployed. Direct unemployment cash benefits (as percentage of GDP) almost tripled from 1991 to 1993. Entitlement rules were subsequently tightened, and benefits were continuously decreasing in real terms. As a result of legislative changes in 2000, other types of income supplements substituted the unemployment cash benefit, and were paid for a shorter period. After 1997 the number of unemployed also started decreasing.

Figure 2: The pension/wage ratio, 1990-2003

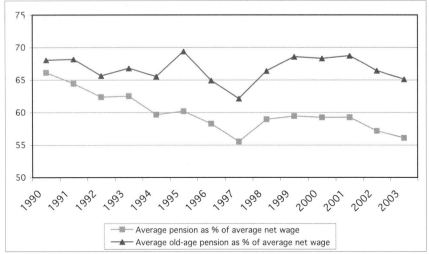

Source: Yearbook of Welfare Statistics, different years.

135

In the first years of transition pensioning offered an escape route for thousands of people loosing their job. In the early 1990s, men at age 55 and women at age 50, threatened by unemployment, tried to get early retirement; mostly, they succeeded. After 1995 the restrictions caused a decrease in the real value of old-age pensions and also the pension/GDP ratio decreased significantly. This ratio started increasing again in 2001.

Cash social assistance covers several different types of assistance, such as permanent and temporary municipal support, funeral aid, benefit to maintain the dwelling, transport support, and assistance to house building belong to this group. Again, in the first years of transition, the share of these benefits in GDP was increasing, then – from 1995 – gradually decreasing. In 2003 a significant rise occurred again.

Beside its social characteristics, family benefits were also paid to increase willingness to raise children. However, the share of these benefits in the GDP was halved over 13 years. In this case – beside the general story – we can identify also a special effect. Under the conservative government (in power from 1998 to 2002), tax allowances served as the main device for helping families with children and this led to the decrease of direct family benefits. At the end of 2002 the socialist-liberal government increased direct family benefits again, redirecting one part of family benefits to the poorest, who do not pay income tax.

Due to its importance, we return to the problem of pensions. In 1990 one-quarter of the population received some kind of pension, including old-age, widow, orphan, disability, and early retirement pension (see Table HU1 in the Annex). The share of old-age pensioners in the total population was only 14% in this year. Because of demographic processes, the share of old-age pensioners slowly increased, reaching 16.5% in 1999. However, because of the increasing and in some cases permanent unemployment, people below the age of retirement tried to retire earlier (in the form of early retirement or disability pension). Consequently, the growth rate of non old-age pensioners was much higher. This resulted in a very high share of persons receiving a pension (as percentage of the total population); in 2003 this share exceeded 30%. In 1990 almost half of the new pensions by own right were old-age pensions, and the other half early retirement pensions and disability pensions. In 1997 the distribution of new pensions was: 30% old-age, 70% early retirement and disability pension. The relation between pre- and disability pensions frequently changed, according to the changing regulation. By 1997 the labour market stabilised, and this synchronized the changes of these two types of pension.

The huge number of pensioners led to serious problems in financing the pension system. In 1997 the Hungarian Parliament passed a new pension bill to reform the whole pension system. This new system – which started operating at the beginning of 1998 – comprised a public pay-as-you-go system (the first pillar), and a new, funded and privately-managed system (the second pillar). A voluntary, funded and privately-managed pillar (the third pillar) already existed before the reform and continues to operate and grow.[3] The retirement rules were also changed, and the statutory retirement age was increased. This caused a change of previous trends, even leading to a small decrease in the share of pensioners after 1999.

As seen from Figure 2, the average net pension is lower than the average old-age pension and there are growing differences between them. With the exception of the post Bokros package period, old-age pensions could more or less maintain their relative value compared to the wages. The causes of the increasing gap between the average pensions and average old-age pensions vary in time. Between 1990 and 1995 the main cause was the growing share of pre- and disability pensioners with lower average income. After two years of narrowing the gap (from 1995 to 1997), the difference between the average

3   On the Hungarian pension reform see e.g. Simonovits (2000), Rocha and Vittas (2001).

level of old-age pensions and the average level of other types of pensions started increasing, because a shorter working history before retirement was increasingly penalized by the new pension rules introduced in 1997.

After 2000 both types of the pension/wage ratio began to decrease again. This is the result of the so-called Swiss indexation of the pensions, which fixes the nominal growth rate of pensions as the average of the nominal growth rate of net wages and the rate of inflation. Consequently, in the years of rapid real wage growth and slower inflation after 2000, this regulation had an adverse impact on pensions.

2   Income structure at the household level

Table 3 shows the changes in household income and GDP for three selected years: 1993, 1997 and 2002 (in the case of GDP using the data of Figure 1). For years before 1993 we do not have comparable household income data.

Table 3:   Changes in household income and GDP (1993=100)

	Median household equivalent income	GDP
1993	100	100
1997	79	111
2002	110	138

Source: Statistical Yearbook of Hungary, 2003 and own computations based on HBS 1993, 1997 and 2002.
On the method of income equalization according to household size see the Technical Annex.

As we have presented in the previous section, before 1995 social protection expenditures and other sources of household income did not follow the huge decline in GDP. As a result of the Bokros package, reduction of household incomes occurred only later, already in the period of growing GDP. Then, between 1997 and 2002 the growth rate of household income exceeded again the growth rate of GDP: median household equivalent income grew by 40% during this period, while GDP by 24%.

Table 4 shows the structure of household disposable income in the first decile, tenth decile and overall (i.e. all households) for the three cross-sections: 1993, 1997 and 2002 (the complete decile structure can be seen in Table HU2 in the Annex). Wages and salaries contain fringe benefits, and also sickness benefit and maternity leave wage compensation, because in 1993 and 1997 these items were not separated from wages in the database.

Wages and salaries have the biggest share in total household disposable income. This share has remained almost stable between 1993 and 1997. Between 1997 and 2002, in the period of economic growth and increasing employment, the share of wages and salaries increased to a small extent.

Pensions amount to about one fourth of household income; their share in household income increased by four percentage points in the 1993-1997 period. This increase was the consequence of the growing share of pensioners, in particular the growing share of non old-age pensioners (see also Table HU1 in the Annex). The other explanation for this increase was the relatively stable real value of pensions in this period. After the stabilization package in 1995, most pensions retained their real value, unlike unemployment and family benefits. The Swiss indexation formula played a great part in this phenomenon. In the 1997-2002 period, the share of pensions in household income has remained almost unchanged.

The third most important component of household income is income from agriculture. Its share in total household income is more than 12% both in 1993 and in 1997, and two third of this share comes from the consumption of own production. The share of consumption of own production within agricultural income fell to 50% in 2002, causing an overall decreasing share of income from agriculture. (These details are not indicated in Table 4.)

In the investigated 10-year period the share of self-employment income in household income more than doubled, and the real change is likely to be bigger, because the wealthiest and the self-employed people are underrepresented in the HBS sample. This process clearly shows the expansion of the market economy.

The fluctuation of the share of income from capital can be explained by the changing role and utilization of the compensation tickets[4] introduced after the change of regime: the sum of the utilized tickets was quite considerable in 1993, but later this sum was negligible. Apart from the effect of the compensation tickets, income from capital followed an unbroken upward curve, but only on a lower level than the self-employment income. As the HBS database contains only that part of interest and dividend income which

[138]

---

4   The Hungarian government did not return nationalized property, most of which involved land forcibly collectivized in the 1950s, to previous owners. Instead, in 1991 the government issued compensation tickets that could be used in the privatization process, to buy shares in business, or to establish new private enterprises.

Table 4: The changing structure of household income

	Wages & salaries	Income from occasional work	Self-employment income	Income from agriculture	Income from capital	Pensions	Unemployment benefits	Family benefits	Other social benefits	Inter-family transfers	Other income	All
First decile												
1993	19.8	2.3	1.4	8.5	0.3	29.4	11.5	20.2	4.1	2.3	0.2	100
1997	22.0	3.8	2.6	9.5	0.2	22.5	10.1	22.2	3.1	3.5	0.5	100
2002	23.3	5.3	4.0	6.8	0.7	26.4	6.2	19.4	3.1	4.1	0.6	100
Tenth decile												
1993	54.4	0.7	3.8	11.7	8.8	10.1	0.7	3.8	0.7	3.7	1.6	100
1997	57.6	0.7	5.4	11.3	4.7	12.5	0.3	3.5	0.6	2.7	0.6	100
2002	49.2	1.2	12.2	10.3	7.6	12.0	0.1	1.0	0.4	5.4	0.6	100
All												
1993	41.1	0.7	2.7	12.5	2.6	24.0	3.0	8.4	1.4	2.6	0.9	100
1997	41.0	1.2	3.1	12.2	1.3	27.8	1.7	6.3	1.4	3.2	0.6	100
2002	43.1	1.8	6.3	8.5	2.0	27.4	0.8	4.2	1.1	4.2	0.6	100

Source: Hungarian HBS 1993, 1997, 2002. The original HBS data set contained only the gross value of the different income sources and the total amount of taxes and social contributions. Generation of the net data by income sources is own computation.

was utilised in household consumption[5] and underreporting is especially high in this field, we can assume that the real value of income from capital is much higher.

The shares of both family and unemployment benefits in household income is continuously decreasing. This decline did not stop after the stabilization period, but continued in the period of dynamic GDP and income growth. The drastic decrease of the share of family benefits cannot be explained by the demographic processes only.

After 1997, not only the share of unemployment benefits, but also the share of other social transfers decreased. In this period the share of unemployment benefits decreased much more than the share of unemployed within the population, that is the average unemployment benefit has fallen. The repeated modification of the rules of unemployment benefits played a great part in this. The reason for these modifications was to stimulate a more intensive job search, however, and consequently, the situation of the permanently unemployed people living in depressed regions considerably worsened, because they did not have any chances to get employed.

The share of occasional work was slightly increasing. This phenomenon is partly connected to the problem of unemployment, since occasional work is becoming to an increasing extent the illegal/black work of unemployed, or other inactive people. Probably, the real extent of occasional work is underestimated.

Interfamily transfers are increasing in importance, due to the increasing number of divorces and allowances within families.[6]

The shape of these general processes varies a great deal across different income segments of society. The share of wages and salaries in household income is dynamically increasing by income deciles. In the analysed 10-year period, the importance of wages and salaries was somewhat growing even among the poorest. However, in the case of the wealthiest the dominance of wages and salaries differs from the average as the importance of self-employment and capital income is considerably increasing, while the share

---

5   In the Household Budget Survey only that part of the interest and dividend is asked which was drawn out from the account and used up in the household consumption in the given year. This is a serious deficiency of the survey.

6   The question may arise that the increasing importance of interfamily transfers is partly due to remittances from abroad. However, regular remittances from family members (e.g. from husbands working abroad) are accounted separately and aggregated into the appropriate income categories (salaries, etc.). Otherwise, the share of foreign income in total household income is around 0.1%.

of wages and salaries decreased by 8 percentage points between 1997 and 2002.

For the poorest households, pensions are the most important income source. The share of pensions in total household income of these households decreased between 1993 and 1997, but in the next period it increased somewhat. During the stabilization, pensions lost the least in real value, as compared to other social protection benefits. In 1997, the share of pensions is much higher in the deciles from 3 to 7 than in the top and bottom ones (Table HU2 in the Annex).

The share of income from agriculture clearly manifests the strong division of the agricultural population. This income type also plays a very important role in income of the poorest, but the decreasing share of consumption from own production affects them in the first place. At the same time, the wealthy agricultural entrepreneur stratum also exists and its income is expanding.

For the poorest households, the role of family benefits is extremely important. As we will see later on, this is a consequence of the fact that households in the poorest income decile have more children and that the share of children in this decile is increasing over time. However, due to numerous social and political actions, these benefits now reach the poorest households more effectively. The role of these benefits in income of the most affluent considerably decreased. We can also see the same phenomenon in the case of unemployment benefits and other social benefits.

The targeting of other social benefits improved between 1997 and 2002, in the sense that a larger share of this income was disbursed to the lowest quintile (see Table HU3 in the Annex). However, even in 2002 only 60% of other social benefits went to the poorer half of the households. This is mostly the consequence of the characteristics of two important components of other social benefits: scholarships and orphan's allowance. Orphan's allowance – constituting one third of other social benefits – is evenly distributed between the poorer and richer part of the households, while scholarships go mainly to households in the highest deciles (cf. Table 11).

For the poorest households, social transfers are the main income source, but due to decreasing unemployment benefits and other allowances they have to accept occasional work and try to start small enterprises in order to earn a living. This process may explain the increasing importance of these two types of income for the poorest households.

141

Finally, we note that interfamily transfers are playing a much more important role in the household budgets of the richest than in that of the poorest households.

To summarize this section, we can conclude that within the sharply decreasing total household incomes in the 1993-1997 period – the result of the Bokros stabilization package – the share of unemployment benefits and other social transfers decreased more than total household income. In the subsequent period (1997-2002), income growth did not re-establish the pre-stabilization income structure.

3   The coverage of social benefits and the socioeconomic status of household members

Social benefits – including pensions – accounted for a little bit more than one-third of total household income in 2002; however their share is decreasing. In this section we investigate how this decreasing amount could reach the target groups. In the second part of the section, we analyse the overall socioeconomic structure of households.

3.1   The coverage of social benefits

"Coverage" denotes the share of the relevant population receiving a given social benefit, for example how many children receive child allowances, how many unemployed receive unemployment benefits etc. Due to the method of the Hungarian household budget surveys we can study the coverage as the share of relevant households (households with children, households with unemployed) receiving benefits.

The ratio of households with pensioners (as percentage of all households) is quite high and in 10 years this ratio increased by a further 3.6 percentage points (Table 5). This can be explained partly by demographic processes: the baby-boom generation was retiring in these years. Another cause was – mainly in the first years after the system change, continuing also between 1993 and 1997 – the growing rate of early and disability retirement. As a result of the new pension legislation in 1997 – that raised the statutory retirement age and reduced the possibilities for early retirement – this process significantly slowed down after 1997.

The coverage of households with pensioners that receive a pension reached 100%, so all of the retired receive some kind of pension, including old-age, widow, orphan, disability, early retirement pensions. Earlier (before 1993) there were some retired people without any pension, due to their social status as agricultural workers without social security.

Table 5:   Coverage of pensions

	A	B
1993	52.3	99.4
1997	54.7	99.9
2002	55.9	100.0

Notes: A: Households with pensioner, as percentage of all households.

B: Percentage of households with pensioners that receive pensions.

Source: Source: HBS 1993, 1997, 2002.

In Table 6 we can observe the share of households with children and also their coverage with family benefits in the different deciles. Column A shows the ratio of families having (a) child(ren) less than 14 years. Due to the declining birth rates, during 10 years the share of families with children decreased from 32% in 1993 to less than 27% in 2002. What is striking, however, is the growing concentration of children in the lowest household income quintile, mainly in the lowest decile. This means that these families were the main losers of the transition process and this tendency was not reversed in the years of economic recovery after 1997. At the top of the income ladder the share of families with children is decreasing faster than the average.

The coverage of family benefits was almost 100% in 1993 and 100% in 2002, while in 1997, mainly in the higher deciles, the coverage was lower. This clearly reflects changes in legislation, especially the legislation on child allowances. Theoretically, in 1993 every family with a child had the right to receive a child allowance, but some administrative steps were needed on the side of the parents. This resulted in the fact that in the first decile about 5 % of the families – with illiterate or functionally illiterate parents, mainly Roma – remained without any family benefit.

During the stabilization process of 1995 the rules for granting child allowances were changed and families above a given income limit became excluded from this type of benefit. Parents had to certify their income before appealing for child allowance. This certification process caused that the coverage is not complete in the lower deciles, in spite of the efforts to help the poorest families. In the case of the highest deciles other forms of family benefits remained in effect: birth grants, allowances for nursing a child, etc. And, of course, false income statements also increased the share of rich families receiving child allowance.

The legislation changed again in 2000: the income ceiling was abolished and families with children received the child allowance without any special administrative steps. Consequently the coverage became 100%.[7]

Table 6:   Coverage of family benefits

	1993		1997		2002	
Decile	A	B	A	B	A	B
1	36.5	95.2	47.4	98.6	45.9	100.0
2	31.1	99.7	34.0	98.3	37.3	100.0
3	29.8	100.0	29.6	98.2	30.7	100.0
4	29.6	97.9	25.9	99.2	26.2	100.0
5	33.5	99.0	25.8	98.9	23.5	100.0
6	35.3	100.0	26.8	96.8	26.5	100.0
7	37.0	99.6	24.5	93.8	20.2	100.0
8	31.2	99.5	26.6	91.1	20.2	100.0
9	30.0	99.4	24.3	89.7	18.9	100.0
10	26.1	100.0	19.1	69.5	17.4	100.0
All	**32.0**	**99.0**	**28.4**	**94.6**	**26.7**	**100.0**

Notes: A: Household with child, as percentage of all households in income decile.
          B: Percentage of households with child, receiving family benefits
Source: HBS 1993, 1997, 2002.

Unemployment benefits were a very important income source in 1993 for some Hungarian households. In the lowest deciles nearly one-third of the households had an unemployed member. This ratio somewhat declined in subsequent years, up to 2002; however the concentration of the unemployed in the lowest deciles became larger. Looking at the average figures, one would think that as the Hungarian economy recovered from the recession, unemployed would find jobs; the truth is that a lot of them chose different forms of inactivity, mainly disability pensioning.

---

7   Survey features also play a role in reaching 100% without any exception, in some cases family allowance was imputed to households with children. The extension of this imputation remained below 1% of the population concerned (personal communication of the experts of the Central Statistical Office).

The coverage of unemployment benefits varied in this period. In 1993 and 2002 it was around 80%, but during the period of economic stabilization its level was only 65% (see Table 7). Comparing this with the results presented in Table 4 (and Table HU2 in the Annex) we can see that between 1993 and 2002 the importance of unemployment benefits in the budget of households with unemployed members sharply decreased. For example, unemployment benefits provided 29% of the income of households with unemployed members belonging to the first income decile in 1993. The same share was only 19% in 2002.

Table 7: Coverage of unemployment benefits

Decile	1993		1997		2002	
	A	B	A	B	A	B
1	37.5	76.4	44.1	70.4	30.3	82.6
2	27.7	84.2	23.2	65.3	15.0	77.4
3	17.6	77.6	13.8	63.6	6.9	80.5
4	13.8	87.9	12.7	72.2	7.6	74.1
5	17.1	84.2	11.2	61.6	3.8	69.7
6	9.5	79.0	8.4	54.4	4.8	81.2
7	13.8	82.3	6.0	48.6	2.7	64.3
8	10.6	80.8	6.5	69.2	2.2	68.4
9	8.4	72.9	4.7	46.3	2.2	71.9
10	5.7	87.6	5.7	71.5	2.0	77.5
All	**16.2**	**80.8**	**13.6**	**65.5**	**7.7**	**78.4**

Notes: A: Household with unemployed member, as percentage of all households in income decile. B: Percentage of households with unemployed member, receiving any kind of unemployment benefits.
Source: HBS 1993, 1997, 2002.

In Hungary there are two main categories of unemployment benefits: unemployment allowances (with subcategories) and income supplement for the unemployed (with changing denomination). Unemployment allowances partially depend on earlier earnings, the maximal entitlement period decreased from 18 to 9 months between 1992 and 2003. After running out of the entitlement period the unemployed can get income supplement, the average amount of which is around half of the unemployment allowances.[8] Our HBS-based unemployment benefit category contains both types of unemployment support.

---

8   The income supplement of the unemployed depends on the per capita income of the family.

Figure 3 – which is based on labour statistics and not on HBS – shows the replacement rate for unemployment allowances strongly declined between 1992 and 1997. At the beginning of 1997 the regulation changed and the lower and upper limits of the monthly allowances were tied to the minimum pension (instead of the minimum wage), which resulted in an increase of the unemployment allowance / net wage ratio. However, in 2000 the regulation became more stringent again, and also the relatively rapid growth of average wages further devaluated the relative value of unemployment allowances.

Altogether the replacement rate for unemployment allowances decreased from 54% to 41% between 1993 and 2002. The HBS-based computations show similar tendencies. The ratio of average unemployment benefits (for recipients only) and average net wages and salaries was 34% in 1993, 25% in 1997 and only 19% in 2002. These ratios are lower than the ratios presented in Figure 3, because in the HBS-based computations unemployment benefits also contain income supplements for unemployed with a lower average value, and wages and salaries also contain fringe benefits.

146

Figure 3: **Replacement rate for unemployment allowances (average unemployment allowance as percentage of average net wage), 1990-2002**

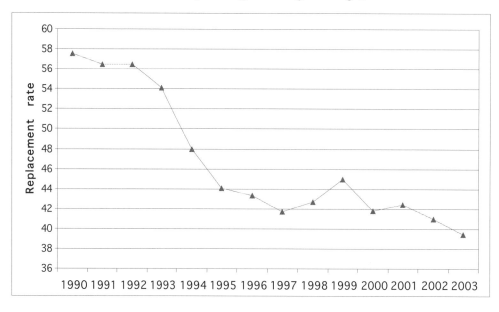

Note: Average unemployment benefits refer to the December average of each year.

Source: Hungarian Labour Statistics (Munkaügyi adattár), HCSO, different years; Hungarian Statistical Yearbook, different years.

Table 8:   Coverage of other social benefits (percentage of households receiving this social benefit)

Decile	1993	1997	2002
1	38.1	32.3	28.9
2	32.7	27.5	22.7
3	28.0	22.7	19.7
4	27.8	25.0	17.0
5	29.1	23.8	14.5
6	26.8	23.0	15.3
7	25.0	17.4	13.7
8	24.1	16.4	13.0
9	25.1	13.8	10.7
10	20.8	12.1	10.1
All	27.8	21.4	16.6

Source: HBS 1993, 1997, 2002.

Other social benefits include temporary or permanent income support for the poor households (paid mainly by local municipalities), scholarships and orphan's allowance. In the early 1990s governments tried to diminish the effect of job losses. In 1993, in the first decile 38.1% of all households received some type of benefit and in the tenth decile only 20.8% did so. By 1997, due to the Bokros package, the average rate of coverage of other social benefits decreased by 6.4 percentage points. Households in every decile felt its effect; however, in the higher income deciles the decrease was more pronounced. We can declare this as a socially fair modification of rights. By 2002 the rate of households covered decreased again. Up to the seventh decile the decrease was significant, whereas in the well-off groups the decrease was smaller. In 2002, just 16.6% of the Hungarian households received some type of other social benefit, as compared to 27.8% in 1993. Comparing these findings with the results presented in Table 4 (and Table HU2 in the Annex) we can see that the average amount of other social benefits did not change significantly in the case of the covered households, only the coverage decreased.

3.2   The socioeconomic structure of household members

Changes in the socioeconomic structure of households since 1993 can be observed in Tables 9 to 11 (and in the more detailed HU3 and HU4 tables in the Annex). The share of the economically active population in the total

147

population remained essentially unchanged between 1993 and 1997. We can see important changes only after growth resumed, i.e. after 1997.

The labour-active population represents a very heterogeneous group, with widely differing labour market status: employees, people active in agriculture in different forms, other self-employed, or persons with occasional income.

The share of employees did not change between 1993 and 1997, but – parallel to the processes presented in Figure 1 – somewhat increased between 1997 and 2002.

The share of self-employed (other than agriculture) slightly increased between 1993 and 2002, mainly in the second half of the period. The total share of people active in agriculture dropped in the same period. There are several distinct subgroups among the active in agriculture. Thus, between 1997 and 2002 the share of employees rose only marginally, whereas the increase in the share of self-employed was significantly higher and the share of co-operative members decreased, due to the almost complete disappearance of co-operatives (see Table HU6 in the Annex, which disaggregates the "active in agriculture" column of Table 9).

Persons with occasional income in Hungary are rare, and represent only 1.2% of the total population in 2002.

In the HBS, which we use, the unemployment status is based on self-declaration. In this context we define people as unemployed if they answer to the question of the survey that they are not employed (and they are not pensioners, students, or they are not on paid child care leave), but they would like to work, that is availability and search criteria are not applied here. The share of unemployed people within the total population decreased from 6.9% in 1993 to 3.3% in 2002, which means a very high, 17.3% unemployment rate[9] in 1993, 15.6% in 1997 and 8.3% in 2002. (The unemployment rates based on the results of Table 9 can be found in Table HU7 in the Annex.)

148

---

9   The "HBS-unemployment rate" is the ratio of unemployed / (non-agricultural, agricultural employed + self-employed + occasional workers + unemployed), according to the HBS survey.

Table 9:   Changes in the socioeconomic structure of household members

	Employees (non-agricult.)	Active in agriculture	Self-employed (non-agricult.)	Persons with occasional income	Unemployed	Pensioners	Persons on paid child care	Dependants	Other	All
First decile										
1993	11.0	1.8	1.4	2.0	17.4	20.6	3.9	40.8	0.9	100
1997	11.5	1.5	2.0	3.5	17.8	15.1	6.1	41.1	1.5	100
2002	11.3	1.9	2.4	2.9	10.6	17.1	6.2	43.8	3.9	100
Tenth decile										
1993	45.7	4.9	3.5	0.4	2.3	16.5	2.6	24.0	0.1	100
1997	47.1	4.4	3.9	0.8	2.4	17.8	1.2	21.9	0.5	100
2002	44.7	4.7	8.1	0.5	0.9	20.0	1.3	19.6	0.2	100
All										
1993	26.6	3.7	2.2	0.6	6.9	26.4	3.3	29.7	0.6	100
1997	26.6	2.9	2.3	1.1	6.1	28.6	3.2	28.5	0.6	100
2002	28.9	2.6	3.7	1.2	3.3	28.9	3.0	27.3	1.3	100

Source: HBS 1993, 1997 and 2002.

The HBS-unemployment rates are consistently higher than the Labour Force Survey (LFS) unemployment rates based on the usual ILO definition. The LFS unemployment rates were 11.3% in 1993, 8.7% in 1997 and 5.8% in 2002. If we lift the search criterion and add the passive unemployed population – those who would like to find a job, but consider that their chances of finding a job are very small and thus do not even try – to the LFS, these rates increase to 13.5%, 10.8% and 8.4% in the three investigated years. The 8.4% value in 2002 is almost identical with the HBS-unemployment rate, however in 1993 and 1997 these rates remain below the HBS-rate. To explain these differences we hypothesize that by 2002 – parallel with the decrease in unemployment – the unemployed status became more definite: somebody had a job, or had no job at all, while in the previous years there were more possibilities to sometimes have a short job (e.g. just an hour in a week, as the ILO definition says).

The share of pensioners increased between 1993 and 1997, which is a consequence of early and disability retirement. As a result of the new pension law in 1998, which raised the retirement age and reduced the possibilities for early retirement, this process significantly slowed down after 1997.

The share of all dependants decreased, mostly caused by a decrease in dependants under age 18; this was caused by demographic processes (see Table 10). Due to the remarkable increase in the number of students, the proportion of dependants above 18 has risen. Between the 1993/1994 and 2001/2002 academic years the number of students in a full-time form of tertiary education increased by 90%![10]

The number of dependants has been gradually decreasing; in 1993 they represented 29.7% of all household members, in 1997 their share was 28.5% and 27.3% in 2002.

Tables 10 and 11 provide a basis for explaining this overall trend by subdividing dependants into four age groups and four educational levels. The decreasing share of younger dependants (i.e. less than 18 years old) is clearly caused by falling fertility rates. Whereas these younger dependants represented 24.9% of all household members in 1993, their share shrank to 21.0% in 2002. On the other hand, the share of dependants in the age group between 18 and 29 years is increasing – a consequence of the large increase in university enrolment. Here, the share of women is greater than men in 1997, due to the fact that more women were enrolled in university education at that time. The characteristics of the two other age groups, from 30 to 59 and 60 years and over, are similar for men, as there are virtually no male

10   See Hungarian Statistical Yearbook 1994, 2002.

dependants aged 30 or over. The share of female dependants decreased in both these age groups.

Due to the early extension of the pension system to the agricultural population, the share of dependants over 30, and especially over 60 years, is negligible.

Examining the structure of household members by socioeconomic status (see again Table HU7 in the Annex), we can see that the unemployment rates – with some insignificant exceptions – show a monotonous decreasing tendency along income deciles. The unemployment rate in the first decile was around 50% both in 1993 and 1997 and it diminished to 36% in 2002. This is caused by the overall decrease in unemployment. However, the relative position of the diminishing unemployed population and their households is worsening. As we can see in Table HU5 in the Annex, 26% of the unemployed belonged to the 1st decile in 1993. By 1997 this share grew to 37%, and in 2002 it reached 42%!

This worsening relative income position of the unemployed can be explained by two factors. As we have seen in the previous subsection the average real value of unemployment allowances related to the net wages strongly decreased. The other factor is the composition effect of the different types of unemployment benefits. In 1993, 75% of unemployment benefit recipients received the higher unemployment allowances, in 2002 this ratio was only 43%.[11] This was caused mainly by shorter entitlement periods for unemployment allowances.

The relative income position of pensioners improved a little bit between 1993 and 1997, but it slowly worsened in the next period (Table HU5). The share of pensioners decreased in the 1st and increased in the 10th decile between 1993 and 2002. This phenomenon mirrors the worsening income position of families with children. Not only the share of pensioners, but – more generally – the share of households without children decreased in the 1st, and increased in the 10th decile, and households with pensioners on average have less children than other households. (Later we discuss the worsening position of children in detail.) Most pensioners can be found in the middle deciles: almost 70% of them are situated in the 3rd to 8th decile.

The high and increasing share of dependants in the lowest deciles is caused again mainly by the worsening position of children. As we have seen in Table 10, most dependants are under age 18. The share of persons on paid child care, who are situated in the first decile increased from 13% to 24% between 1993 and 1997 (Table HU5). This process continued at a

151

---

11   See Yearbook of Welfare Statistics, HCSO, different years.

slower pace in the period of economic growth as well, inflation being one of the causes for the devaluation of child-related benefits.

If we would use expenditure deciles instead of income deciles we could observe that the share of the self-employed is strictly increasing moving from the lower expenditure deciles to the upper ones. The situation of self-employed tends to improve through time. They try to suppress information on their true income figures from the Tax Office and the CSO as well, however, in the case of consumption-related questions, they are not consistent in declaring their income and their expenditure. The consumption stated as their firm's cost is declared as household expenditure and this data is not consistent with their declared household income. In the case of other social groups we do not find this systematic gap between income and expenditure positions. Nevertheless even the less reliable income data show the rapid growth of self-employed among the richest. In most cases inactive persons get into the tenth decile as family members of an employee or a self-employed. Thus, the self-employed pushed back the employees on the income ladder, resulting in the decrease of employees in the tenth decile.

152

On the other hand, there is a growing share of self-employed also in the first decile. For many, becoming entrepreneur was an involuntary switch, an escape from unemployment.

The agricultural workers in Hungary may be employees, co-operative members and self-employed. Table HU6 in the Annex shows that the agricultural population is very heterogeneous. Within the poor agriculturally active population, employees form the majority, while in the tenth decile agricultural entrepreneurs dominate.

We have seen that the improving educational level of the Hungarian population is strongly influencing the socioeconomic structure of households. Now, we give a more detailed analysis of the educational level, by income deciles (see Table 11). This will lead us to the issue discussed in the next section, namely income inequality.

The share of household members (between 25 and 64 years) who attained only the primary educational level or lower level (equal or less than 8 years in schooling) decreased by almost 14 percentage points between 1993 and 2002. The rate of decrease was somewhat higher in the upper income deciles than in the lower ones. The higher the income decile, the lower the share of persons with only primary education.

Table 10: The share of dependants, by age groups and gender
(as percentage of all persons)

	Less than 18	18 to 29	30 to 59	60 +	All
1993					
Men	12.5	1.4	0.1	0.0	14.0
Women	12.3	1.4	1.2	0.8	15.7
All	24.9	2.7	1.3	0.8	29.7
1997					
Men	11.4	2.0	0.2	0.0	13.6
Women	10.9	2.3	1.1	0.5	14.8
All	22.4	4.3	1.3	0.5	28.5
2002					
Men	10.8	2.6	0.1	0.0	13.4
Women	10.2	2.5	0.8	0.3	13.8
All	21.0	5.1	0.9	0.3	27.3

Source: HBS 1993, 1997, 2002.

Table 11: Attained educational level of persons aged between 25 and 64 years,
by income deciles

	Primary	Vocational	Secondary	Tertiary	All
1993					
Decile					
1	62.4	25.5	10.2	1.9	100.0
2	52.1	26.9	17.5	3.7	100.0
3	54.0	24.3	19.0	2.7	100.0
4	47.8	28.7	20.4	3.1	100.0
5	45.9	27.6	21.1	5.4	100.0
6	41.7	28.5	23.5	6.3	100.0
7	37.7	28.0	26.6	7.7	100.0
8	31.7	22.4	32.2	13.7	100.0
9	23.4	21.9	33.5	21.2	100.0
10	15.2	14.5	38.8	31.5	100.0
All	39.7	24.5	25.2	10.7	100.0
2002					
Decile					
1	53.3	31.8	12.4	2.6	100.0
2	37.7	42.0	17.7	2.6	100.0
3	33.4	37.7	24.6	4.3	100.0
4	28.1	39.7	27.2	5.1	100.0
5	28.7	38.7	25.9	6.8	100.0
6	22.4	35.8	31.6	10.2	100.0
7	20.2	34.2	31.5	14.0	100.0
8	16.7	31.2	35.0	17.1	100.0
9	12.2	23.9	36.9	27.1	100.0
10	6.4	17.7	34.3	41.6	100.0
All	25.9	32.8	27.7	13.6	100.0

Source: HBS 1993 and 2002.

The share of persons with an attained vocational school educational level increased between 1993 and 2002. At the same time, the proportion and even the absolute number of young people attending vocational school has been continuously decreasing, showing that the share of persons with this attained educational level will start to decrease in the near future. The distribution of these persons by income deciles was more uniform in 1993 than in 2002. In 2002 their concentration was higher in the lower income deciles.

The share of persons with a secondary school educational level stagnated between 1993 and 1997, and grew in the next period. However, their share was decreasing in the top decile, while the share of persons with tertiary education has been continuously increasing. In 2002, 40% of the persons situated in the 10th income decile had attained a tertiary education level. This is the educational level where the income differences are really large and are increasing. In the investigated period the share of people with tertiary educational level increased, and this growth will accelerate in the near future because of the huge expansion in tertiary education.

The differences in educational level obviously influence the income positions. Table 12 presents the relative equivalized income of the population aged between 25 and 64 years, by attained educational level.

Table 12:   Relative equivalized income by education levels of persons aged between 25 and 64 years

Education level	1993	1997	2002
Primary	0.86	0.84	0.78
Vocational	0.94	0.92	0.90
Secondary	1.12	1.12	1.10
Tertiary	1.37	1.43	1.44
All	1.00	1.00	1.00

Source: HBS 1993, 1997, 2002.

It is important to notice that the relative income position of persons with primary and vocational school is continuously worsening, while the highly educated could further improve their relative position. The differences between the returns of education are very large, and increasing. Our simple statement is in line with the results of modelling returns of education in Halpern-Kőrösi (1998), or Kertesi-Köllő (2001).

4   Income inequality

Numerous investigations have focused on earnings and income inequalities in Hungary in recent years. Most empirical studies used the Hungarian Household Panel database of Tárki, and later their Hungarian Household Monitor,[12] others used the Household Budget Survey,[13] and the Hungarian Household Rotation Panel extracted from the HBS.[14] We emphasize the comprehensive work of Tóth (2004), who followed the pattern of inequalities from 1987.

At this point a comment on the differences of the two main Hungarian data sources is appropriate. The samples of the Tárki survey always show higher inequalities than the HBS. This is mainly caused by the fact that the sample of the Tárki contains more rich people than the sample of the "official" Central Statistical Office. However, the trends are the same in both cases; in this sense our results do not differ from the results of the above referred works. For the sake of comparability with other countries and other parts of our study we apply the HBS sample.

4.1   Income inequality: income distribution across income quintiles

Table 13 shows the distribution of the total household disposable income by income quintiles, as well as the ratio of income of the top quintile and bottom quintile. According to this Q5/Q1 measure, inequality in 1997 decreased from its peak in 1993, and further decreased between 1997 and 2002. Does this really mean that income inequality is decreasing generally between 1993 and 2002? This would contradict all of the previously mentioned results.

The explanation lies in the changing family structure. Analysing the changes in family size and the changes in income positions of the same households in time, we can see that moving in time, an ever larger proportion of households with many children is concentrated in households belonging to the bottom income decile. Consequently, using equivalized income,[15]

---

12   Atkinson (2003), Atkinson and Micklewright (1992), Förster and Pellizzari (2000), Förster et al. (1999), Galasi (1998), Spéder and Habich (1999), Heinrich (1999), Medgyesi et al. (2000), Rutkowski (2001), Lokshin and Ravallion (2000), Révész (1994), Spéder (1998), Tóth (2004), Tóth et al. (1994), Van de Walle et al. (1994).

13   Collins and Redmond (1997), Kattuman and Redmond (1997, 2001), Milanovic (1998, 1999), Pudney (1994), Redmond and Kattuman (2001).

14   Kapitány and Molnár (2002, 2004), Molnár and Kapitány (2006a, b).

15   Technical and methodological issues are described in the Technical Annex.

i.e. taking into account each person with his household equivalent income instead of total household income we obtain a more realistic picture. Table 14 shows the growing inequalities in the investigated period. Between 1993 and 1997 the growth is very small; it is due mainly to the worsening relative position of the people in the first quintile. After the first years of transition the growth of inequalities slowed down. Between 1997 and 2002 the growth of the Q5/Q1 ratio is somewhat larger, stemming from the growing relative income of the top quintile. This means that the richest families gained more from the large income increase between 1997 and 2002 than the others.

While the average family size in the first decile was 2.17 in 1993 and 2.55 in 2002, the average equivalized family size in the tenth decile was only 2.05 in 1993, and is decreasing in the investigated time period. Between 1993 and 1997 the structure of the poorest households had been significantly re-arranged; thus, within households belonging to the first income decile the share of families having many children increased considerably, suggesting increased child poverty (see Table 15).

156

Table 13: Distribution of the total income of households, by household income quintiles

Quintile	1993	1997	2002
1	11.2	12.2	12.7
2	14.2	14.7	14.9
3	18.3	17.8	17.9
4	23.1	22.5	21.6
5	33.3	32.9	33.0
All	100.0	100.0	100.0
5/1	2.97	2.69	2.60

Source: HBS 1993, 1997, 2002.

Table 14: Distribution of the equivalized income of households, by household income quintiles

Quintile	1993	1997	2002
1	11.4	10.9	10.9
2	15.1	15.1	15.0
3	18.0	18.2	17.8
4	21.9	22.2	21.7
5	33.7	33.6	34.7
All	100.0	100.0	100.0
5/1	2.97	3.07	3.18

Source: HBS 1993, 1997, 2002.

Table 15:   Average equivalized household size by selected household
            income deciles

Decile	1993	1997	2002
1	2.17	2.45	2.55
2	2.04	2.14	2.22
. . .	. . .	. . .	. . .
9	2.20	2.01	1.99
10	2.05	1.97	1.89
All	**2.12**	**2.05**	**2.07**

Source: HBS 1993, 1997, 2002.

4.2   *Decomposition of income inequality*

Describing income inequality, Q5/Q1 ratios measure only the differences
between the top and bottom quintiles. Investigating the whole income distribution, Table 16 presents Gini coefficients and their Rao-decomposition.[16]

After 1997 not only the Q5/Q1 ratio of the equivalized income but
also the Gini coefficient increased further. According to the Q5/Q1 ratio the
increase in inequality was almost the same between 1997 and 2002 as in the
preceding period. The increase in the Gini coefficient – which is more sensitive to changes in the middle of the income distribution than at the tails – was
somewhat smaller in the second time period than in the first one.[17]

The Gini-indices (see Milanovic, 1998; Atkinson and Micklewright,
1992) for both the pre- and post-transition period in Hungary suggest that in
Hungary the inequality increase was relatively smaller than in other transition countries. Analysing the connection between the inequality measures
based on monthly and annual data, we can surmise that the Gini-indices
for the 1980s were overestimated in the literature.[18] We must also mention
that after the transition, people in extreme poverty and people who are the

---

16   Rao (1969). The decomposition expression is: $G = \Sigma\, s_k C_k$, where G is the Gini coefficient,
     s_k is the share of the given income source in total income, and C_k is the concentration
     coefficient.

17   After the receding of the direct effects of the stabilization package passed in 1995, i.e.
     between 1996 and 1998, the income inequalities stagnated. That is the presented increase
     in the Gini coefficient actually occurred between 1993 and 1996 in the first time period,
     and between 1998 and 2002 in the second one (see Kapitány and Molnár, 2002).

18   As is well-known (see Shorrocks, 1978), the normally used inequality measures applied
     on a longer period containing a shorter one, show lower inequality for the longer period.
     That is, the inequality based on yearly income is necessarily lower than that based on
     monthly income.

most affluent are more or less missing in the samples. Consequently, the
inequality growth between the pre- and post transition period in Hungary
is underestimated.

Table 16: Decomposition of income inequality

	1993	1997	2002
Concentration coefficients			
Wages and salaries	0.3524	0.3654	0.3177
Income from occasional work	0.0861	-0.0804	-0.0233
Income from self-employment (non agriculture)	0.3670	0.3492	0.4611
Income from agriculture	0.2585	0.2672	0.2860
Income from capital	0.7535	0.7502	0.7973
Pensions	0.0302	0.1190	0.1182
Unemployment benefits	-0.2779	-0.3792	-0.4890
Family benefits	-0.0372	-0.1225	-0.2627
Other social benefits	-0.0925	-0.0450	-0.1014
Interfamily transfers	0.3023	0.2156	0.2925
Other	0.4866	0.2795	0.3668
All (Gini coefficient)	**0.2170**	**0.2306**	**0.2369**
Income shares			
Wages and salaries	0.4215	0.4219	0.4429
Income from occasional work	0.0073	0.0127	0.0185
Income from self-employment (non agriculture)	0.0282	0.0323	0.0644
Income from agriculture	0.1263	0.1242	0.0868
Income from capital	0.0251	0.0135	0.0201
Pensions	0.2185	0.2543	0.2528
Unemployment benefits	0.0304	0.0172	0.0089
Family benefits	0.0926	0.0715	0.0477
Other social benefits	0.0142	0.0144	0.0107
Interfamily transfers	0.0268	0.0319	0.0416
Other	0.0092	0.0060	0.0056
All	**1.0000**	**1.0000**	**1.0000**

Note: The income shares in this table differ slightly from the income shares presented in Table 4. In Table 4 the "point of reference" was the household, whereas in Table 16 the "point of reference" is the household member, so that a three-member household is counted three times.

Source: HBS 1993, 1997, 2002.

Table 16 unambiguously indicates that not only inequality of income, but
also inequality of earnings showed an unbroken upward trend throughout

the first period, between 1993 and 1997. During this period inequality was somewhat neutralized by different kinds of social transfers. This process, analysed by Kattuman and Redmond (2001) and Rutkowski (2001), continued after 1997.

The stabilization package in early 1995 went hand in hand with a reduction in the real value of various social transfers, primarily through inflation. That is why rising wage inequalities between 1993 and 1997 appear in the inequality of household incomes without the counter-effect of other factors.[19]

Decomposing the Gini coefficient, the concentration coefficient of salaries and wages remarkably exceeds the value of the Gini coefficient, the inequality of total disposable income. As we see in the second part of Table 16, the biggest proportion of household incomes is wages and salaries, they play a fundamental role in determining overall income inequalities.

As we know from the literature,[20] inequality of wages and salaries considerably increased in the first transition years. This increase slightly continued between 1993 and 1997; however, between 1997 and 2002 we can see a large decrease in wage inequality, as the concentration coefficient of wages and salaries significantly decreased in this period. Between 1993 and 1997, in the period of falling real income, the concentration coefficients of self-employment income, income from agriculture, capital income, and wages and salaries did not change much. However, in the next period, in the period of growth, the concentration coefficients of capital income and self-employment income increased, showing that these incomes are becoming more concentrated among the rich. The concentration coefficient of income from capital is quite high, but because of the small share of this type of income, its contribution to total inequality is small. But we stress again that income from capital is undoubtedly underestimated in our sample.

Behind the changes of concentration coefficients of income in agriculture we can observe two opposite processes. The concentration coefficient of income in market agricultural production was about 0.42, in 1993 and in 1997, and it is higher than the concentration coefficient of income from non-agricultural self-employment. It increased to 0.46 in 2002, similar to the value of the concentration coefficient for income from non-agricultural

---

19   Kapitány and Molnár (2002) showed that this rise in wage inequalities occurred mainly between 1994 and 1995.

20   See Blanchflower (2000, 2001), Kattuman and Redmond (2001), Rutkowski (2001), Kertesi and Köllő (2001), Köllő (2001), Köllő and Vinczer (1999), Kolosi et al. (1999, 2004).

self-employment. During this period, the concentration coefficient of the consumption from own production was low, 0.165 in 1993 and 0.185 in 1997, and decreased to 0.105 in 2002. As we have mentioned earlier, the relative extent of the consumption from own production decreased significantly between 1997 and 2002. This decrease took place mainly in households belonging to the higher income deciles.

With the exception of 1997 the concentration coefficients of interfamily transfers also remained above the overall Gini, so we can conclude that these transfers did not contribute to improving the relative position of the poor.

The concentration coefficient of pensions has a positive sign throughout the whole investigated period, and increased considerably between 1993 and 1997. That is, pensions were distributed more unequally in 1997 than in 1993. In the period of large relative decline (1993-1997), the share of pensions in household income also increased, because many people moved from unemployment to retirement. In this period, pensions retained their relative value, in contrast with the other social transfers.

Absolute income equalizers are: unemployment benefits, family benefits, and other social benefits. Unemployment benefits have the largest negative concentration coefficient among the three groups of social benefits, and their absolute value is continuously increasing. This means that unemployment benefits are being increasingly concentrated among the poorest. At the same time their share is decreasing, therefore its absolute (negative) contribution to total income inequality is not very high.

This process can be partly linked to the slight increase of the share of occasional work, and with the change of the sign of its concentration coefficient from positive to negative, since occasional work is becoming more and more the purview of unemployed people in the informal sector. The income situation of the unemployed is deteriorating in spite of the fact that the unemployment benefits are more and more concentrated among the poor; these benefits, however, do not enable households from moving out of poverty.

The role of family benefits as an absolute income equalizer increased to an extraordinary extent in the investigated period. As we have seen, families with children suffered mostly from the relative income fall, and they benefited the least from the resumption of economic growth. In many cases, the living costs of the poorest can be maintained with family benefits. However, the large decrease in the value of the concentration coefficient between 1997 and 2002 shows that family benefits reached the poorest households to a greater extent in this period than before. The equalizer effect of other social benefits is relatively small.

Now, we turn back to the problem of education and income inequalities, confining ourselves only to wages and salaries. Table 17 presents the average (net) wage for wage-earners aged between 25 and 64 years, by educational level. A comparison with Table 12 (which presented equivalized income by education levels) leads us to interesting observations.

Table 17: Relative average net wages and salaries by education levels of wage-earners aged between 25 and 64 years

Education level	1993	1997	2002
Primary	0.75	0.71	0.72
Vocational	0.91	0.86	0.86
Secondary	1.06	1.07	1.00
Tertiary	1.50	1.54	1.52
All	1.00	1.00	1.00

Source: HBS 1993, 1997, 2002.

It is natural that the wage difference between highly- and less-educated people is far larger than the income difference. However, in the case of wages and salaries the growth of these differences has stopped after 1997. The only exception is the case of persons with secondary education. Their average wage previously was above the overall average, but in 2002 it fell to the average. In spite of the fact that highly-educated wage-earners somewhat lost their advantage to the average, the differences between them and persons with secondary education increased further. This process is connected to the expansion of tertiary education, described in section 3.2.

These results can also partly explain the diminishing concentration coefficient of wages and salaries between 1997 and 2002 (see Table 16).

5   Risk of poverty

In this section we shall present some results on income poverty incidence. The risk of poverty significantly increased between 1993 and 1997, then between 1997 and 2002 its level stagnated, or slightly decreased (see Table 18). We measure poverty as the percentage of persons with a given characteristic (pensioners, elderly, unemployed etc) who live in households with household equivalent income below a given income threshold. Three income poverty lines are used, i.e. 40, 50 and 60% of the median equivalent household income.

Table 18:   Poverty incidence in 1993, 1997, and 2002 (in per cent)

Poverty line as % of median equivalent household income	1993	1997	2002
All persons			
40	1.0	1.8	1.6
50	3.0	5.5	5.3
60	6.5	10.3	10.0
Pensioners			
40	0.7	0.7	0.6
50	1.6	1.8	2.3
60	4.4	4.7	5.5
Children < 14			
40	0.9	3.0	2.9
50	3.6	9.0	9.2
60	8.0	15.0	16.8
Children <14 with family member on paid child care			
40	0.5	4.7	4.9
50	2.8	12.9	14.9
60	8.3	21.5	26.4
Unemployed			
40	3.8	7.3	8.6
50	10.3	20.1	24.4
60	19.0	33.1	35.4
Persons 60+			
40	0.6	0.2	0.2
50	1.3	0.7	1.4
60	4.0	2.4	4.1

162

Source: HBS 1993, 1997, 2002.

Regarding the risk of poverty, the position of the unemployed is the worst and deteriorated in time as well. Between 1997 and 2002 the risk of poverty for the total population decreased somewhat, but – with the exception of pensioners and children at the 40% poverty line – the risk of poverty for all other groups presented in Table 18 increased further. Between 1993 and 1997, a quite large increase in risk of income poverty occurred for children, regardless of the poverty threshold considered. This was caused by a drastic deterioration of living conditions of families with many children, and is partly connected to the worsening status of the Roma population.[21]

After 1998, the nominal value of the income-independent (i.e. universal) family support did not change (the inflation rate in these years was around 10%), but a tax allowance was introduced for children. This allowance could be drawn on only above a given income threshold and – up to a relatively high income level – was proportional to income. Thus the risk of poverty of children under age 14 increased a little bit further in the period of overall income growth.

A special subgroup of children are children whose mother (or, admittedly very seldom, father) is on paid child care. Their poverty incidence (together of course with their parents') is the second worst, preceded only by the unemployed. One of the parents (usually the mother) can remain at home with her/his child for three years after the birth of the child. The type and the amount of paid child care depend on the previous employment status and – in case of being previously employed for a longer while – on previous earnings. For unemployed women paid child care is a better option than receiving unemployment income supplement. In the case of previously employed persons the opportunity cost of remaining at home strongly depends on previous earnings. With relatively high wages it is not financially beneficial to remain at home on paid child care. These facts explain the high poverty incidence of children with parents on paid child care. Their position strongly deteriorated not only between 1993 and 1997 but also between 1997 and 2002, caused by the decreasing real value of child care allowances.

The risk of poverty of dependants above age 18 increased to a small extent (not shown in the table). This is a very heterogeneous group. As we have seen, in the group of relatively rich families the number of university students (who are dependants) increased heavily. At the same time the position of other dependants was worsening.

Pensioners and persons above age 60 show different trends in risk of income poverty. This difference is caused by younger pensioners, persons in disability- or early retirement pension. The poverty incidence of pensioners below age 60 at the 60% poverty line, was 6.9% in 1993, 9.4% in 1997 and 9.7% in 2002. The trends are similar also in the case of the other two poverty thresholds.

---

21   On poverty and education of Roma children, see Kertesi and Kézdi (2005)

As seen from Table 18, the poverty incidence, i.e. risk of income poverty, has remained fairly stable for the whole population in the second investigated period, between 1997 and 2002. If we set the poverty threshold at 60% of the median equivalent household income, we observe that in 2002 only 10% of all persons lived in households whose equivalent income was below the poverty threshold, which represents a huge increase in comparison to 1993, but a slight improvement in comparison to 1997. That the risk of income poverty increased for the unemployed is not surprising, in view of the decrease of coverage of unemployed persons and the decrease in the value of unemployment benefits disbursed. The risk of poverty is rather high for children.

Table 19 shows the poverty incidence for the same three poverty thresholds in case of the elderly subgroup, i.e. persons aged 60 and above. As seen from this table, marital status is important for both genders, but the poverty incidence is typically much higher for unmarried (divorced, single, widowed) than for married women. The same also holds for the comparison between unmarried and married men, however, the difference here is not as large as in the case of women.

Because of the relatively high level of old-age pensions the poverty incidence for persons above age 60 is low at the 40% and 50% poverty thresholds and in this respect there are no significant differences between men and women. But in the case of the higher (60%) threshold the difference between men and women and mainly between unmarried men and women is already quite large. This difference is decreasing in time. In 1993 the ratio of the average pension of men and women above age 60 was 1.33, while in 2002 it was only 1.21.

Child poverty is much lower in two-parent households than in single-parent households (Table 20). The analysis according to the type of household shows that a high number of children increases the odds of being poor, and in the case of single-parent households and of cohabitation partnership the likelihood of poverty is extremely high. The position of children in families with unmarried couples is significantly worse than that in single-parent families. We suppose that the causal connection is the opposite: in the case of the poorest families the cohabitating couples do not get married, the mothers officially remain in single-parent status, because in this case they can get slightly higher family benefits.

Table 19:   Poverty incidence for persons aged 60 or above (in per cent)

Poverty line as % of median equivalent household income	1993	1997	2002
Married women			
40	0.6	0.1	0.2
50	1.0	0.4	0.9
60	2.6	1.3	2.9
Unmarried women			
40	0.6	0.3	0.1
50	1.7	1.2	1.8
60	6.0	3.9	5.1
Married men			
40	0.5	0.1	0.2
50	0.9	0.4	1.1
60	2.9	1.6	3.5
Unmarried men			
40	1.3	0.0	0.3
50	2.1	0.3	2.0
60	3.9	1.9	4.5

Source: HBS 1993, 1997, 2002.

Table 20:   Poverty incidence for children (less than 14 years old), in per cent

Poverty line as % of median equivalent household income	1993	1997	2002
Children in two-parent families with married couple			
40	0.5	2.6	2.1
50	2.9	7.5	7.4
60	6.9	13.2	14.5
Children in single-parent families			
40	2.1	1.9	5.9
50	6.1	5.8	14.2
60	11.9	13.1	24.4
Children in two-parent families with unmarried couple			
40	3.9	8.9	6.5
50	10.4	30.1	19.1
60	18.0	38.0	27.9
Distribution of children by family type			
Two married parents	86.2	82.1	79.5
Single parent	9.0	10.6	10.6
Two unmarried parents	4.6	7.2	9.4
Other	0.3	0.1	0.5
All	100.0	100.0	100.0

Source: HBS 1993, 1997, 2002.

The decrease in the number of marriages is caused by the transformation of long-term partnership forms. People living in a long-term partnership often choose to cohabit, either before or instead of getting married, also in order to obtain more advantageous family benefits. The share of people living in cohabitation partnership is higher in the case of poorer households. The decrease in the number of legal marriages leads to the decrease of the share of children who are living in a married and two-parent family, and to an increasing share of children who have parents living in non-marital long-term partnership where one of the parents is only a step-parent.

6   Concluding remarks

We may interpret the stabilization package of 1995 as the final act of the first period of transition; a gentle rise of inequalities took place besides a major shrinking of real incomes. Some social groups became the victims of the 1995 stabilization, mostly those who could not cope with the uncertainty and disadvantages of the transition. In this respect we mention three, partly overlapping groups: households with unemployed family members, households with many children, and households with persons on paid child care.

Analysing the changes of family size and the changes of income position of the same households in time, we can see that moving in time, an ever larger proportion of households with many children is concentrated in the bottom income decile. Between 1993 and 1997 the structure of the poorest households was significantly rearranged, and within households belonging to the first income decile the share of families having many children drastically increased. Broken family structures (single-parent families or families with unmarried couples) increase the risk of child poverty.

Within the sharply decreasing total household incomes between 1995 and 1997 – the result of the Bokros stabilization package – the share of unemployment benefits and other social transfers was decreasing more than total household income. In the subsequent period, income growth did not re-establish the pre-stabilization income structure.

The inequality of earnings and income followed an unbroken upward trend throughout the first period, between 1993 and 1997. During this period the inequality of primary incomes was moderated by different kinds of social transfers. The absolute income equalizers are unemployment benefits, family benefits, and other social benefits. Unemployment benefits and other social benefits are increasingly more concentrated among the poorest households.

After 1997 income inequalities slightly increased, and a significant number of the losers of the previous period did not recover. We may argue that the social policy of the years of growth improved the situation of the population around the lower middle of the income ladder, but this policy could not reach the poorest.

7   References

Atkinson, A.B. (2003) Income Inequality in OECD Countries: Data and Explanations. ifo Working Paper, No. 881. http://ssrn.com/abstract=386761

Atkinson, A.B./Micklewright, J. (1992) *Economic Transformation in Eastern Europe and the Distribution of Income*. Cambridge: Cambridge University Press.

Collins, G./Redmond, G. (1997) 'Poverty in the UK and Hungary: Evidence from household budget surveys', Working Paper No. 9703, Department of Applied Economics, University of Cambridge.

Blanchflower, D.G. (2000) 'Self-Employment in OECD Countries', NBER Working paper 7486, Cambridge.

Blanchflower, D.G. (2001) 'Unemployment, Well-being, and Wage Curves in Eastern and Central Europe', *Journal of the Japanese and International Economies* 15: 364-402.

Förster, M.F./Pellizzari, M. (2000) Trends and Driving Factors in Income Distribution and Poverty in the OECD Area. OECD, Labour Market and Social Policy Occasional Papers No. 42. http://ssrn.com/abstract=243521

Förster, M.F./Szívós, P./Tóth, I.Gy. (1999) 'Welfare Support and Poverty: The Experiences of Hungary and the Other Visegrad Countries', pp. 293-309 in: Kolosi, Tóth/Vukovich (1999).

Galasi, P. (1998) 'Income Inequality and Mobility in Hungary, 1992-96', *Innocenti Occasional Papers*, Economic and Social Policy Series, 64, Florence, UNICEF, 1998.

Halpern, L./Kőrösi, G. (1998) 'Labour Market Characteristics and Profitability: An Econometric Analysis of Hungarian Exporting Firms, 1986–95', *Economics of Transition* 6 (1): 145-162.

Heinrich, G. (1999) 'When average is not good enough: An analysis of income inequality in transition', UNU/Wider and CERT, Heriot-Watt University.

Jenkins, S.P. (1995) 'Accounting for inequality trends: decomposition analyses for the UK, 1971-86', *Economica* 62: 29-63.

Kapitány, Zs./Molnár, Gy. (2002) Inequality and Mobility Analysis by the Hungarian Rotation Panel, 1993-98. Institute of Economics, Hungarian Academy of Sciences, Discussion Papers MT-DP. 2002/4, p. 42. http://econ.core.hu/doc/dp/dp/mtdp0204.pdf

Kapitány, Zs./Molnár, Gy. (2004) 'Inequality and Income Mobility in Hungary, 1993-1998', *Europe-Asia Studies* 56 (8): 1109-1129.

Kattuman, P./Redmond, G. (1997) 'Income Inequality in Hungary, 1987-1993', DAE Working Paper No. 9726.

Kattuman, P./Redmond, G. (2001) 'Income Inequality in Early Transition: The Case of Hungary 1987-1996', *Journal of Comparative Economics* 29 (1): 40-65.

Kertesi, G./Köllő, J. (2001) 'Economic Transformation and the Revaluation of Human Capital, Hungary 1986-1999', Budapest Working Papers on the Labour Market, BWP 2001/4, Budapest: Institute of Economics and Corvinus University.

Kertesi, G./Kézdi, G. (2005) 'Roma children in the transformational recession. Widening ethnic schooling gap and Roma poverty in post-communist Hungary', Budapest Working Papers on the Labour Market, BWP 2005/8, Budapest: Institute of Economics and Corvinus University.

Kolosi, T./Tóth, I. Gy./Vukovich, Gy. (eds.) (1999) *Social Report 1998*. Budapest: TÁRKI.

Kolosi, T./Tóth, I. Gy./Vukovich, Gy. (eds.) (2000) *Social report 2000* (in Hungarian). Budapest: TÁRKI.

Kolosi, T./Tóth, I. Gy./Vukovich, Gy. (eds.) (2004) *Social Report 2004*. Budapest: TÁRKI.

Köllő, J. (2001) 'The Patterns of Non-employment in Hungary's Least Developed Regions', BWP 2001/1., Budapest: IE and BUE.

Köllő, J./Vincze, M. (1999), 'Self-employment, Unemployment and Wages: Regional evidence from Hungary and Romania', BWP 1999/7, Budapest: Institute of Economics and Corvinus University.

KSH (various years), *Household Budget Survey*. Budapest: HCSO.

KSH (various years), *Hungarian Statistical Yearbook 2002*. Budapest: HCSO.

Lokshin, M./Ravallion, M. (2000) 'Short-Lived Shocks with Long-Lived Impacts? Household Income Dynamics in a Transition Economy', mimeographed, World Bank, WPS 2459, October 2000, 26 p.

Medgyesi, M./Szívós, P./Tóth, I. Gy. (2000) 'Poverty and inequalities: generational shifts' (in Hungarian), in: Kolosi, T./Tóth, I. Gy./Vukovich, Gy. (eds.) (2000).

Milanovic, B. (1998) *Income, Inequality and Poverty during the Transition from Planned to Market Economy*. Washington D.C.: World Bank.

Milanovic, B. (1999) 'Explaining the increase in inequality during transition', *Economics of Transition* 7 (2): 299-341.

Pudney, S. (1994) 'Earnings Inequality in Hungary: A Comparative analysis of Household and Enterprise Survey Data', *Economics of Planning* 27/3: 251-276.

Redmond, G./Kattuman, P. (2001) 'Employment polarisation and inequality in the UK and Hungary', *Cambridge Journal of Economics* 25: 467-480.

Révész, T. (1994) 'An Analysis of the Representativity of the Hungarian Household Budget Survey Samples', Discussion Paper on Economic Transition, No. DPET 9403, University of Cambridge.

Rocha, R./Vittas, D. (2001) 'Pension Reform in Hungary: A Preliminary Assessment', *World Bank Policy Research Working Paper*, No. 2631.

Rutkowski, J.J. (1996) 'High Skills Pay Off: the Changing Wage Structure During Economic Transition in Poland', *Economics of Transition* 4 (1): 89-112.

Rutkowski, J. J. (2001) 'Earnings Mobility during the Transition. The Case of Hungary', *MOCT--MOST: Economic Policy in Transitional Economies* 11 (1): 69-89.

Simonovits, A. (2000) 'Partial Privatization of a Pension System: Lessons from Hungary', *International Journal of Development* 12: 519-529.

Shorrocks, A.F. (1978) 'Income Inequality and Income Mobility', *Journal of Economic Theory* 19: 376-393.

Spéder, Zs. (1998) 'Poverty Dynamics in Hungary during the Transformation', *Economics of Transition* 1: 1-21.

Spéder, Zs./Habich, R. (1998) 'Loser and Winner: Processes and Outcomes during the Transformation in a Comparative Perspective'. Paper presented at the Conference of Interaction between Politics and Economics in the Post Socialist Transition, Collegium Budapest, Budapest.

Tóth, I. Gy./Andorka, R./Förster, M./Spéder, Zs. (1994) 'Poverty, Inequalities and the Incidence of Social Transfers in Hungary, 1992-3'. Budapest: TÁRKI.

Tóth, I. Gy. (2004) 'Income Composition and Inequalities, 1987-2003', pp. 72-92 in: Kolosi, T./ Tóth, I. Gy./Vukovich, Gy. (eds.) (2004) *SocialReport 2004*. Budapest: TÁRKI.

Van de Walle, D./Ravallion, M./Gautam, M. (1994) 'How Well Does the Social Safety Net Work? The Incidence of Cash Benefits in Hungary, 1987-89', LSMS Working Paper No. 102. Washington: The World Bank.

169

Annex

Table HU1:   The share of pensioners in the population, 1990-2003

Year	Share of pensioners in the population, %	Share of old-age pensioners in the population, %
1990	24.9	14.1
1991	25.7	14.6
1992	26.9	15.0
1993	27.7	15.2
1994	28.5	15.5
1995	29.1	15.7
1996	29.6	16.0
1997	30.1	16.3
1998	30.5	16.4
1999	31.0	16.5
2000	30.8	16.4
2001	30.5	16.3
2002	30.5	16.3
2003	30.4	16.3

Source: Hungarian Statistical Yearbook, different years.

Table HU2: The structure of household income sources, by income deciles (horizontal structure)

Deciles	1	2	3	4	5	6	7	8	9	10	Total
1993											
Wages & salaries	19.8	23.1	29.2	31.5	34.2	39.7	41.9	45.8	50.1	54.4	41.1
Income from occasional work	2.3	0.8	0.7	0.5	0.6	0.8	0.5	0.5	0.7	0.7	0.7
Self-employment income	1.4	1.5	2.5	2.2	1.8	2.3	2.0	2.7	4.3	3.8	2.7
Income from agriculture	8.5	10.3	10.3	11.2	13.4	12.8	14.2	14.7	13.7	11.7	12.5
Income from capital	0.3	0.3	0.2	0.7	0.6	0.7	1.2	1.5	2.5	8.8	2.6
Pensions	29.4	35.2	36.5	35.3	31.8	28.6	25.3	21.4	17.5	10.1	24.0
Unemployment benefits	11.5	9.0	4.7	4.1	3.5	1.8	2.1	1.8	1.1	0.7	3.0
Family benefits	20.2	14.1	11.1	10.2	9.9	8.9	8.2	7.3	5.5	3.8	8.4
Other social benefits	4.1	2.8	2.0	1.6	1.5	1.4	1.1	1.0	0.8	0.7	1.4
Interfamily transfers	2.3	2.4	2.3	2.4	2.1	2.5	2.1	2.5	2.7	3.7	2.6
Other income	0.2	0.4	0.5	0.5	0.6	0.7	1.3	0.7	1.1	1.6	0.9
All	100.0	100.0	100.0	100.0	100.0	100.0	100.0	100.0	100.0	100.0	100.0
1997											
Wages & salaries	22.0	31.4	27.3	31.1	34.2	35.8	41.8	44.1	47.2	57.6	41.0
Income from occasional work	3.8	1.5	3.1	1.5	0.7	1.3	1.0	0.5	0.9	0.7	1.2
Self-employment income	2.6	3.3	2.7	2.1	2.2	2.4	2.2	2.4	3.3	5.4	3.1
Income from agriculture	9.5	9.9	12.0	10.5	11.2	12.1	12.9	14.4	15.1	11.3	12.2
Income from capital	0.2	0.2	0.3	0.4	0.3	0.4	0.4	1.1	0.8	4.7	1.3
Pensions	22.5	29.9	37.6	39.0	38.3	36.1	31.6	28.1	24.0	12.5	27.8
Unemployment benefits	10.1	4.5	1.9	2.2	1.5	1.0	0.6	0.8	0.4	0.3	1.7
Family benefits	22.2	13.1	8.8	7.8	6.3	5.3	4.3	3.6	3.0	3.5	6.3
Other social benefits	3.1	2.3	1.8	2.0	2.2	1.5	1.4	1.2	0.6	0.6	1.4
Interfamily transfers	3.5	3.4	3.5	2.9	2.7	3.5	3.3	3.2	3.7	2.7	3.2
Other income	0.5	0.5	0.9	0.4	0.4	0.5	0.5	0.5	1.0	0.6	0.6
All	100.0	100.0	100.0	100.0	100.0	100.0	100.0	100.0	100.0	100.0	100.0
2002											
Wages & salaries	23.3	35.2	37.7	37.5	40.7	42.4	44.3	47.3	50.6	49.2	43.1
Income from occasional work	5.3	2.8	2.4	1.9	1.8	1.4	1.2	1.4	1.4	1.2	1.8
Self-employment income	4.0	3.9	4.0	3.9	3.2	5.3	4.3	5.1	7.7	12.2	6.3
Income from agriculture	6.8	8.9	7.4	8.7	7.3	8.0	7.6	8.6	8.6	10.3	8.5
Income from capital	0.7	0.1	0.4	0.3	0.3	0.6	0.7	0.7	1.2	7.6	2.0
Pensions	26.4	30.7	35.3	36.9	37.4	33.3	34.0	28.6	22.7	12.0	27.4
Unemployment benefits	6.2	2.2	1.0	1.0	0.5	0.6	0.3	0.2	0.1	0.1	0.8
Family benefits	19.4	9.5	6.6	4.8	4.1	3.2	2.2	2.2	2.0	1.0	4.2
Other social benefits	3.1	2.3	1.2	1.3	1.2	0.9	0.9	1.0	0.5	0.4	1.1
Interfamily transfers	4.1	4.0	3.7	3.6	3.3	4.0	3.7	3.9	4.2	5.4	4.2
Other income	0.6	0.5	0.2	0.3	0.2	0.3	0.7	1.0	0.8	0.6	0.6
All	100.0	100.0	100.0	100.0	100.0	100.0	100.0	100.0	100.0	100.0	100.0

Source: Hungarian HBS 1993, 1997, 2002.

172

Table HU3: The distribution of household income sources across income deciles (vertical distribution)

Deciles	1	2	3	4	5	6	7	8	9	10	Total
						1993					
Wages & salaries	2.4	3.5	4.8	5.7	7.2	9.2	11.1	13.6	17.1	25.4	100.0
Income from occasional work	16.1	6.4	6.1	5.2	7.1	10.4	7.3	8.2	13.7	19.6	100.0
Self-employment income	2.5	3.4	6.2	5.9	5.6	8.0	8.1	12.1	21.7	26.5	100.0
Income from agriculture	3.4	5.1	5.6	6.6	9.3	9.8	12.3	14.4	15.3	18.1	100.0
Income from capital	0.7	0.8	0.6	2.0	2.1	2.5	5.0	7.2	13.7	65.5	100.0
Pensions	6.2	9.1	10.3	10.9	11.5	11.4	11.5	10.9	10.2	8.1	100.0
Unemployment benefits	19.6	18.9	10.7	10.3	10.3	5.9	7.7	7.3	5.0	4.3	100.0
Family benefits	12.1	10.4	8.9	9.0	10.3	10.1	10.7	10.6	9.2	8.7	100.0
Other social benefits	14.8	12.4	9.8	8.4	9.4	9.5	8.7	9.1	8.4	9.5	100.0
Interfamily transfers	4.3	5.6	5.9	6.7	7.0	8.9	8.7	11.7	14.3	26.9	100.0
Other income	1.4	2.9	3.6	3.8	5.4	7.7	15.0	9.0	16.5	34.8	100.0
Total income	5.0	6.2	6.7	7.4	8.7	9.6	10.9	12.2	14.0	19.2	100.0
						1997					
Wages & salaries	3.0	5.1	4.7	5.7	7.1	8.1	10.8	12.7	15.6	27.2	100.0
Income from occasional work	16.9	7.8	17.8	9.4	5.0	9.4	8.3	4.6	9.4	11.4	100.0
Self-employment income	4.7	7.1	6.1	5.1	5.8	7.1	7.6	9.0	14.2	33.4	100.0
Income from agriculture	4.3	5.4	7.0	6.5	7.8	9.2	11.2	14.0	16.7	17.9	100.0
Income from capital	0.9	1.1	1.8	2.3	1.9	3.1	3.2	9.9	8.0	67.8	100.0
Pensions	4.5	7.2	9.6	10.6	11.7	12.1	12.1	11.9	11.7	8.7	100.0
Unemployment benefits	33.6	17.9	8.1	10.0	7.6	5.7	3.9	5.5	3.6	4.0	100.0
Family benefits	19.5	13.8	9.9	9.4	8.5	7.8	7.3	6.7	6.3	10.8	100.0
Other social benefits	12.2	10.7	9.2	10.6	12.9	9.5	10.8	10.1	6.1	7.9	100.0
Interfamily transfers	6.1	7.1	7.7	6.9	7.1	10.3	10.9	12.0	15.6	16.4	100.0
Other income	4.7	5.4	10.6	5.6	5.2	7.1	9.1	10.2	22.0	20.2	100.0
Total income	5.6	6.7	7.1	7.6	8.5	9.3	10.6	11.8	13.5	19.4	100.0
						2002					
Wages & salaries	3.1	5.6	6.3	6.7	8.0	9.3	10.3	12.6	15.6	22.4	100.0
Income from occasional work	17.1	10.5	9.4	8.0	8.5	7.2	6.9	8.7	10.6	13.1	100.0
Self-employment income	3.7	4.3	4.6	4.8	4.3	7.9	6.8	9.3	16.2	38.0	100.0
Income from agriculture	4.6	7.2	6.2	7.9	7.3	8.9	9.0	11.7	13.5	23.7	100.0
Income from capital	2.1	0.2	1.5	1.2	1.1	2.6	3.7	3.9	8.0	75.6	100.0
Pensions	5.6	7.7	9.2	10.4	11.5	11.5	12.5	12.0	11.0	8.6	100.0
Unemployment benefits	42.9	17.7	8.6	8.9	4.7	6.3	3.4	2.9	2.2	2.5	100.0
Family benefits	26.8	15.6	11.2	8.7	8.2	7.3	5.3	6.1	6.4	4.5	100.0
Other social benefits	17.0	14.7	8.2	9.4	9.3	8.1	8.6	11.1	6.9	6.6	100.0
Interfamily transfers	5.8	6.6	6.4	6.6	6.6	9.2	9.0	10.7	13.6	25.5	100.0
Other income	5.9	5.9	3.0	4.7	2.7	5.7	11.9	19.9	17.8	22.4	100.0
Total income	5.8	6.9	7.2	7.7	8.4	9.5	10.1	11.5	13.3	19.6	100.0

Source: Hungarian HBS 1993, 1997, 2002.

Table HU4: The structure of household members, by socioeconomic status and income deciles (horizontal structure)

Deciles	1	2	3	4	5	6	7	8	9	10	Total
1993											
Employees (non-agricultural)	11.0	14.6	19.1	20.3	23.3	27.9	28.6	35.2	39.3	45.7	26.6
Active in agriculture	1.8	2.5	3.8	2.7	3.8	3.8	4.4	4.4	4.5	4.9	3.7
Self employed (non-agricult.)	1.4	1.7	2.2	2.3	1.6	1.9	2.4	2.0	3.6	3.5	2.2
Persons with occasional income	2.0	0.9	0.6	0.4	0.2	0.4	0.3	0.2	0.1	0.4	0.6
Unemployed	17.4	13.0	7.5	6.2	6.7	3.8	5.1	3.9	3.3	2.3	6.9
Pensioners	20.6	28.8	33.1	33.8	31.3	29.0	26.6	24.2	21.3	16.5	26.4
Persons on paid child care	3.9	4.5	3.1	3.8	3.4	3.4	3.0	2.5	2.6	2.6	3.3
Dependants	40.8	32.8	29.8	29.9	29.4	29.5	29.2	26.8	24.9	24.0	29.7
Other	0.9	1.4	0.8	0.6	0.5	0.3	0.4	0.9	0.4	0.1	0.6
All	100.0	100.0	100.0	100.0	100.0	100.0	100.0	100.0	100.0	100.0	100.0
1997											
Employees (non-agricultural)	11.5	19.0	18.8	21.2	24.1	26.7	32.1	34.0	37.4	47.1	26.6
Active in agriculture	1.5	2.3	3.0	2.0	2.7	2.6	2.6	3.9	4.4	4.4	2.9
Self employed (non-agricult.)	2.0	2.9	2.0	1.7	1.8	2.0	2.0	1.6	2.7	3.9	2.3
Persons with occasional income	3.5	0.9	2.6	0.7	0.3	0.6	0.5	0.0	0.5	0.8	1.1
Unemployed	17.8	9.6	6.0	6.0	5.0	3.6	2.3	2.6	1.9	2.4	6.1
Pensioners	15.1	24.2	33.1	36.1	36.3	36.8	32.7	31.1	27.5	17.8	28.6
Persons on paid child care	6.1	4.9	3.4	4.1	2.6	2.5	2.5	2.5	1.5	1.2	3.2
Dependants	41.1	35.1	30.5	27.5	26.9	25.0	24.9	24.1	23.2	21.9	28.5
Other	1.5	1.1	0.6	0.6	0.5	0.3	0.2	0.1	0.8	0.5	0.6
All	100.0	100.0	100.0	100.0	100.0	100.0	100.0	100.0	100.0	100.0	100.0
2002											
Employees (non-agricultural)	11.3	20.5	24.0	25.6	28.9	30.5	34.6	37.4	41.1	44.7	28.9
Active in agriculture	1.9	2.2	1.4	2.6	1.9	2.6	2.8	2.9	3.0	4.7	2.6
Self employed (non-agricult.)	2.4	2.8	2.9	3.3	2.2	3.6	3.2	4.4	5.3	8.1	3.7
Persons with occasional income	2.9	1.5	1.5	0.9	0.9	0.8	0.7	0.9	0.4	0.5	1.2
Unemployed	10.6	5.5	2.9	3.1	1.7	2.0	1.1	0.9	0.9	0.9	3.3
Pensioners	17.1	26.2	31.4	34.9	36.9	32.8	36.0	30.4	27.0	20.0	28.9
Persons on paid child care	6.2	4.3	4.0	3.3	2.3	2.3	1.0	1.8	1.5	1.3	3.0
Dependants	43.8	35.2	30.5	25.5	24.0	24.6	20.1	21.0	20.5	19.6	27.3
Other	3.9	1.9	1.5	0.9	1.0	0.8	0.5	0.3	0.3	0.2	1.3
All	100.0	100.0	100.0	100.0	100.0	100.0	100.0	100.0	100.0	100.0	100.0

Source: Hungarian HBS 1993, 1997, 2002.

174

Table HU5:   The distribution of household members (by socioeconomic status) across income deciles (vertical distribution)

Deciles	1	2	3	4	5	6	7	8	9	10	Total
						1993					
Employees (non-agricultural)	4.4	5.3	6.7	7.1	8.9	10.8	11.4	14.0	15.2	16.3	100.0
Active in agriculture	5.3	6.6	9.5	6.9	10.5	10.5	12.7	12.8	12.6	12.7	100.0
Self employed (non-agricult.)	6.5	7.1	9.1	9.6	7.1	8.8	11.5	9.2	16.7	14.6	100.0
Persons with occasional income	38.2	15.7	10.7	7.1	3.3	7.8	5.1	3.7	1.2	7.3	100.0
Unemployed	26.4	18.1	10.0	8.3	9.8	5.7	7.9	6.0	4.9	3.2	100.0
Pensioners	8.2	10.5	11.6	11.9	12.1	11.3	10.7	9.7	8.3	5.9	100.0
Persons on paid child care	12.6	13.1	8.8	10.7	10.4	10.7	9.7	8.1	8.3	7.5	100.0
Dependants	14.4	10.6	9.3	9.3	10.1	10.2	10.4	9.6	8.6	7.7	100.0
Other	15.5	20.6	12.0	9.0	7.2	5.1	6.4	15.0	7.2	1.9	100.0
						1997					
Employees (non-agricultural)	5.4	7.6	6.9	7.4	8.7	9.6	11.9	12.5	13.5	16.5	100.0
Active in agriculture	6.4	8.3	10.2	6.4	8.9	8.6	8.9	13.4	14.8	14.2	100.0
Self employed (non-agricult.)	10.9	13.6	8.6	7.2	7.5	8.4	8.9	7.2	11.8	16.1	100.0
Persons with occasional income	39.0	8.8	22.4	6.1	2.6	5.4	4.8	0.0	4.2	6.7	100.0
Unemployed	36.6	16.6	9.5	9.2	7.8	5.6	3.8	4.2	3.1	3.7	100.0
Pensioners	6.6	8.9	11.2	11.7	12.2	12.3	11.3	10.7	9.3	5.8	100.0
Persons on paid child care	23.6	16.1	10.3	11.8	7.7	7.3	7.8	7.7	4.5	3.4	100.0
Dependants	18.1	13.0	10.4	9.0	9.1	8.4	8.7	8.3	7.9	7.2	100.0
Other	28.4	18.5	8.5	8.4	7.5	3.9	3.2	1.7	12.5	7.6	100.0
						2002					
Employees (non-agricultural)	5.1	7.8	8.2	8.4	9.5	10.4	11.2	12.4	13.4	13.6	100.0
Active in agriculture	9.6	9.6	5.3	9.7	7.1	9.9	10.4	11.0	11.2	16.2	100.0
Self employed (non-agricult.)	8.4	8.3	7.6	8.4	5.7	9.6	8.1	11.3	13.5	19.1	100.0
Persons with occasional income	32.5	14.0	12.7	6.9	7.6	6.5	5.6	7.7	3.1	3.4	100.0
Unemployed	42.1	18.4	8.7	8.9	4.9	6.0	3.2	2.7	2.6	2.5	100.0
Pensioners	7.7	10.0	10.7	11.5	12.2	11.2	11.7	10.1	8.8	6.1	100.0
Persons on paid child care	27.3	15.8	13.3	10.7	7.5	7.7	3.2	5.7	4.7	4.0	100.0
Dependants	21.0	14.2	11.0	8.9	8.4	8.9	6.9	7.4	7.1	6.3	100.0
Other	40.4	16.3	11.6	7.1	7.9	6.5	3.8	2.6	2.3	1.5	100.0

Source: Hungarian HBS 1993, 1997, 2002.

Table HU6:   Distribution of the agricultural population (% of total population;
disaggregation of the third column of Table 9)

	Employees	Members of agricultural cooperatives	Self-employed in agriculture	Active in agriculture, total
First decile				
1993	1.1	0.5	0.2	1.8
1997	0.9	0.2	0.4	1.5
2002	1.3	0.1	0.7	1.9
Tenth decile				
1993	2.5	1.7	0.8	4.9
1997	1.8	1.3	1.3	4.4
2002	1.3	0.2	3.3	4.7
All				
1993	1.8	1.3	0.6	3.7
1997	1.5	0.9	0.5	2.9
2002	1.4	0.1	1.1	2.6

Source: HBS 1993, 1997, 2002.

Table HU7:   HBS unemployment rates

Deciles	1	2	3	4	5	6	7	8	9	10	Total
1993	51.7	39.8	22.5	19.4	18.8	10.1	12.6	8.6	6.4	4.1	17.3
1997	49.1	27.6	18.5	19.0	14.7	10.0	5.8	6.2	4.1	4.1	15.6
2002	36.4	16.9	8.8	8.7	4.7	5.0	2.6	2.0	1.8	1.6	8.3

Source: Based on Table HU3, dividing the number of unemployed by the sum of employed, active in agriculture, self-employed, occasional workers and unemployed.

Chapter 5

The Transition Process and Changes in Income, Income Inequality and Poverty: The Case of Romania

Manuela Sofia Stănculescu / Lucian Pop

Poverty and inequality measurement in Romania

Until 1994, poverty and inequality were considered a political taboo in Romania. Between 1991 and 1994, only the Research Institute for the Quality of Life (RIQL) developed a programme focused on poverty and anti-poverty policies and carried out surveys on an annual basis. In 1992, RIQL issued the first calculation of an absolute poverty line using the normative method. The first comprehensive analysis of poverty and inequality was released in 1995 (Zamfir, 1995), providing an overview of the work of the RIQL team.

After 1994, the national expertise in the field of poverty and inequality has been greatly developed, mainly in relation to programmes of international agencies. Beginning with 1995 the Integrated Household Survey (IHS), designed with international expertise, and implemented by the Romanian National Institute for Statistics (NIS) became functional. In 1996, both the World Bank and UNDP, together with national experts, started to develop a methodology for poverty and inequality measurement. In 1997, within the UNDP Poverty Alleviation Project, different research teams of the National Institute for Statistics, and the Romanian Academy analysed the outcomes of five different methods [1] (with two or three corresponding lines) and five

---

[1] The World Bank method (a combination between the caloric and food expenditure weight methods, the NIS caloric scale of equivalence, food line and poverty line), the normative method (RIQL version – RIQL scale of equivalence, subsistence line and decency line), the relative poverty methods (NIS version – modified OECD and NIS caloric scales of equivalence, poverty lines – 40%, 50%, and 60% of the average consumption expenditures per adult equivalent), and the multidimensional model (TFR method, described in Cheli et al., 1994).

scales of equivalence. Needless to say, each method (line and equivalence scale) proved to have its advantages and its limitations. Regardless of the methodology, however, the subsistence poverty rates ranged between 23% and 33% of the population, but between 28% and 52% when the superior poverty line was used.

The main outcome of the project was an "official" methodology (the NIS version of the relative method and the NIS caloric scale of equivalence), which was used in most subsequent poverty assessments in the 1999-2001 period (UNDP, 1998 and 1999a).

In parallel, the World Bank initiated a series of studies on rural poverty (Chircă and Teşliuc, 1999) and on rural community poverty. In 1999 the first comprehensive analysis of poverty trends and the system of social protection was issued (Teşliuc and Pop, 1999), followed by subsequent studies (e.g. Teşliuc et al., 2001; CASE, 2004). In 2001, with World Bank support, a first study on post-socialist underclass and urban poor zones was also undertaken (Stănculescu and Berevoescu, 2004).

In 2002, the World Bank, the Anti-Poverty and Social Inclusion Commission (CASPIS) and the National Institute of Statistics jointly developed a new measurement methodology (Teşliuc et al., 2003), which is currently used by the Romanian Government in the design of social policy regulations and programmes.

Irrespective of the methodology, nearly all previous studies on inequality and poverty in Romania used the population consumption expenditures as the welfare indicator. The present study is based on incomes so that the results presented below are not necessarily consistent with those of the previous studies.

This is an empirical study based on micro-data at the household level from four nationally representative surveys carried out by the National Institute for Statistics, namely the Integrated Household Survey (for 1995 and 1997) and the Family Budget Survey[2] (for 2001 and 2004) (see the Technical Annex).

---

2   Similar to the IHS (1995-2000), the FBS is conducted (since 2001) on a monthly basis on a sample of approximately 3,000 households (an annual sample includes about 36,000 households). FBS preserves the IHS modules on expenditures and incomes. However, adjustments to the Eurostat definitions and classifications were made.

1 Changes in GDP, wages, pensions and social protection expenditures

For analysing changes in income, income inequality and poverty during transition, we selected four points fairly well spread in time: 1995 was a year of apparent recovery after the first depression (1988-1992) and it was also the year when the first national household budget survey was available; 1997 was the first year of the second depression (1997-1999); 2001 marked the beginning of economic recovery; 2004 was the year when the national output reached the 1989 level. 2004 was also the year when the European Commission concluded its report, assessing that Romania complies with the criterion of being a functioning market economy.

Table 1 describes the general context in which households operated in the four selected years: 1995 – GDP increase and significant decrease of inflation; 1997 – GDP decline, high inflation and significant drop in household gross income; 2001 – GDP started to grow reaching back the 1997 level, inflation considerably reduced, but household gross income was still low, lower than in 1997 and much lower than in 1995; 2004 – significant GDP growth, substantial decrease of inflation and increase of household gross income, but the agricultural sector was seriously hit by massive floods.

179

Table 1: The general context in which households operated during transition

Year	Real GDP growth (1989=100) (1)	Annual inflation rate (2)	Real average gross income of households (1995=100) (3)
1989	100	3.3	
1990	94.4	5.1	
1991	82.2	170.2	
1992	75.0	210.4	
1993	76.1	256.1	
1994	79.1	136.7	
1995	84.7	32.3	100
1996	88.0	38.8	104.7
1997	82.6	154.8	84.4
1998	78.2	59.1	79.3
1999	77.2	45.8	71.0
2000	78.9	45.7	68.3
2001	83.3	34.5	79.5
2002	87.6	22.5	81.9
2003	92.2	15.4	85.8
2004	99.9	11.9	104.7

Source: (1) Computations based on Table EBRD in UNICEF, Innocenti Social Monitor 2004 for 1990-1998 and Eurostat (http://epp.eurostat.cec.eu.int), Table a_gdp_k for 1999-2007; (2) NIS, Statistical Yearbook; (3) Computations based on IHS (1995-2000) and FBS (2001-2004).

The difficult economic transformation resulted in a very large decrease in real wages in the first years of transition: in 1993, the average real wage represented only 58.9% of its 1990 level. After a short period of recovery, during the second recession period, real wages fell down again to 56-58% of their 1990 level. Since 2000 wages have continuously increased, yet reaching in 2004 only 78.3% of the 1990 level (see Table 2).

Table 2:   The dynamics of wages in Romania, 1990-2004

Year	Index of average real wage (1990=100)	Gross minimum wage as % of average wage	Share of wages in GDP (%) (1)
1990	100	59.2	0.550
1991	81.5	78.2	0.443
1992	70.8	62.7	0.390
1993	58.9	62.1	0.365
1994	59.1	38.0	0.342
1995	66.5	35.5	0.356
1996	72.7	30.2	0.339
1997	56.2	39.6	0.281
1998	58.4	33.6	0.368
1999	57.0	29.5	0.296
2000	59.4	46.7	0.357
2001	62.4	46.4	0.376
2002	63.9	46.2	0.364
2003	70.8	51.7	0.346
2004	78.3	51.7	0.342

Source: NIS, Statistical Yearbook; (1) NIS. In 1998 the methodology was changed from ESA79 to ESA95.

The large drop in real wages was accompanied by a considerable decrease in employment. Unlike wages, however, employment kept on falling even after the economic recovery, which started in 2000 (see Chapter 1). The major decrease of employment was concentrated at the level of employees. Furthermore, the chaotic wage evolution by types of activities, sectors, professions, jobs, and areas of residence resulted in substantial changes of the structure of employees by wage groups. On the one hand, the share of employees earning the minimum wage or less increased from 3.5% in 1994 to 6.1% in 1998, and 31.7% in 2004. On the other hand, the proportion of employees earning monthly wages that exceed two monthly average wages increased from 5% in 1994 to about 17% in 1998, afterwards decreasing to 9% in 2004.

In addition, the decrease in the real minimum wage was much greater than the decrease in the real average wage. In 1999, the minimum wage reached its lowest value, only 29% of the 1989 level and only 29.5% of the average wage (compared to 65.4% in 1989); between 2000 and 2003, the minimum wage increased to 59% of its 1989 level and 51.7% of the average wage. Over the entire 1994-1999 period, the minimum wage was even lower than the average unemployment benefit.

Due to these negative developments, the share of (gross) wages in gross total income of households decreased from 62.8% in 1989 to 43.8% in 1995, 37.9% in 1997, and reached a minimum of 36.3% in 2000 (NIS data). Once the economy recovered, the trend reversed, and the share has increased.

Social benefits only to a lesser degree replaced the diminished contribution of wages to the household budget. After 1990 Romania faced two tendencies: on the one hand, huge social costs (mainly related to massive retirement, rise in unemployment and high poverty), and, on the other hand, decreasing funding available for social protection. In the first years of transition, Romania adopted a "prudent attitude: a slow economic reform and a low social protection" (Zamfir, 1997: 31; see also Milanovic, 1998). However, the solid economic reforms implemented after 1996, the reform of the mechanisms for collecting contributions (the system became fully operational only in 2001) as well as the drastic change of the social assistance system after 2001 led to significant improvements in recent years.

As the budgetary resources increased, social expenditures as share in GDP have also increased, but remain among the lowest in Europe. The current social protection system is widespread – it amounts to about 10% of the GDP, reaching 83% of the population – and substantially contributes to poverty reduction, with a large share of the impact being due to pensions (World Bank, 2003) and child allowances (Zamfir, 2005).

Table 3 presents the basic trends of the most important expenditure categories within the system of social protection. The largest part of these expenditures goes to social insurance, with increasing expenditures on pensions and decreasing expenditures on cash unemployment benefits.

Table 3:   Social protection expenditures, as percentage of GDP

Year	Social ex-penditure (1)	Social protection expenditure (2)	Unemploy-ment cash benefits (3)	Pensions (4)	Social assistance (5)
1989	14.2	9.5	0	5.2	n.a.
1990	16.6	11.0	0	6.5	2.7
1991	17.0	10.1	0.3	5.9	1.4
1992	16.5	9.8	0.7	5.9	1.0
1993	15.2	9.1	0.9	5.6	0.8
1994	15.5	9.5	1.0	5.6	0.7
1995	16.0	10.0	1.0	5.8	0.8
1996	15.7	9.3	0.7	5.7	0.7
1997	15.9	10.0	1.3	5.4	1.2
1998	17.3	10.5	1.4	5.8	1.3
1999	18.4	10.8	1.5	6.9	0.9
2000	17.2	10.4	1.2	6.4**	0.7
2001	18.2	11.0	0.8	6.5**	0.8
2002	18.1	10.5	0.7	7.3	1.2
2003	18.4	10.4	0.8	7.0	1.0
2004 (p)	19.4	11.5	0.8	7.4	1.0

Notes: (1) Social expenditures covered both from state and local budgets. We did not adopt the ESSPROS classification because it was not yet available in Romania. (2) Social protection expenditures include administrative expenses and refer to all social expenditures, except those for the education and health sectors. (3) Unemployment cash benefits include unemployment benefit, allowance for vocational integration and support allowance. (4) Pensions also include pension-related expenditures, health insurance for pensioners and administration costs of the pension system. (5) Social assistance includes family benefits paid from the state budget: state allowances for children, allowances for family place-ment, newborn allowances, benefits for wives of conscripts, emergency benefits and benefits paid from the local budgets: social aid (means-tested for the poor), birth indemnities, and emergency benefits. Thus, family benefits are included in the social assistance expenditures.

Source: Romanian Government, Joint Memorandum on Social Inclusion 2005 (JIM); Calculations based on data published by NIS, Ministry of Public Finance and (**) Ministry of Labour, Social Solidarity and Family; (p) Projection.

In the field of social assistance, the introduction of the Guaranteed Minimum Income (GMI) in 2002 is considered the most important reform. Social aid was first introduced in 1995, under the financial responsibility of the local governments. Insufficient local budgets led to the failure of the social assist-ance system in 2000, when expenditures on social aid represented only 6% of those corresponding to the first months of implementation. Consequently, in 2002, the GMI replaced the former system. Since the introduction of the

GMI,[3] the share of social assistance expenditure in GDP has increased more significantly, but the resources allocated are considered to be insufficient to meet the needs (Zamfir, 2005).

Table 4 shows the main trends in the pension/wage ratio. The replacement rate, expressed by the ratio between the average pension (all types) and average wage, declined between 1990 and 2000, and then varied in the narrow band of 32-35%. However, the ratio between the average old-age pension with due complete stage and average wage was much higher; after 2000, it ranged around 55-58%. Furthermore, these two ratios followed different patterns. Both ratios declined considerably between 1990 and 1996 and stabilized in a narrow band after 2000. But in the period 1997-1999, while the ratio between the average pension and average wage declined (from 41.1% to 34.9%), the ratio between the average old-age pension with due complete stage and the average wage increased (from 52.1% to 60%). The decrease in the former ratio was mainly due to the large number of early/ anticipated retired people (receiving old-age pensions with due incomplete stage) associated with massive redundancies implemented in this period.

Real pensions decreased much more than real wages: in 2000, the average real pension represented only 44% of the 1990 level; in 2004, the average real wage reached 78% of its 1990 level, the average real pension reached only 57.7% of its 1990 level.

The situation of pensions is an aggregate result of several negative tendencies. First, the large increase in the number of pensioners due to the legal provisions encouraging early/anticipated retirement as alternative to redundancy, due to the inclusion of 1.7 million retired farmers in the system, but also because of a considerable increase in the number of disability pensioners. Second, the insufficient resources for funding the system, due to the low (and decreasing) number of contributors and the low (but improving) collection rate.[4]

While the total number of pensioners (survivors and disability pensioners included) increased from 3.5 million persons to more than 6 million between 1990 and 2004, the number of employees (the main contributors) declined within the same period, from over 8 million to about 6 million,

183

---

3   The GMI scheme is means-tested and consists of granting to beneficiaries the difference between the standard level of minimum income set by law and the disposable income of the person/family, under specific conditions. When GMI started to be implemented, the benchmark minimum revenue was set at 36% of the minimum gross wage in the economy.

4   For instance, in 2001, the collection rate (proportion of collected contributions out of the total due contributions) was only 77% (Toma, 2004).

but only about 4.5 million were contributing to the system. Third, the pension system was highly inequitable. In the transition context, the pension calculation method inherited from the socialist period led to serious discrepancies between high and low pensions: in 2001, the highest pension in Romania was 42 times the average pension, while the lowest pension represented only 0.015% of the average pension. As part of the pension reform introduced in 2000 (and implemented beginning with April 2001), a new calculation method was introduced and a process of pension recalculation was adopted in 2001 (for a 3-year period), aimed at reducing these differences. The recalculation and realignment was less successful than expected and large variations still persist. A new mechanism was initiated in 2004 to recalculate all the pensions granted before April 2001.

Table 4:   The real pension and the pension/wage ratio, Romania 1990-2004

Year	Average real pension of state social insurance pensioners (1990=100) (1)	Average social insurance pension (all types) as % of average net wage (2)	Average old-age pension with due complete stage as % of average net wage	Average farmer's pension as % of average net wage
1990	100.0	46.5	62.6	14.4
1991	74.3	44.5	52.8	7.2
1992	63.1	43.6	53.9	4.6
1993	56.3	45.0	56.0	6.5
1994	55.0	43.2	54.9	8.6
1995	61.4	41.8	53.0	7.8
1996	63.1	39.5	50.1	8.1
1997	50.3	41.1	52.1	10.9
1998	49.2	38.4	49.5	9.9
1999	47.2	34.9	60.0	9.4
2000	44.0	33.8	57.9	8.8
2001	46.6	34.5	58.2	9.0
2002	48.2	35.2	58.6	9.1
2003	51.6	32.3	54.7	8.0
2004	57.7	34.1	56.6	12.3

Notes: Since 1 July 2000, monthly average pension includes monthly average pension, supplementary pension, health social insurance contribution and tax for the amount exceeding the legal threshold. Since 1 January 2003, the amounts for pensions do not include the health social insurance contribution.

Source: Calculations based on NIS, Statistical Yearbook 1994, 2000, 2005; (1) Including the pensions of the Ministry of National Defence, the Ministry of Administration and Interior and the Romanian Intelligence Office system, which comply to a special retirement scheme. (2) All types of pensions include old-age pension with due complete or incomplete stage, pension for disability, for farmers, for survivors, for war invalids and their widows, and for social support.

Table 5A: The socioeconomic structure of household members, by income deciles

		Employees	Non-agricultural self-employed	Active in agriculture	Unemployed	Pensioners	Dependants 0-17 years	Dependants 18+ years	All population
First decile	1995	7.6	2.7	20.6	9.6	13.4	34.0	12.0	100
	1997	8.6	2.8	20.2	10.5	11.2	33.3	13.5	100
	2001	4.4	3.8	23.9	11.4	11.4	32.8	12.3	100
	2004	4.8	5.3	19.0	11.4	12.1	32.4	15.0	100
Tenth decile	1995	50.5	3.8	4.6	1.7	14.5	18.1	6.8	100
	1997	46.1	3.7	5.0	2.1	16.4	18.7	7.9	100
	2001	49.1	3.4	3.1	2.1	17.9	16.2	8.3	100
	2004	51.2	4.8	3.8	1.7	15.5	15.7	7.4	100
All	1995	28.6	1.7	10.0	5.5	20.8	24.7	8.8	100
	1997	28.2	1.8	9.5	5.1	21.6	23.9	9.8	100
	2001	24.3	2.4	10.4	6.7	24.0	21.9	10.2	100
	2004	26.0	3.3	9.3	5.4	23.9	21.2	10.9	100

Table 5B: The distribution of household members (by socioeconomic status) across income deciles

		Employees	Non-agricultural self-employed	Active in agriculture	Unemployed	Pensioners	Dependants 0-17 years	Dependants 18+ years	All population
First decile	1995	3.3	19.6	25.4	21.3	7.9	16.9	16.8	12.3
	1997	3.8	19.0	26.6	25.7	6.5	17.5	17.3	12.6
	2001	2.4	20.4	29.7	21.8	6.1	19.3	15.6	12.9
	2004	2.4	20.4	26.1	27.1	6.5	19.6	17.6	12.8
Tenth decile	1995	15.3	19.5	4.0	2.7	6.1	6.4	6.6	8.7
	1997	14.4	17.9	4.7	3.7	6.7	6.9	7.1	8.8
	2001	17.9	12.5	2.6	2.8	6.6	6.6	7.2	8.9
	2004	17.1	12.5	3.5	2.8	5.6	6.4	5.9	8.6
All	All years	100	100	100	100	100	100	100	100

Source: IHS 1995, 1997 and FBS 2001, 2004.

2   Socioeconomic structure at the household level

This section focuses on the economic activity of household members, while the next sections will concentrate on income, income inequality and poverty. Changes in the socioeconomic structure at the household level (Table 5) reflect the macro tendencies described in Chapter 1: the decreasing activity rate and share (number) of employees, the increasing share (number) of pensioners as well as the increase in the rate of unemployment between 1997 and 2001.

There are discrepancies between data presented in Table 5 and data from other statistical sources, notably the Labour Force Survey (LFS). For example, according to the IHS/FBS data, the activity rate[5] declined from 58% in 1997 to 55% in 2004, while according to the LFS,[6] it declined from 65% to 54.8%, during the same period. These discrepancies result mainly from our decision to use the IHS/FBS[7] item on occupational status for the computations presented in Table 5, which allows the interviewed persons to choose (from a short list) the status that they think to be the most appropriate for their situation.

Consequently, Table 5 is based on different concepts than the LFS. For instance, in the IHS/FBS data from Table 5, "unemployed" refers to all persons who declared themselves as such, regardless of whether they are registered or not at the Agencies for Employment, if they do receive or not some form of unemployment compensation, or if they comply or not with the ILO criteria for unemployment. In common language, self-declared unemployed is synonymous with "I am looking for a job". On the other hand, casual workers or informal workers, which in the LFS would be recorded either as employees or as self-employed, in the household budget survey may choose a different status. Under these conditions, the widespread[8] situations

---

5   Number of all active persons (employed and unemployed) divided by the population 15 years and over.

6   The LFS is available in Romania only beginning with 1996. For this reason, here we do not use the year 1995. Figures provided here come from the time series recalculated based on the 2002 Census (NIS, 2005).

7   The Romanian IHS/FBS includes also an extended chapter on work, but for Table 5 we chose keeping people's point of view, without performing any statistical corrections.

8   In 2001, in Romania, out of the total employment aged 15 years or more, 12% were wage-earners without work contract, 14% combined a formal main activity with at least one additional activity (mostly informal), and 23% were self-employed (the large majority being pensioner-farmer or unemployed-farmer active in subsistence agriculture) (Stănculescu, 2005).

of unemployed-farmer, pensioner-farmer, multiple jobholders as well as the well-developed informal sector represent major sources of discrepancy. As a result, in the IHS/FBS data used in Table 5, the activity rate is lower and the inactivity rate is much higher than the ones from the LFS. In a systematic manner, the IHS/FBS data from Table 5 imply somewhat smaller figures for employees, but considerably smaller figures for self-employed[9] and considerably larger figures (almost double) for unemployed,[10] compared to the LFS statistics. For example, for 2001, the IHS/FBS data (Table 5) imply the following figures: 5.4 million employees, 2.9 million self-employed, and 1.5 million unemployed, while the corresponding figures provided by LFS are: 5.9 million, 4.6 million, and 0.75 million for the ILO unemployed (0.83 million for registered unemployed) respectively.

During the entire period, the activity rate of households in the poorest income decile was the lowest, whereas the most affluent households (the tenth income decile) had the highest activity rate; households from all other income deciles had activity rates between these two extremes, following the rule: the higher the income decile, the higher the activity rate. The distributions of household members according to socioeconomic status by income deciles vary between the limits set up by the extreme deciles, shown in Table 5B. Thus, the share of employees is the lowest in the poorest (first) income decile and the highest in the most affluent (tenth) income decile. In contrast, the share of people active in agriculture, of unemployed, and of dependants are the highest in the poorest households and the lowest in the most affluent ones. Two socioeconomic statuses, however, make up distinctive cases, namely non-agricultural self-employed and pensioners.

According to the LFS, the total self-employment (not including unpaid family workers) accounted for 20% of employment in 1997, 24% in 2001, and 18% in 2004. Yet, the agricultural self-employment represented 90% (in 1997-2001) to 85% (in 2004) of total self-employment. The proportion of non-agricultural self-employment, although small, increased from 2% of total employment in 1997, to 2.7% in 2004. This trend is visible also in the IHS/FBS data (Table 5A).

---

9   In this paragraph, self-employed includes also unpaid family workers. According to the NIS methodology for LFS, in a farmer household, the household head is recorded as self-employed, while the other active members are recorded as unpaid family workers. During the entire period of transition, 80-90% of the self-employed and over 95% of the unpaid family workers were doing agriculture.

10   Based on IHS/FBS, the unemployment rate was 11.4% in 1997, 15.3% in 2001, and 12.3% in 2004, compared with 5.8%, 6.4%, and 8% respectively – the ILO unemployment rates according to the LFS.

Figure 1:   The distribution of non-agricultural self-employed by income deciles

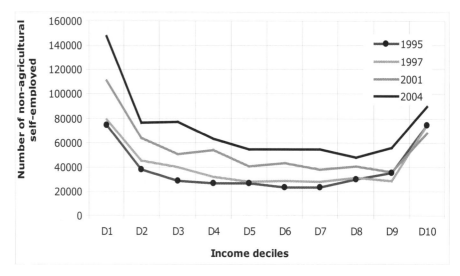

Source: IHS 1995, 1997 and FBS 2001, 2004.

More important, however, is the U-shaped distribution of the non-agricul-tural self-employed by income deciles (Figure 1), which is rather stable in time, although the proportion of non-agricultural self-employed in the tenth income decile declined to a level of 12-13% since 2000. This distribution indicates that non-agricultural self-employment was concentrated among the poorest and among the most affluent. These results are confirmed by other studies (e.g. Neef and Stănculescu, 2002); however, there is a trend after 2000 to move towards the poorest.

The share of pensioners in total population increased gradually from 22.5% in 1995 to 28% in 2004, according to NIS data. This growing trend is also observed in the IHS/FBS data (Table 5A). Unlike the other socioeco-nomic groups, pensioners are concentrated in the middle (third to eighth) income deciles. Both within the poorest and the most affluent households, pensioners were underrepresented, during the entire period 1995-2004.

Finally, the group of dependants slightly decreased from 33.5% of the total population in 1995 to 32.1% in 2004.

The structure of dependants by gender and age categories (Table 6) shows that several types of economic dependency can be identified. The dependency of children represents the dominant type of economic depend-ency, accounting for 74% of all dependants in 1995, and 66% in 2004. The decreasing share of dependant children (0-17 years) is clearly caused by falling fertility rates; whereas they represented 24.7% of all household members in 1995, their share shrank to 21.2% in 2004. Noteworthy, in Romania many children (0-17 years) live in the poorest households: almost a third of all children are from households found in the first or second income decile (see Table RO4).

Table 6:   Shares of dependants by gender and age groups
(as percentage of total population)

		0 to 17 years	18 to 29 years	30 to 59 years	60 + years	All
1995	Men	12.5	2.2	0.3	0.1	15.1
	Women	12.2	3.2	2.3	0.8	18.4
	All	24.7	5.4	2.6	0.8	33.5
1997	Men	12.0	2.2	0.2	0.1	14.5
	Women	11.8	3.6	3.0	0.8	19.2
	All	23.9	5.7	3.2	0.9	33.7
2001	Men	11.2	2.3	0.2	0.1	13.8
	Women	10.7	3.5	3.3	0.8	18.3
	All	21.9	5.8	3.5	0.8	32.1
2004	Men	10.7	2.2	0.2	0.0	13.2
	Women	10.5	3.8	3.9	0.7	18.9
	All	21.2	6.0	4.2	0.8	32.1

Source: IHS 1995, 1997 and FBS 2001, 2004.

The dependency of young people (18-29 years) is much lower, accounting for 16% of all dependants in 1995, and 19% in 2004 respectively. However, the share of young dependants in all household members is increasing mainly as a consequence of the large increase in university enrolment. The share is greater for women than for men; on the one hand, because more women are enrolled in university education, and, on the other hand, because young mothers delay entering the labour market.

The third type of economic dependency relates to working-age household members doing domestic work. In this respect, the 30-59 age group is the most relevant; this group accounted for 8% of all dependants in 1995, and 13% in 2004. During the entire period, more than 90% of all dependants in the age group 30-59 years were women. Many of them used to work at the beginning of transition, but lost their jobs and retreated to the niche of

Table 7A: The structure of household income in the first decile, tenth decile and in all households

		Wages/ salaries	Self-employment	Income from agriculture	Income from capital	Pensions	Unemployment benefits	Family benefits	Other social benefits	Inter-family transfers	Other income	All
First decile	1995	17.8	8.4	44.2	0.1	13.4	5.4	6.2	1.8	1.6	1.0	100
	1997	16.7	7.4	43.1	0.1	13.1	3.1	11.3	2.3	2.3	0.7	100
	2001	10.5	13.0	44.0	0.1	14.5	3.2	9.8	1.5	2.2	1.1	100
	2004	12.5	11.8	34.1	0.1	17.3	1.3	7.4	10.2	2.6	2.6	100
Tenth decile	1995	48.2	12.9	23.4	1.0	5.7	0.2	0.4	0.4	5.2	2.6	100
	1997	44.6	10.4	23.9	2.7	6.8	0.3	0.9	0.4	4.2	5.8	100
	2001	57.0	4.3	17.7	1.3	9.9	0.2	0.6	0.5	4.7	3.7	100
	2004	56.2	6.4	14.7	2.7	7.6	0.2	0.4	0.5	5.1	6.1	100
All	1995	45.5	5.8	25.0	0.4	15.9	1.4	1.5	0.7	2.5	1.3	100
	1997	40.8	4.9	27.1	0.8	16.7	0.9	3.0	1.0	2.4	2.4	100
	2001	42.0	4.0	24.6	0.4	19.9	1.2	2.2	0.9	2.8	2.0	100
	2004	42.9	5.2	20.1	0.8	19.1	0.9	1.6	1.7	3.2	4.6	100

Table 7B: The distribution of household income in the first decile, tenth decile and across all households

		Wages/ salaries	Self-employment	Income from agriculture	Income from capital	Pensions	Unemployment benefits	Family benefits	Other social benefits	Inter-family transfers	Other income	All
First decile	1995	1.5	5.7	6.9	1.2	3.3	15.6	16.1	9.8	2.4	2.9	3.9
	1997	1.8	6.4	6.8	0.5	3.4	13.9	16.2	9.8	4.1	1.3	4.3
	2001	1.0	13.3	7.4	1.2	3.0	11.2	18.6	7.3	3.3	2.2	4.1
	2004	1.2	9.1	6.8	0.3	3.6	6.1	18.7	24.3	3.2	2.2	4.0
Tenth decile	1995	24.4	51.1	21.5	59.0	8.2	3.4	5.9	12.0	48.0	45.8	23.0
	1997	24.2	46.7	19.5	74.5	8.9	7.8	6.7	8.7	38.4	53.7	22.1
	2001	29.4	23.3	15.7	69.9	10.8	3.3	6.2	13.5	36.2	39.0	21.7
	2004	29.3	27.7	16.4	80.1	8.9	4.3	6.3	6.5	35.8	29.8	22.4
All	All years	100	100	100	100	100	100	100	100	100	100	100

Notes: Wages include social security benefits for temporary disability, maternity and child leave. Other income includes income from redundancy, sale of hard currency, in-kind products such as electricity, coal, etc. Income from agriculture refers both to sales and (counter-value of) self-consumption of food produced by household members.

Source: IHS 1995, 1997 and FBS 2001, 2004.

domestic work. Thus, data reveal the increasing dependency rate of women in the 30-59 age group. Whereas they represented 2.3% of all household members in 1995, their share increased to 3.9% in 2004. In other words, in 2004 some 850 thousand women in the 30-59 age group were dependants. Since 2004, some active labour market measures for the reinsertion of persons older than 45 years were being introduced.

The fourth, and last, type of economic dependency refers to elderly (aged 60 years or over) with no pension. This situation is specific to women, as there are virtually no men-dependants aged 60 years or over. Compared to the other three types of dependency, elderly dependency is minor in Romania; between 1995 and 2004, the share of women-dependants aged 60 and over remained rather constant at about 2-3% of all dependants and 0.8% of all household members (about 160 thousand persons).

3   Income structure at the household level

Both the aggregate trends in various income sources (wages, pensions and social protection disbursements) and the changes in the socioeconomic structure of household members give a sense of the drastic changes of the household income structure. For instance, as a consequence of the decrease in the number of employees and the declining real wages, the share of wages in total household income dropped during the second recession (1997-1999) and slightly increased during the period of economic recovery (after 2000).

Tables 7a and 7b show the main changes in income structure at the household level, in the period 1995-2004. It would be much more interesting to study these changes starting with the pre-transition period, to capture the "tectonic changes" (Milanovic, 1998) from the first years of transition. As IHS/FBS was not operational before 1995, for comparisons we will use the rather indicative statistics provided by the NIS.

Without doubt, the change that most affected the income structure of Romanian households was the huge fall in the share of cash income. Since the years of the first depression (1988-1992), the share of cash income in total household income was drastically reduced. In 1995 already, cash income represented only 72% of total household income, compared to 86% in 1989;

in 1997, it was even lower, reaching a low 68% of total household income (NIS data in UNDP, 1999b). Thus, between 1990 and 1997, cash incomes were being substituted with in-kind ones, particularly consumption of home-grown products, which gained an increasing share. The share of income from agriculture[11] in total household income increased from 14% in 1989 to 27% in 1997 (Table 7A). With the economic recovery, which started in 2000, the trends have reversed: the share of cash income in total income has increased, while the share of in-kind incomes from agriculture has decreased.[12] Yet, in-kind incomes from agriculture still accounted for as much as 20% of the total household income in 2004, and have always been particularly high (more than 50%) in the case of peasants and rural households.

As expected, the household income structure differs considerably across income deciles (Table 7A). While the poorest households (first decile) have the lowest share of cash income (about 50% of total income), the most affluent households (tenth decile) have the highest share of cash income. For the poorest households, income from agriculture and social benefits (including pensions) represent the main sources of income; they make up more than 70% of their total disposable income. In contrast, these income sources accounted for only 30% (in 1995) to 23.4% (in 2004) of the total income for the most affluent households. Income from agriculture and social benefits accounted for about 44% of the total income, for all households. The most affluent households, instead, rely more on wages and income from self-employment; between 1995 and 2004 these incomes represented more than 60% of their total income. For comparison, the corresponding share for all households varied between 51% and 45% of the total household income. In conclusion, the main sources of income for Romanian households are wages, income from agriculture and pensions. Whereas wages (and paid labour incomes) are specific to the top stratum of the social structure, incomes from agriculture are specific to the bottom ones.

This means that neither the poor households have no wage incomes, nor that the well-off households have no incomes from agriculture. Households from the first income decile also have fewer wage-earners, with much lower wages compared to households from the tenth decile. During the

---

11   In the period 1995-2004, the in-kind income accounted for 78-83% of the agricultural income (see Technical Annex).

12   The decreasing share of income from agriculture is confirmed by macro data, which show the decreasing share of agriculture in GDP. In 1997, this share amounted to 18% of GDP, decreasing to 11.7% of GDP in 2003 (UNDP, 2005a).

entire 1995-2004 period, the average wage per wage-earner from the poorest households was more than three times lower than the average wage per wage-earner from the affluent households. In contrast, households from the tenth decile had much fewer members active in agriculture, but with much higher incomes from agriculture. The average income from agriculture per active member from the affluent households was 20 times (in 1995), 24 times (in 2001), and 18 times (in 2004) higher than the average income from agriculture per active member from the poorest households. This considerable income gap results from the difference between subsistence and market-oriented agriculture. The numerous persons from poor households active in agriculture engage in subsistence agriculture, providing only in-kind incomes that cover at most food consumption of the household, whereas the few persons active in agriculture from affluent households perform market-oriented agriculture on large surfaces of (leased) land, with modern equipment and technology.

Recapitulating, households from the first income decile have a large share of persons active in agriculture, unemployed, children, dependants, and also an increasing number of non-agricultural self-employed. Accordingly, their most important income sources are agriculture and social benefits. In addition, self-employment incomes increased their share – from 8.4% in 1995 to 11.8% in 2004 – in the total disposable income of these poorest households. On the other hand, households from the tenth income decile have a large share of employees and non-agricultural self-employed, though the share of the latter is decreasing. Accordingly, between 1995 and 2004, for these affluent households, the share of wages in the total disposable income increased from 48% to 56%, whereas the share of self-employment incomes decreased sharply from 12.9% to 6.4%. Furthermore, in 1995, a non-agricultural self-employed from the tenth income decile earned on average nine times more than one from the first decile. This ratio decreased to five in the year 2004, but this might be due to under-reporting, particularly as a large part of the income of the non-agricultural self-employed is informal, and not officially registered (see Ilie, 2004). However, this considerable income gap results mainly from the difference between various types of non-agricultural self-employment. Non-agricultural self-employed are small entrepreneurs in the trade and service sector. As Neef (2004) described it, while the poor perform mainly unskilled or low-skilled services as a survival strategy, self-employed from the well-off households perform highly

193

specialized services for firms in a market-oriented manner. The former just survive, the latter accumulate experience and capital for setting up a business with high development potential.

Therefore, from the poorest to the most affluent households in Romania, labour-related incomes – be it wages, income from self-employment or agriculture – are the main contributors to the total household budget. Nonetheless, as we have shown above, these income sources are rather polarized. The situation is similar with respect to other primary income sources. Income from capital[13] is a modest income source, with a small contribution to household disposable income, even for the most affluent ones, which in relative terms benefit the most from it.

Between 1995 and 2004, interfamily transfers (receipts from persons other than household members, including remittances from abroad) were a small contribution to household disposable income. Nevertheless, this contribution was larger than that of income from capital, even for the most affluent households. For the poorest, during 1995-2001, remittances contributed more to household disposable income than the category of "other social benefits". The share of these benefits in household disposable income overtook the share of remittances only after the social assistance system was reformed in 2002. At the level of all households, during the entire period, the share of remittances in household income was higher than the shares of all social benefits other than pensions. Thus, during the most difficult years of transition, kinship/social networks rather than the social assistance system provided a more reliable safety net for poor households.

For the entire population, kinship/social networks provided a significant buffer. In addition, as shown above and as many previous studies underlined, in Romania, agriculture, although seriously under-performing in economic terms, provided also a social safety net during the restructuring process. Starting from here and keeping in mind the public controversy over how much we may or not speak about "welfare dependency" in Romania and how much the Romanians protect themselves or wait for the state to provide social protection, we performed a simple exercise.

Based on the household income structure (Table 7A), we determined a proxy for the *balance of protection,* as ratio between *state-protection* (sum of shares of all social benefits, including pensions) and *self-protection* (share

---

13   Income from real estate and other leases, from dividends, interest and sale of shares.

of income from agriculture[14] + share of interfamily transfers). Basically, this indicator shows whether the state effort for cushioning the population against the transition shock was higher (balance>1), equal (balance=1) or lower (balance<1) than people's efforts for self-protection (by growing their own food and by investing in social networks). For a comprehensive picture, we determined the protection balance both for Romania and Bulgaria.[15] The distribution of the indicator of protection balance by income deciles for Romania and Bulgaria is shown in Figure 2.

Two remarks are useful. First, "self-protection" as determined here represents also a proxy of the informal sector, particularly if non-agricultural self-employment would be included. Second, in both countries, the inclusion of non-agricultural self-employment within self-protection drags down the curve, but does not change its shape. Thus, in Romania, the major changes would be located in the extreme income deciles – the poorest and the richest – that is, the values of protection balance for poor and rich households would be even lower than shown in Figure 2. In contrast, in Bulgaria, only in the two highest income deciles – ninth and tenth – self-protection would be higher than social protection provided by the state. Although we decided not to include income from non-agricultural self-employment in Figure 2, it is important to note the major role as transition shock absorber played by the informal sector in Romania as compared to Bulgaria.

Figure 2 shows that, in Romania during the postcommunist transition, the households' welfare is definitely a personal achievement. Even for the middle-income deciles, in which the pensioners are concentrated, the share of agriculture and support received through kinship/social networks was almost equal to the share of social benefits. For the poorest, the state support was clearly insufficient, particularly during the years of economic depression. Nonetheless, the situation started to improve after 2002, when both the pension system and the social assistance system were reformed. Taking into consideration that children (0-17 years) are more concentrated among poor households (see Table RO4), the need for further efforts to provide the poor with real social inclusion opportunities becomes clear.

195

---

14   Thus, the indicator assumes that 100% of agricultural incomes are "self-protection" (growing own food). In fact, the share of in-kind income ("self-protection") in agricultural income was 78-83% in Romania and 83-89% in Bulgaria (see Technical Annex).

15   The comparison between Romania and Bulgaria is also influenced by a lower share of farmers in the latter country (see chapter on Bulgaria, this volume).

Figure 2: Protecting against the transition shock: balance (ratio) at the
household level between state's and households' efforts

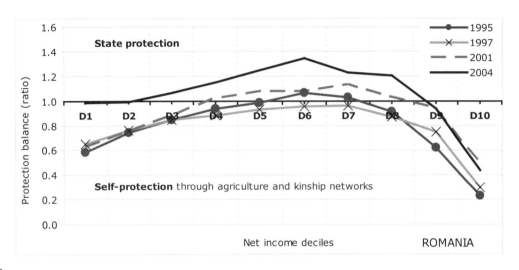

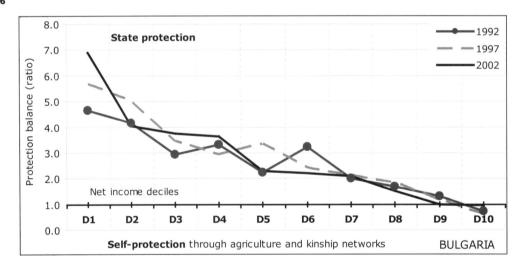

Source: Romania: IHS 1995, 1997 and FBS 2001, 2004. Bulgaria: BHBS, 1992-2002. Note: State protection = share of all social benefits, including pensions, in total household disposable income. Self-protection = share of income from agriculture and interfamily transfers in total household disposable income. Protection balance = State protection/Self-protection. Thus, a protection balance larger/smaller than 1 indicates that the state effort to protect the population was higher/lower than people's efforts to protect themselves.

Coming back to the interfamily transfers, one may observe that, consistently, the rich households were the largest recipients of remittances; Table RO2 shows that out of all incomes from interfamily transfers, the most affluent 20% of the households (the top two deciles) received more than 60% in 1995 and about 50% during 1997-2004. In Romania, this is not a statistical aberration, but reflects the strong kinship networks developed and strengthened as a response to the state socialist "economy of shortage" (Kornai, 1980). Most Romanian households are embedded in "diffuse mixed households" (Mihăilescu, 1996), which basically are kinship networks with no clear boundaries and the redistribution of resources as main function. Diffuse mixed households proved very effective not only in mastering the permanent shortages of goods and services during the socialist period, but also in dealing with the turbulences of postcommunist transformation. Most of these kinship networks include households both from rural and urban areas. The typical kinship network[16] has a rural nucleus, usually formed by elderly parents and their grown-up sons and daughters, who have not left the village, plus other relatives. Sons and daughters who left the village make up the urban parts of the network. Typically, the rural nucleus provides the urban relatives with food products. In return, the urban members provide other products or services, such as help in case of illness, accommodation in the city, help in work on the weekends or, more rarely, help with money. The richer the members of the network, the higher the amount/value of goods exchanged, which explains why the richest are also the greatest recipients of remittances.

197

---

16   Just for illustration: "We have two hectares of land, a vegetable garden, a cow, three pigs and poultry. Since we got back the land, we have worked it, but we have not sold the products, not even when we had more than we need. We give them to my brothers, who left for the city. One lives in Găeşti (city, 18 km), the other in Odorheiul Secuiesc (city, 300 km). Both are workers in industry. (…) When we need money, my brothers have always helped, they have never turned us off. When my father was ill, they sent medicines and the one from Găeşti took him to the hospital. They also help us with work in agriculture (on the weekends and holidays). The far away one comes less. Even so, we share with them what we obtain, irrespective of how much they have helped us in work." (Excerpt from an interview taken in 1999, in a Romanian village, within the research project *The Economic Potential of the Informal Economy in Romania*, financed by the Volkswagen-Stiftung, Germany. For more, see Neef and Stănculescu, 2002).

3.1   Social benefits and their coverage[17]

Pensions[18]

As shown in Table 7A, the share of pensions in total household income increased between 1995 and 2004, from 15.9% to 19.1%. The share of pensioners (as percentage of all household members) also increased, as shown in Table 5A. Pensioners are concentrated in the middle-income deciles – from the third to the eighth income decile. To a lesser degree, this is also valid for pensions, which are concentrated from the fifth to the ninth decile.

In both the poorest and the richest households, pensioners are under-represented. However, the pensioners from the poor households have an average pension three times lower than pensioners from the most affluent households. This reflects the different work history of the pensioners from the first and tenth income deciles; also, in the first (and second) decile, farmer's pensions are strongly concentrated.

198

Table 8:   Coverage of pensions

		1995	1997	2001	2004
Relevant households, as % of all households	All income deciles	33.6	34.2	36.0	37.2
	First decile	37.1	29.4	31.3	30.6
	Tenth decile	17.5	20.7	18.8	18.9
% of relevant households that receive pensions, in:	All income deciles	95.3	95.3	96.6	97.2
	First decile	85.1	83.0	84.9	88.0
	Tenth decile	95.2	95.9	97.5	97.4
% of all households that receive pensions, in:	All income deciles	47.7	48.3	52.9	53.0
	First decile	41.4	34.8	36.4	39.7
	Tenth decile	28.4	32.5	34.7	31.4

Source: IHS 1995, 1997 and FBS 2001, 2004. Note: Relevant households refer to households with at least one member of retirement age, which according to the most recent law on social security (implemented since 2001) is 65 years or more for men and 60 years or more for women.

Furthermore, as Table 8 shows, during the entire period 1995-2004, the coverage of pensions for households in the first income decile is much lower than for households in the tenth decile and for all households: more than 12% of the relevant poorest households do not receive pensions, compared to less

---

17   In this section, coverage refers to the proportion of relevant households (i.e. with pensioners, with children or with unemployed) that receive a given social benefit (i.e. pensions, family benefits or unemployment benefits).

18   Include old-age pension with due complete or incomplete stage, pension for disability, for farmers, for survivors, for war invalids and their widows, and for social support.

than 5% of all relevant households. This rather low coverage of pensions for the poorest is related to the major structural problem of rural areas and old-age farmers, for whom the situation has been unclear, particularly as they have not paid social contributions.

The coverage of pensions in Romania is lower than, for example, in Slovenia (see chapter on Slovenia, this volume). However, due to the 2001 pension reform, the share of relevant households that receive pensions increased for all relevant households (from 95.3% in 1995, to 97.2% in 2004) and for the poorest households (from 85.1% in the first income decile in 1995, to 88% in 2004). The newly introduced social allowance for single old-age persons is expected to further improve the situation.

With respect to pensions, however, Table 8 also shows that in Romania there is a large discrepancy between the share of relevant households (as determined here) and the share of households that actually receive the relevant benefit. For instance in 2004, 37.2% of all households had at least a member entitled to social insurance old-age pension, according to the law. However, the share of households that actually received pensions was much higher (53%). In the previous section on changes of income we have already mentioned that in 2000 a new pension law (effectively implemented since 2001) was passed, which changed the pension calculation method, but also increased the retirement age from 55 to 60 years for women and from 60 to 65 years for men. Thus, before 2001, the retirement age was five years lower than the one used for the estimations presented in Table 8. This, however, does not explain the gap between the share of relevant households and share of households that actually received pensions in the years 2001 and 2004. Consequently, we turn to another possible explanation for this gap. Namely, the widespread social practices, during the restructuring process, related to anticipated retirement and disability retirement as alternatives to redundancy/unemployment. Due to these practices, the effective retirement age (determined for 2001-2003) decreased to 52-53 years (Preda et al., 2004). The effects of these social practices together with the various types of social pensions (not work-related, thus not related to a given retirement age) account for the gap under discussion.

A final remark on pensions: households that received pensions were, during the entire period, concentrated in the middle-income deciles. For instance, in 2004, their share in all households was increasing from 39.7% in the first decile to more than 62% in deciles fourth to sixth, then gradually decreasing to 31.4% in the tenth decile. Thus, leaving the labour market through early retirement (be it anticipated or for disability), although it resulted in a lower pension (than the one for old-age with due complete stage), represented an efficient survival strategy, since most households with no member of retirement age but receiving pensions have been found in the middle-income deciles. Why is the share of households with no member of retirement age but receiving pensions lower in the first decile as compared to the other deciles? First, because households in the first decile are younger and, consequently, had less access to the survival strategy of early retirement. Second, because most elderly households in the first decile had marginal positions on the labour market even during the socialist regime, so they either had no access to this survival strategy or had access but obtained low pensions, insufficient to escape poverty.

In conclusion, on the whole the Romanian social protection system covered the old-age related social risks rather well between 1995 and 2004.

Unemployment benefits

Unemployment benefits include unemployment benefit, labour market entry benefit and (cash) support allowances.

Unemployment benefits were introduced in 1991, with an amount set at 43% of the net average wage. Following its introduction, the benefits gradually declined in real terms. In 1994 they were raised, and in 1997 these benefits amounted to 39% of the net average wage and as much as 136% of the minimum wage.

Figure 3: The average real value of unemployment benefit and the unemployment benefit/minimum wage ratio

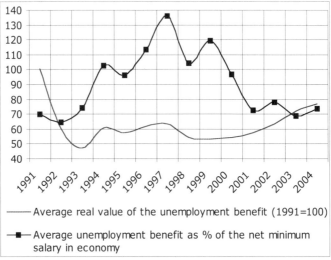

Source: NIS, *Statistical Yearbooks*.

The unemployment benefit became lower than the minimum wage only in 2001. In 2002, the unemployment system was reformed.[19]

Between 1995 and 2004, the share of unemployment benefits in total household income (Table 7A) and the share of unemployed in all household members (Table 5A) followed the same pattern: 1995-1997, decreased; 1997-2001, increased; and 2001-2004 decreased. Yet, overall, while the share of unemployed in all household members in 2004 reached the 1995 level (5.4%), the share of unemployment benefits in total household income was lower in 2004 (0.9%) compared to 1995 (1.4%).

Table 9:   Coverage of unemployment benefits

Income deciles:		D1	D2	D3	D4	D5	D6	D7	D8	D9	D10	Total
A	1995	24.9	22.3	19.2	16.7	12.8	10.3	9.0	7.1	7.2	3.9	13.3
	1997	26.2	19.7	16.2	13.8	10.8	9.2	7.2	7.2	4.9	4.9	12.0
	2001	29.1	23.5	21.7	19.6	17.0	14.3	11.8	8.3	7.1	5.0	15.7
	2004	29.6	18.6	18.1	14.7	11.8	9.2	8.8	7.8	6.5	4.1	12.9
B	1995	57.2	60.0	59.7	65.1	62.2	62.2	63.8	64.2	59.0	53.2	60.7
	1997	32.4	40.8	47.0	49.6	49.6	45.6	49.8	52.9	53.3	45.3	43.9
	2001	32.2	44.0	46.3	48.3	49.3	52.2	50.5	54.8	49.3	44.8	45.3
	2004	7.7	15.5	26.4	33.6	37.2	30.7	33.0	41.0	38.4	32.9	24.8
C	1995	14.7	14.1	11.9	11.4	8.4	6.6	5.9	4.9	4.4	2.3	8.5
	1997	8.7	8.3	7.8	6.9	5.4	4.3	3.6	3.8	2.7	2.2	5.4
	2001	9.3	10.3	10.0	9.5	8.4	7.5	5.9	4.6	3.5	2.3	7.1
	2004	2.3	2.9	4.8	5.0	4.5	2.9	2.9	3.3	2.5	1.3	3.2

Notes: A: Relevant households (i.e. households with unemployed member/s) as percentage of all households.
B: Percentage of relevant households that receive unemployment benefits.
C: Percentage of all households that receive unemployment benefits.

Source: IHS 1995, 1997 and FBS 2001, 2004. Note: Relevant households refer to households with at least one member self-declared unemployed.

It is useful to reiterate that in this study the status of unemployed is self-declared.[20] Thus, the contradiction between the distribution of unemployed across income deciles (Table 5B) and the distribution of unemployment

---

19   Since 2002, unemployment benefits are provided for a total duration of 270 days (9 months); the beneficiary receives 75% of the minimum gross wage in the first 6 months and 50% for the remaining period. After the period for which they are entitled to unemployment benefits, those who are still without a job can receive support allowances for a period of maximum 18 months, up to 60% of the previously paid benefits.

20   Thus, unemployed differs here from both registered unemployed and ILO unemployed.

benefits across income deciles (Table 7A) is only apparent. We refer to the fact that while most (self-declared) unemployed were constantly concentrated in the lowest four income deciles (particularly in the first and the second), the unemployment benefits moved from the lowest four income deciles in 1995-2001 to the middle-income ones (third to fifth) in 2004 (see Tables RO4 and RO2).

Unlike the case of pensions, virtually all households that receive unemployment benefits are households with unemployed, thus belonging to the relevant group of households.

The coverage of unemployment benefits considerably decreased between 1995 and 2004. In 1995, households with unemployed represented 13.3% of all households and 60.7% of these households were receiving unemployment benefits. In 2004, the share of households with unemployed was about the same (12.9%), but only 24.8% of these were receiving unemployment benefits. This decreasing coverage is also observed in the macro-data on the number of registered unemployed receiving benefits. Thus, while 77.6% of the registered unemployed were recipients of unemployment benefits in 1995, the share decreased to 45.1% in 2003 (UNDP, 1999b and 2005a).

During the entire period, the lowest coverage of unemployment was for households in the first income deciles, thus among the poorest. In their case, also, the coverage of unemployment decreased the most. In 1995, 57.2% of households with unemployed in the first income decile received unemployment benefits. In 2004, that share was only 7.7%, which is extremely low. This is a result of the fact that the first decile concentrates (self-declared) unemployed from rural areas, who are not eligible for unemployment benefits either because they own arable land, or because they have been active in the informal sector and, consequently, have not paid social insurance.

In conclusion, between 1995 and 2004, the Romanian unemployment system reduced the protection against the social risk of job (and income) loss, particularly for the poor.

Family benefits

The system of family benefits changed several times between 1995 and 2004. After the reform of the social assistance system (beginning with 2002), family benefits expanded and diversified, including both cash benefits and support programmes in goods and services. Cash benefits include child allowance, which is universal,[21] and a series of other benefits based on means-testing. Child allowance represents the main family benefit and is provided for more than 4.2 million children.

Child allowance together with the newly introduced complementary allowance (for families with children and modest income) and allowances for single-parent families accounted for 0.64% of GDP,[22] in 2004. Other family benefits, namely family placement allowance and newborn allowance, have had a much lower number of beneficiaries. These are not included in our analysis.

Table 10:   Coverage of family benefits

Income deciles:		D1	D2	D3	D4	D5	D6	D7	D8	D9	D10	Total
A	1995	47.0	43.3	40.1	36.9	35.5	34.2	33.6	31.7	33.8	29.2	36.5
	1997	50.3	41.7	38.1	37.7	34.6	32.7	31.5	31.7	29.9	29.9	35.8
	2001	50.3	40.9	35.5	33.1	30.8	30.1	28.8	29.9	28.8	28.3	33.7
	2004	48.1	37.2	31.7	31.4	29.2	27.7	27.1	28.7	28.2	26.5	31.6
B	1995	88.0	92.0	91.0	89.1	89.3	88.5	86.4	85.1	82.7	77.0	87.3
	1997	90.9	93.3	92.5	93.0	91.7	91.9	90.7	90.7	90.0	83.6	91.0
	2001	94.7	97.1	95.6	96.6	96.3	96.3	96.0	94.2	92.7	91.2	95.2
	2004	95.7	97.3	97.1	96.4	95.2	96.3	95.8	95.3	94.3	91.6	95.6
C	1995	45.5	44.6	41.2	38.0	36.5	34.5	33.5	31.2	32.4	26.5	36.4
	1997	49.9	43.9	40.5	40.4	36.9	34.7	33.5	33.2	31.8	29.8	37.5
	2001	52.7	45.2	39.8	38.9	36.0	34.6	34.9	34.9	32.2	30.8	38.0
	2004	54.5	46.6	41.6	41.2	36.9	35.6	34.9	34.7	34.5	30.6	39.1

Notes: A: Relevant households (i.e. households with child/children) as percentage of all households.
B: Percentage of relevant households that receive family benefits.
C: Percentage of all households that receive family benefits.
Source: IHS 1995, 1997 and FBS 2001, 2004. Note: Relevant households refer to households with at least one child 0-14 years.

As shown in Table 7A, the share of family benefits in household disposable income had a trend similar to that of the child allowance in real terms.[23]

---

21   Child allowance is granted to all children 0-16 years and can be extended until the age of 18 if the child is enrolled in a form of education recognized by law or if it is disabled.
22   Between 1990 and 2001, the child allowance accounted for 76% of all social assistance expenditures.
23   Compared to the 1989 level (1989=100), the real value of the child allowance was 34 in 1995, 69 in 1997, 48 in 2001, and 33 in 2004.

Family benefits, particularly the universal child allowance, have a good coverage and achieve the widest coverage of households in the first income decile (Table 10). Furthermore, after 1995, the coverage of family benefits increased for households in all income deciles, reaching (in 2004) more than 95% of all households with children.

Nonetheless, a recent study on child welfare (Zamfir, 2005) showed that there is a polarization tendency between children from poor (first consumption quintile) and from rich (fifth consumption quintile) families. The level of polarization is much higher among the school-age (8-16 years) children than among children aged 0-7 years, because much more than others, children from poor families do not attend compulsory education and, consequently, do not qualify for the child allowance. Even so, among all family benefits, the child allowance has had the highest impact on absolute poverty alleviation during the period 1995-2004 (e.g. Teşliuc et al., 2001; Zamfir, 2005).

Other social benefits

This is an eclectic category of benefits, which includes scholarships, benefits for the disabled (other than disability pensions), allowances for war veterans and their widows, allowances for political persecutes, social aid (GMI), and other social assistance allowances.

Table 11:   Coverage of other social benefits (percentage of households receiving this benefit)

Income deciles	D1	D2	D3	D4	D5	D6	D7	D8	D9	D10	Total
1995	8.8	9.7	9.4	8.3	8.0	6.8	6.1	6.2	5.2	5.3	7.4
1997	18.5	23.8	25.3	23.2	24.2	22.4	22.1	19.3	16.6	12.8	20.8
2001	7.4	8.4	8.5	7.8	7.0	6.8	6.5	6.0	5.8	4.3	6.8
2004	32.9	24.4	18.4	14.6	11.3	9.8	8.0	7.9	7.4	5.3	14.0

Source: IHS 1995, 1997 and FBS 2001, 2004.

The share of other social benefits in total household disposable income varied according to the changes in the social assistance system; overall, it increased from 0.7% in 1995 to 1.7% in 2004 (Table 7A). Especially for the poorest households in the first income decile, the system reform in 2002 resulted in a considerable increase of the share of these social benefits from 1.5% in 2001 to 10.2% of household disposable income in 2004.

The coverage of other social benefits also increased, as a consequence of the reform of the social assistance system. In 2004, 14% of all households were recipients of other social benefits, with a much higher share of poorest houdseholds receiving this benefit (32.9%).

All social benefits

The reform of the social protection system led to significant changes at the household level. The share of social benefits (not including pensions) in household disposable income increased; for households in the first income decile it amounted to 13.4% in 1995, and to 19% in 2004 (see Table RO1). Family benefits and other social benefits (but not unemployment benefits) were increasingly distributed towards the poorest households (see Table RO2).

The coverage of social benefits (not including pensions) also expanded (Table 12), particularly due to the large increase in the number of recipients of social assistance benefits.

Table 12:   Coverage of all social benefits not including pensions (percentage of households receiving this benefit)

Income deciles	D1	D2	D3	D4	D5	D6	D7	D8	D9	D10	Total
1995	55.7	56.2	52.8	49.7	46.9	43.2	42.0	39.5	39.2	32.4	45.8
1997	63.3	62.1	60.3	58.7	56.8	53.3	52.4	50.0	46.9	41.3	54.5
2001	60.1	54.3	50.2	47.9	44.9	43.0	42.8	42.2	39.4	35.8	46.1
2004	63.8	55.3	51.4	50.3	44.8	42.3	41.0	42.1	41.2	35.4	46.8

Source: IHS 1995, 1997 and FBS 2001, 2004.

Thus, the latest reforms significantly improved the Romanian system of social protection, compared to the first years of transition.[24]

---

24   In the first years after 1989, unlike other CEE countries, Romania made a relatively modest effort in social protection, which did not compensate the social costs of transition (e.g. Zamfir, 1997; Milanovic, 1998). As a result, the absolute poverty "exploded" from an estimated 4% in 1989 to 20% in 1993, evaluated against a poverty line determined on the 1993 consumption of the poorest (World Bank, 1997). Subsequently, under the shock of the second depression (1997-1999), lack of reform of the social protection system resulted in a further increase of poverty up to 36% of the population in 2000, measured by per adult equivalent consumption according to the WB/CASPIS/NIS methodology (World Bank, 2003).

The system funding is low as compared to EU countries and there still are corrections to be made. For instance, in 2004, the poor households (due to their high number of children) were much better covered by the child allowance system than by social aid (GMI), which is specifically designed for the poorest families. In 2003-2004, in spite of the much larger number of poor, the GMI-related expenditure in Romania (about 0.2% of GDP, for about 5 million poor) was similar to the EU-25 average expenditure for means-tested "last resort" programmes. For many benefits, the amount disbursed is still low, insufficient for poor households to escape poverty. In spite of the fact that over 80% of households receive a social protection benefit (including pensions), the (consumption) absolute poverty rate in Romania, although decreasing, was as high as 18.8%[25] in 2004, much higher than in any other CEE country. Nonetheless, during 1995 and 2004, the Romanian social protection system provided a satisfactory coverage for old-age and demographic social risks (pensions and child allowances), and after 2001 has been expanding and increasingly targeted toward the poor.

4 Income inequality

In Romania, as in other CEE countries in postcommunist transition, income inequality significantly rose during the years of the first economic depression. However, during 1997-1999, i.e. the second economic recession, absolute poverty increased but inequality decreased. After 2000, as the economy started to recover, absolute poverty gradually declined, but inequality rose again, reaching levels somewhat higher than in 1995.

Thus, in 2004, the income of the richest 20% of the households was 3.9 times higher than the income of the poorest 20% of the households, matching the EU-25 and EU-15 averages.[26] Yet, according to the Laeken social inclusion indicators[27] (NIS, 2006a), when self-consumption is not taken into account, the quintile share ratio shown in the last row of Table 13 changes significantly. Thus, without self-consumption, the quintile share indicator

25 Absolute poverty determined by per adult equivalent consumption according to the WB/CASPIS/NIS methodology (CASPIS and NIS data).

26 Ratios ranged in 2004 from 3.3 in Slovenia to 7.2 in Portugal (Eurostat).

27 NIS uses the same income concept – household disposable income (including self-consumption) – but a different equivalence scale, namely the modified OECD scale, which gives a weight of 1.0 to the first adult, 0.5 to other household members aged 14 or over, and 0.3 to each child aged less than 14 years.

is almost twice as high, 7.1 rather than 3.9, which although decreasing from 8.5 in 2000 still represents one of the highest quintile ratios in Europe.

Table 13: Distribution of household disposable income by quintiles

Quintile	1995	1997	2001	2004
Q1	9.53	10.23	9.84	9.47
Q2	14.09	14.48	14.21	13.96
Q3	17.38	17.77	17.67	17.37
Q4	22.03	21.88	22.53	22.41
Q5	36.97	35.64	35.76	36.80
All	100	100	100	100
Top 20%/bottom 20%	3.88	3.49	3.63	3.89

Source: IHS 1995, 1997 and FBS 2001, 2004.

The Gini coefficient of income inequality rose from 0.21 in 1989 (Teşliuc et al., 2001) to 0.306 in 2004 (Table 14), which is in range with the other countries from South Eastern Europe, but is higher than the EU average. Nonetheless, in the absence of in-kind income from agriculture (self-consumption), income inequality was much higher, but with a declining trend; the Gini coefficients decreased from 0.378 in 2000 to 0.363 in 2004 (NIS, 2006a). Accordingly, during the entire period, income inequality was also much higher in the rural areas than in the urban ones, particularly with respect to cash income (total household disposable income without self-consumption).

Table 14: Gini coefficients of income inequality (household disposable income)

Based on the distribution of:	1995	1997	2001	2004
Households	0.3070	0.2815	0.2907	0.3060
Individuals	0.3093	0.2889	0.2988	0.3106

Source: IHS 1995, 1997 and FBS 2001, 2004.

As a result of all these inequalities, several gaps have emerged or widened: (1) wide gaps between rural and urban areas, but also (2) between larger cities and medium-sized or small towns (in particular formerly mono-industrial) as well as (3) between large, central and developed villages close to cities and small, peripheral, remote and poor villages, with a high proportion of elderly population. In addition, (4) large regional gaps between the developed capital and Western regions and the poor North-East and South regions. The main causes of these inequalities are, apart from the profound structural reforms, poor performances of the social protection system before 2001 and the distorted distribution of budgetary resources (e.g. Zamfir, 2005; Pascariu et al., 2003).

4.1 Sources of income inequality

Income inequality is a complex issue, but in this section, we focus only on two factors influencing overall income inequality. First, we analyse whether a given income source increases or decreases overall income inequality. Following that, we briefly analyse the relationship between household human capital and household income.

Decomposition of income inequality

The Gini coefficient of income inequality is decomposed using the Rao analytical decomposition:

$$G = \sum s_k C_k$$

where G is the Gini coefficient of income inequality, s_k is the share of income source k in total income, and C_k is the concentration coefficient of income source k. Table 15 presents the values of the concentration coefficients and the values of the income shares for 1995, 1997, 2001 and 2004.

This decomposition does not have a clear and unique meaning in the sense of allocating "contributions" of a particular income source to overall income inequality. However, it can be shown[28] that the amount of the increase or decrease in the Gini coefficient depends on (a) the difference between the concentration coefficient of a given income source and the Gini coefficient and (b) the share of a given income source in total income. Income sources, whose concentration coefficients are higher than the Gini coefficient increase income inequality in the following sense: a 1% increase of the mean value of the given income source, assuming a uniform 1% increase for every household receiving this income source, would result in an increase in the Gini coefficient. Similarly, for income sources whose concentration coefficient is less than the value of the Gini coefficient of income inequality,

---

28   See Technical Annex.

an increase in the mean value of the given income source (assuming again a uniform proportional increase) would cause a decrease in the Gini coefficient. As stated, the amount of this increase/decrease also depends on the share of the given income source in total income, i.e. the higher the share, the greater the impact on the Gini coefficient. Secondary income sources (social or private transfers) are labeled relative income equalizers if their concentration coefficients are less than the Gini coefficient, meaning that the poor receive relatively more of this income source than the rich. If these concentration coefficients are negative, they are labeled absolute income equalizers, as the poor even in absolute terms receive more of this income source than the rich.

Table 15:   Decomposition of income inequality

	1995	1997	2001	2004
Concentration coefficients				
Wages and salaries	0.4026	0.3907	0.4657	0.4605
Non-agricultural self-employment	0.4941	0.4537	0.1146	0.2318
Income from agriculture	0.2092	0.1996	0.1499	0.1754
Income from capital	0.6501	0.8263	0.7858	0.8587
Pensions	0.1648	0.1915	0.2155	0.1872
Unemployment benefits	-0.1993	-0.1304	-0.1262	-0.0055
Family benefits	-0.1284	-0.1080	-0.1497	-0.1489
Other social benefits	0.0367	-0.0016	0.1198	-0.2189
Interfamily transfers (remittances)	0.5769	0.4559	0.4415	0.4422
All (income Gini)	0.3093	0.2889	0.2988	0.3106
Income shares				
Wages and salaries	0.4719	0.4280	0.4387	0.4582
Non-agricultural self-employment	0.0602	0.0522	0.0430	0.0561
Income from agriculture	0.2520	0.2768	0.2518	0.2120
Income from capital	0.0041	0.0082	0.0040	0.0078
Pensions	0.1485	0.1573	0.1896	0.1883
Unemployment benefits	0.0142	0.0099	0.0124	0.0092
Family benefits	0.0169	0.0341	0.0248	0.0182
Other social benefits	0.0072	0.0097	0.0084	0.0181
Interfamily transfers (remittances)	0.0251	0.0238	0.0275	0.0319
All income	1.0000	1.0000	1.0000	1.0000

Source: IHS 1995, 1997 and FBS 2001, 2004. Note: Gini coefficients based on household disposable income. There are slight differences between the income shares in this table and those presented in Tables 7A and RO1. In this table, income shares were determined based on the distribution of all individuals in households across income deciles, while in Tables 7A and RO1 these were determined based on the distribution of all households across income deciles.

During the 1995-2004 period, wages were the largest "contributor" to income inequality. Wages held the highest share in household income and had a high (and rising) concentration coefficient; we have already showed in a previous section that both wage-earners and higher wages are concentrated in the higher (household) income deciles.

Income from agriculture was relatively more concentrated among low-income households, as can be seen from the rather moderate concentration coefficient. As presented in section 3, there are two types of recipients of income from agriculture: (1) the majority of farmers who do subsistence agriculture and are concentrated in the lower (household) income deciles and (2) a small group of farmers who develop a profitable agri-business (mostly informal) and are concentrated in the higher income deciles. However, as the economy started to recover, its share in household income decreased and, at the same time, its concentration coefficient decreased (except for the period 2001-2004).

The "contribution" of income from non-agricultural self-employment to overall income inequality seriously decreased between 1995 and 2001; in 1995 its concentration coefficient was much higher than the overall Gini coefficient (0.4941 vs. 0.3093), whereas in 2001 it was much lower (0.1146 vs. 0.2988). In other words, this income source in 1995 and 1997 acted in the direction of increasing the overall income inequality, whereas in the subsequent years it reversed its impact and acted in the direction of decreasing the overall income inequality. The most plausible explanations, beside under-reporting of self-employment income, relate to the distribution of non-agricultural self-employed, following a U-shaped curve (see section 2) and the income gap between self-employed providing unskilled/low-skilled services and those providing highly specialized services for companies (see section 3).

Interfamily transfers constantly have very high concentration coefficients. The widespread kinship networks, discussed in section 3, and mostly the pursuit of the wealthier households, provide the main explanation for this phenomenon.

Income from capital had high concentration coefficients, but even larger relative increases in the share of this income source would have a small impact on the overall Gini, due to the small share of income from capital in total household income.

During the entire period 1995-2004, in Romania – unlike Bulgaria – pensions were not an absolute income equalizer, which means that the poor households did not receive (in absolute terms) more of this income source than the rich ones. Nonetheless, pensions were a relative income equalizer. The concentration coefficients for pensions had a positive sign. Thus, pensions – basically earnings-related income – were unequally distributed but less so than total income and much less than wages and salaries. The concentration coefficients for pensions were, however, larger for Romania than for Hungary or Slovenia; this is also quite possibly caused by the structural problems of the Romanian rural areas and old-age farmers, that is the large number of farmers receiving very low pensions (see Table 4). The latest implemented reforms in 2001 resulted in a decrease in the concentration coefficient, possibly implying that the redistributive character of pensions has increased.

Out of the social benefits other than pensions, only family benefits were absolute income equalizers during the entire period – the poor received more of this income source than the rich – in spite of the fact that the most important benefit (child allowance) is universal. Thus, family benefits "contributed" most to the reduction of overall income inequality.

Unemployment benefits represented a significant income equalizer only until 2001. After the social protection system was reformed, the concentration coefficient of the unemployment benefits remained negative but increased from -0.1262 in 2001 to -0.0055 in 2004. So, one can also say that unemployment benefits in 2004 had a lower impact on poverty alleviation.

Finally, other social benefits (which include means-tested social assistance benefits targeted to the poor families, such as GMI) became a significant absolute income equalizer only after the social assistance system was reformed (after 2002). Figure 4 presents the main effect of this reform: in 2004, other social benefits "contributed" to the reduction of income inequality by being much better targeted to the poor.

In conclusion, compared to the other three countries included in this volume, income inequality in Romania is relatively high but rather stable. Between 1995 and 2004, the social protection system as a whole had a rather mixed performance. The pension system provided protection against old-age risks for a large number of persons; the pension reform, started in 2001 (Law no.19/2000) and planned to be completed in 2014, led to some positive effects. The unemployment system changed its focus from passive to active measures, established a correct relation between unemployment benefits and minimum wage, but at the household level, had a low coverage and lost its role of significant income equalizer. The reforms of the social assistance system implemented since 2002 had some positive impact on the reduction of income inequality. The Achilles' heel has always been the "rural problem":

old-age farmers, unemployed-farmers, and the children and young from rural areas with poor access to education relevant for obtaining a sustainable position on the formal labour market.

Figure 4: Distribution of "other social benefits" across (household) income deciles (in per cent), 1995-2004

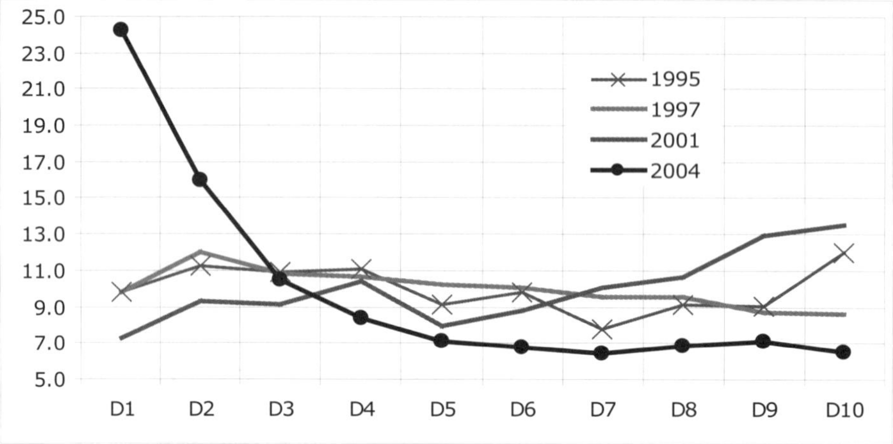

Source: IHS 1995, 1997 and FBS 2001, 2004. "Other social benefits" than pensions, unemployment benefits, and family benefits.

Human capital and income

Human capital represents a decisive factor for a household's income-generating capacity. This fact is well-documented in the case of Romania: education is a strong correlate of poverty, as it represents the factor with the largest positive effects both on income and consumption (e.g. Zamfir, 1995; UNDP, 1999a; World Bank, 2003; Stănculescu and Berevoescu, 2004; Ilie, 2004).

In this section, we use as proxy for household human capital the attained education level of all household members aged 25-64 years. Table 16 shows that, as a rule, the higher the household human capital, the higher the household disposable income. During the entire period, individuals with primary education have mainly belonged to poor households (low income deciles), those with vocational education have been more numerous in low-middle and middle income deciles, those with secondary education have been prevalent in middle and middle-up income deciles, and individuals with tertiary education have been concentrated in the affluent households (high income deciles). On the one hand, this distribution mirrors the distribution of people active in agriculture across income deciles. On the other hand, this distributional pattern provides an explanation for the large income gaps between employees and self-employed from the low and the high income deciles.

Table 16: **Attained level of education of household members aged 25-64 years, by (household) income deciles (%)**

Income deciles	Educational level				All	Urban		Rural	
	Primary	Vocational	Secondary	Tertiary		Primary	Tertiary	Primary	Tertiary
1995									
1	68	15	15	1	100	54	2	75	0
2	60	20	19	1	100	46	1	71	0
3	55	22	23	1	100	40	2	68	0
4	51	21	25	2	100	36	4	66	1
5	46	21	30	3	100	32	4	63	1
6	41	22	33	4	100	29	6	59	2
7	36	22	35	7	100	27	9	55	2
8	31	19	40	10	100	21	13	55	3
9	24	17	42	16	100	16	20	48	6
10	19	11	39	30	100	9	37	50	9
Total	42	19	31	8	100	27	12	63	2
2004									
1	56	24	19	1	100	45	2	62	0
2	44	28	27	1	100	33	2	51	1
3	37	31	30	1	100	25	3	47	1
4	32	31	35	3	100	21	4	43	1
5	27	31	39	3	100	18	4	39	1
6	23	31	40	6	100	15	7	38	3
7	21	28	44	7	100	14	10	34	3
8	15	24	48	13	100	9	15	28	6
9	11	20	48	20	100	6	24	28	8
10	6	10	39	44	100	2	51	23	17
Total	27	26	37	10	100	15	16	43	3

Source: IHS 1995, 1997 and FBS 2001, 2004. Note: Primary includes no education, primary and lower secondary education (up to 8 years of schooling). Vocational refers to vocational and apprenticeship education. Secondary refer to high-school, post high-school and foremen education.

If before 1990 the urban-rural education gap was narrowed, after 1990 the trend reversed and the gap has widened. Data in Table 16, showing the educational attainment of household members, are highly consistent with data on the labour force. According to the LFS data (NIS, 2006b), most of

213

the rural labour force has low levels of education. For instance, in 2005 (4th quarter), nearly 38% of the rural labour force had achieved less than primary education (ISCED 1), a further 28% completed only the ISCED 2 level (with no qualification either), while just 1.5% graduated from university. This is due to three factors: (1) the labour force in agriculture is old and also poorly educated; (2) lack/scarcity of financial resources impedes rural young people from continuing their education since most of the vocational as well as high schools are based in cities and the education-related costs (transport, accommodation etc.) are very high; (3) young people who attended higher education left villages in favour of urban areas or, more recently, in favour of a Western country. In contrast, more than half of the urban labour force has an upper secondary education, and 12% have attained tertiary education.

Between 1995 and 2004, the attained educational level of household members aged between 25 and 64 years has been rising. The share of persons with primary education has sharply decreased from 42% in 1995 to 27% in 2004, while the proportion of those who attained tertiary educational level increased from 8% in 1995 to 10% in 2004. Yet, most improvements were concentrated among the better-off households and in the urban areas.

Table 17 shows the influence of the educational level on one's income position, i.e the average equivalized income of the labour-active population by attained educational level. The relative income position of persons with primary and vocational education has continuously worsened, while that of highly-educated people has significantly improved. The differences between returns to education have been large and are increasing.

Table 17: Relative equivalized income by education levels of labour-active persons aged between 25 and 64 years

	1995	1997	2001	2004
Primary	0.82	0.82	0.76	0.71
Vocational	0.92	0.92	0.89	0.87
Secondary	1.12	1.09	1.08	1.07
Tertiary	1.68	1.57	1.73	1.81
All	1	1	1	1

Source: IHS 1995, 1997 and FBS 2001, 2004.

In addition, in Romania, (1) most children (0-17 years) belong to low-income households (see Table RO4); (2) children from rural areas have a higher risk of poverty than children from urban areas (see section 5); (3) access to secondary education of children from rural areas is very poor: in 2004,

31.9% of children from rural areas, aged 15-18 years, were not enrolled in any form of education (Zamfir, 2005); (4) merely 2% of the 18-24 age group from rural areas are enrolled in tertiary education; (5) the rate of early school-leavers not in education increased from 19.7% of the 18-24 age group in 1997 to 23.4% in 2004, which is high in the European context (e.g. 18.1% for EU-15 and 16% for EU-25, Eurostat); and (6) the lifelong learning system is underdeveloped and, consequently, adult's participation rate in education and training is among the lowest in the European Union. Given that education is probably the strongest correlate of poverty, all the above-mentioned trends show that a focus on rural education and on continuous training for adults could substantially contribute in breaking the vicious poverty circle, in which otherwise some half a million Romanian children would be entrapped.

5   Risk of income poverty in Romania

The risk of poverty is assessed on the basis of the concept of relative poverty, which is poverty measured in relation to national living standards; the rationale for this definition is that people whose living standards (either income or expenditure) fall far below the national average are at risk of being excluded from the advantages and benefits considered normal in a given society.

Economic growth results in rising household incomes, improving the overall living conditions of the population and consequently also of the poor. On the other hand, rising inequality results in an increasing number of socially excluded people. The two factors work in opposite direction, so that it is possible that even if in absolute terms many poor would be better off than they were at the beginning of the period of economic growth, in relative terms they would not be. Thus, relative measures of poverty are weak in reflecting poverty developments over time, particularly during periods of drastic structural changes.

Nonetheless, in this volume, for the comparisons between the four countries – Bulgaria, Hungary, Romania and Slovenia – we focus on the risk of relative income poverty of four social groups, namely the elderly (60 years or more), children (0-14 years), pensioners and the unemployed. However, taking into consideration Romania's specific features, we also focus on the large social group of people active in agriculture, in the rural areas, and on the Roma ethnic minority.

We measure relative poverty using three poverty lines,[29] namely 40, 50 and 60% of the median[30] household equivalent disposable income (including self-consumption). The results are presented in Table 18.

Data in Table 18 clearly indicate that during the entire period 1995-2004:

(1) About 20% of the population lived in households whose equivalent income was less than 60% of the median equivalent income.

(2) The risk of income poverty has been consistently higher in rural areas (about 1.3 to 1.5 times higher), irrespective of the social group considered.

Table 18:   Risk of income poverty (in per cent)

Poverty lines as % of median household equivalent income	All households				Rural households			
	1995	1997	2001	2004	1995	1997	2001	2004
All persons								
40	6.8	5.8	7.1	7.2	10.7	8.3	11.1	10.3
50	12.6	11.2	12.9	13.4	19.1	16.2	20.1	19.7
60	19.9	18.5	20.2	20.6	28.7	26.0	30.7	30.1
Children 0-14 years								
40	9.9	8.7	11.8	12.1	15.3	12.5	17.1	15.8
50	17.7	16.1	20.1	21.0	26.6	23.7	29.1	28.3
60	26.9	25.4	29.3	29.9	38.4	35.9	41.8	40.3
Persons 60+ years								
40	4.7	2.7	3.0	3.1	7.0	3.7	4.4	4.2
50	10.0	6.7	7.6	7.6	14.1	8.8	11.0	10.6
60	17.2	13.2	14.7	14.3	22.5	16.7	20.3	20.0
Unemployed								
40	12.0	14.0	13.4	17.9	14.8	16.5	16.2	24.3
50	21.8	23.5	21.7	27.9	25.7	27.8	26.5	37.2
60	34.2	34.9	32.4	37.9	38.7	40.0	39.2	48.3
Active in agriculture								
40	15.2	12.5	16.9	14.0	15.5	12.7	17.0	13.9
50	26.0	23.7	29.7	27.1	26.6	24.2	29.7	27.3
60	37.8	36.8	43.4	41.3	38.6	37.5	43.6	41.5
Pensioners								
40	3.7	2.1	2.3	2.8	5.7	2.9	3.5	4.0
50	8.1	5.5	6.1	7.0	12.0	7.4	9.2	9.9
60	14.4	11.2	12.3	13.3	20.1	14.4	17.7	18.9

Source: IHS 1995, 1997 and FBS 2001, 2004.

29   The standard poverty line, used for instance by the EU, is 60% of the median equivalent income.

30   Relative poverty measurement is sensitive to inequality: a rise/decline in inequality determines an increase/decrease of the number of people in relative poverty. However, if the poverty line is defined as a percentage of the median income, then changes in the distribution of income among people above the median affect measured income inequality, but leave the number of people in poverty unchanged.

(3) The risk of income poverty for children has been high. In 2004, 30% of children lived in households with an equivalent income less than 60% of the median household equivalent income, compared to 20.6% of all persons or 14.3% of persons aged 60 years or more. Children from single-parent households are in the most difficult situation (Table 19). Their risk of poverty increased sharply between 1997 and 2004, so that 43% of children from single-parent households (about 155 thousand children) in 2004 lived in households whose equivalent income was less than 60% of the median household equivalent income. As a response to this situation, a (means-tested) support allowance for single-parent families was introduced in early 2004; by the end of the year more than 200 thousand single-parent families took up this benefit.

Table 19: Risk of income poverty for children 0-14 years, by household type (in per cent)

Poverty lines as % of median household equivalent income	Single-parent household						Two-parent household		
	Per cent			Thousand			Per cent		
	1997	2001	2004	1997	2001	2004	1997	2001	2004
40	12	15	19	35.8	55.4	71.0	7	12	11
50	19	27	31	57.4	101.8	114.5	14	19	20
60	31	38	43	92.6	143.8	155.5	23	28	29

Source: IHS 1995, 1997 and FBS 2001, 2004.

(4) The unemployed and people active in agriculture represent the social groups with the highest risk of income poverty in Romania. Only these two groups have had a higher risk of poverty than children. The risk of income poverty for the unemployed increased between 1995 and 2004, due to the decrease in coverage, weaker targeting and decrease in the value of unemployment benefits, discussed in section 4.

(5) The risk of income poverty for persons aged 60 years or more has been low. Pensioners had a similar situation, although the two groups only partially overlap. A closer look at the risk of poverty for four elderly subgroups (according to gender and marital status, see Table 20) shows that only among the non-married elderly (unmarried, divorced, separated or widow), women aged 60 years or more had a higher risk of income poverty during the 1995-2004 period. However, their risk of income poverty has constantly been lower than that of children.

Table 20: Risk of income poverty for population aged 60 years or more, by gender and marital status (in per cent)

Poverty lines as % of median household equivalent income	Women				Men			
	1995	1997	2001	2004	1995	1997	2001	2004
Married*								
40	3	2	2	2	3	2	2	2
50	8	5	6	5	7	5	5	5
60	14	11	12	11	13	11	11	11
Non-married**								
40	8	4	5	5	6	4	4	3
50	15	10	11	12	12	8	8	7
60	25	18	21	21	16	13	13	13
All persons 60+ years								
40	6	3	3	4	4	2	2	2
50	12	8	9	9	8	6	6	6
60	20	15	17	17	14	11	11	11

Source: IHS 1995, 1997 and FBS 2001, 2004. Note: (*) Including consensual unions. (**) Including never married, divorced, separated and widow.

Figure 5: Risk of income poverty by ethnic groups (in per cent)

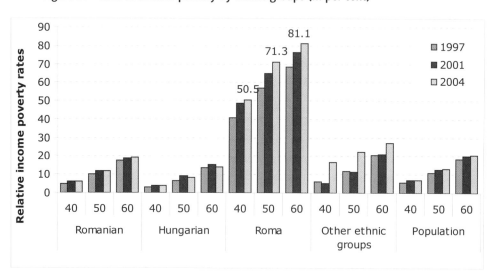

Source: IHS 1995, 1997 and FBS 2001, 2004. Note: Ethnicity is self-declared.

The Roma population constitutes a distinct case, as the Roma ethnic group faces various forms of social exclusion (Zamfir and Zamfir, 1993; Preda, 2002; UNDP, 2005b). The risk of income poverty was extremely high for the Roma population and increased from 1997 and 2004, when 81.1% of all Roma lived in households with income below 60% of the median household equivalent income (Figure 5). Thus, in spite of the big efforts to improve the Roma's social conditions made over the last decade by the government, political parties and non-governmental organizations, the risk of poverty for the Roma population has remained a chronic problem. This increasing risk of social exclusion and income poverty has been caused by the interplay of several factors.

The Roma situation has worsened immediately after 1990. By the year 1992, 63% of the Roma families were in absolute poverty [31] and another 18% had a total income greater than the subsistence minimum but not enough for a decent life (Zamfir and Zamfir, 1993). On the one hand, the Roma's educational attainment has been very low. The level of illiteracy is extremely high, and 18% of adult Roma men and 28% of adult women cannot read. Only some 5% of Roma adults have attained high school or college. Only about half of the children in the age group 7-18 years has been enrolled in school (Zamfir and Preda, 2002). Consequently, the level of professional qualification has been extremely low, which, combined with discriminatory stereotypes – Roma are "the last to be hired and the first to be fired" – has caused a very precarious employment situation since the first years of transition.

In the last 50 years, traditional trades were greatly discouraged by the former socialist regime and hence disappeared among most of the Roma population. Other minor opportunities traditionally exploited by the Roma, such as buying empty bottles, paper or scrap metal and returning them for refunding or selling clothes are time-consuming, poorly rewarded, extremely unstable, reinforce marginality and are not covered by the social security system. Furthermore, the land was reinstated in accordance with the ownership structure that existed before the formation of the socialist agricultural cooperatives. As a result, most Roma do not own land, and those who own some have plots less than half of a hectare (Sandu and Stănculescu, 1999).

The income of Roma families is low mostly due to the following factors. First, the very small share of working-age persons who are employed combined with the fact that most women do not work, or earn only insignifi-

219

---

31   Absolute poverty measured using the normative method, RIQL version, RIQL scale of equivalence, and two poverty lines related to subsistence and decent life.

cant amounts from occasional jobs, mostly in agriculture. Second, the Roma families have a large number of children. Third, the small number of Roma pensioners combined with the fact that most of them receive only low pensions due to their former jobs either in agriculture or as unskilled workers. Therefore, most Roma households end up relying on child allowance and irregular, low-level informal incomes. This pattern of informal, unskilled and occasional activities in the Roma case leads to the self-reproduction of the human capital deficit and entraps the family in poverty for generations.

6   Concluding remarks

In Romania, the "tectonic changes" from the first years of postcommunist transition were followed after 1995 by a second "socioeconomic quake". Compared to the egalitarian society before 1989, both poverty and inequality "exploded" (Zamfir, 1995). The economy started to recover only after ten years of transition. The social costs are still being paid, particularly as for the entire period before 2000 the social protection system had a relatively good performance only with respect to social risks related to old age. After 2001, the social protection system was reformed, expanded and improved in many respects. Nevertheless, the system performance for risks related to unemployment is still very poor, so that in the 1995-2004 period the income position of unemployed has considerably worsened. However, estimates based on the absolute approach show a much lower risk of poverty for unemployed and their households (e.g. World Bank, 2003 and 2007).

Both absolute (e.g. World Bank, 2003 and 2007) and relative (Table 18) poverty rates are disproportionately high for children and the young (18-24 years), for people with low educational attainment, and for the rural population, particularly people active in agriculture. These social groups are precisely those who benefited least from the recent economic growth. The rural population was less adversely affected by the second economic recession (1997-1999), but in the period 2000-2004 it also gained less from economic revival compared to the urban population (CASE, 2004). People active in agriculture were relatively less hit by losses than other groups during the second recession, but in 2000-2004 they also benefited less from the economic recovery, particularly compared to skilled self-employed and employees in industry and services, who benefited the most (CASE, 2004). Children and the young lost more during the second recession and they benefited less from economic recovery (Zamfir, 2005).

In conclusion, the fact that the Romanian social protection system as a whole had a rather poor performance in absorbing the social transformation shock before 2000, although important, is history that cannot be changed. At present, the major concern is whether the newly reformed system of social protection is capable of ensuring spillover of the benefits of economic growth in an equitable and sustainable way.

7 References

CASE (2004) *Operationalizing Pro-Poor Growth. Case of Romania*, World Bank Report, Warsaw.

Cheli, Ghellini, Lemmi and Pannuzi, in *Statistics in Transition*, 5(1), 1994)

Chircă, Ct. and Teşliuc, E. (coord.) (1999) *From Poverty to Rural Development*, Bucharest: World Bank and National Institute for Statistics.

Ilie, S. (2004) *Inegalităţi în distribuirea veniturilor şi politica socială a veniturilor*, Ph.D Thesis, Bucharest: University of Bucharest, Faculty of Sociology and Social Assistance.

Kornai, J. (1980) *Economics of Shortage*, Amsterdam: North-Holland Publishing Company.

Mihăilescu, V. (1996) 'Două sate în tranziţie. Tipuri strategice dominante în lumea rurală', in *Revista de Cercetări Sociale* 3, p. 3-24.

Milanovic, B. (1998), *Income Inequality and Poverty during the Transition from Planned to Market Economy*, Washington D. C.: World Bank.

Neef, R. and Stănculescu, M.S. (eds.) (2002) *The Social Impact of Informal Economies in Eastern Europe*, Aldershot: Ashgate.

Neef, R. (2004) 'Economic conditions for households' informal activities in the different sectors', in Neef, R. and Adair, Ph. (eds.), *Informal Economies and Social Transformation in Romania*, p. 119-132, Munster: LIT Verlag.

NIS, *Statistical Yearbooks* 1994, 2000 and 2005, Bucharest.

NIS (2005) *Labour Force in Romania. Employment and Unemployment – Recalculated time series based on the 2002 Census*, Bucharest.

NIS (2006a) *Social Inclusion Indicators 2004*, Bucharest.

NIS (2006b) *Labour Force in Romania. Employment and Unemployment in the fourth quarter 2005*, Bucharest.

Pascariu, G. (coord.), Stănculescu, M. S., Jula, D., Luţaş, M. and Lhomel, E. (2003) *EU Cohesion Policy and Romania's Regional Economic and Social Development*, Pre-accession Impact Studies I, Bucharest: European Institute of Romania, http://www.ier.ro.

Preda, M. (2002) 'Caracteristici ale excluziunii sociale specifice pentru populaţia de romi din România', in Zamfir, C. and Preda, M. (eds.) *Romii in Romania*, p. 283-301, Bucharest: Expert.

Preda, M. (coord.), Dobos, C. and Grigoras, V. (2004) *Romanian Pensions System during the Transition: Major Problems and Solutions*, Pre-Accession Impact Studies II, Bucharest: European Institute of Romania, http://www.ier.ro.

Romanian Government (2005) *Joint Memorandum on Social Inclusion 2005*, Bucharest.

Sandu, D. and Stănculescu, M.S. (1999) *Rebuilding Community Space*, World Bank Report, Bucharest.

Stănculescu M. S. and Berevoescu I. (coord.) (2004) *Sărac lipit, caut altă viaţă! Fenomenul sărăciei extreme şi al zonelor sărace în România*, 2001, Bucharest: Nemira.

Stănculescu M. S. (2005) 'Working Conditions in the Informal Sector', in *South-East Europe Review for Labour and Social Affairs*, 8/3, p. 79-94.

Teşliuc, C. M. and Pop, L. (1999) 'Poverty, Inequality, and Social Protection', in Ruhl, C. and Dăianu, D. (eds.), *Economic Transition in Romania: Past, Present and Future*, p.173-245, Bucharest: CEROPE and World Bank.

Teşliuc, C. M., Pop L. and Teşliuc, E. (2001) *Sărăcia şi sistemul de protecţie socială*, Bucharest: Polirom.

Teşliuc, E., Pop, L. and Panduru, F. (2003) *Poverty in Romania: Profile and Trends during the 1995-2002*, World Bank Poverty Assessment, Bucharest: World Bank.

Toma, C. (2004) 'The Collection of Pension Contributions in Romania', in Fultz, E. and Stanovnik, T. (eds.), *The Collection of Pension Contributions: Trends, Issues, and Problems in Central and Eastern Europe*, p. 197-246, Budapest: International Labour Office.

UNDP (1998) *Methods and Instruments for Poverty Measurement*, Wagner P., Chircă Ct., Zamfir C., Molnar M., Pârciog S. (coord.), Poverty Alleviation Project, Bucharest: UNDP.

UNDP (1999a), *Poverty in Romania 1995 – 1998, Vol. I. Coordinates, Dimensions and Factors*, Stănculescu, M. S. (ed.), Poverty Alleviation Project, Bucharest: UNDP.

UNDP (1999b) *National Human Development Report*, Bucharest: UNDP.

UNDP (2005a) *National Human Development Report*, Bucharest: UNDP, www.undp.ro.

UNDP (2005b) *Faces of poverty, faces of hope. Vulnerability profiles for decade of Roma inclusion countries*, Bratislava: United Nations Development Programme. http://vulnerability.undp.sk/

UNICEF (2004) *Social Monitor 2004*, Innocenti Social Monitor CEE/CIS/Baltic States.

World Bank (1997), *Romania: Poverty and Social Policy*, Report No. 16462-RO, World Bank.

World Bank (2003) *Romania: Poverty Assessment*, Report No. 26169-RO, Bucharest: World Bank.

World Bank (2007) *Romania: Poverty Monitoring Analytical and Advisory Assistance Program*, Report No. 40120-RO, Bucharest: World Bank.

Zamfir, C. (ed.) (1995) *Dimensiunile Sărăciei*, Bucharest: Expert.

Zamfir, C. (1997) 'Social insurance and social assistance in countries in transition', in *Romanian Journal of Sociology*, VIII/ 2, p. 18-65.

Zamfir, E. and Zamfir C. (eds.) (1993) *Ţiganii între ignorare and îngrijorare*, Bucharest: Alternative.

Zamfir, C. and Preda, M. (eds.) (2002) *Romii în România*, Bucharest: Expert.

Zamfir, C. (coord.) (2005) *Understanding the Dynamics of Poverty and Development Risks on Children in Romania*, UNICEF Report, Bucharest.

Annex

Table RO1: The structure of household income sources, by income deciles (horizontal structure)

	D1	D2	D3	D4	D5	D6	D7	D8	D9	D10	Total
1995											
Wages and salaries	17.8	29.3	34.7	38.4	41.8	45.2	48.5	52.5	58.5	48.2	45.5
Non-agricultural self-employment	8.4	5.5	3.8	3.6	3.2	2.7	2.6	3.2	3.8	12.9	5.8
Income from agriculture	44.2	35.4	31.4	28.0	25.9	23.4	22.1	20.5	19.9	23.4	25.0
Income from capital	0.1	0.2	0.1	0.2	0.2	0.1	0.2	0.3	0.3	1.0	0.4
Pensions	13.4	18.4	20.9	21.9	22.7	23.0	21.6	18.3	12.0	5.7	15.9
Unemployment benefits	5.4	3.7	3.0	2.5	1.7	1.1	0.9	0.7	0.6	0.2	1.4
Family benefits	6.2	3.8	2.7	2.1	1.7	1.4	1.2	1.0	0.8	0.4	1.5
Other social benefits	1.8	1.5	1.2	1.1	0.8	0.8	0.5	0.6	0.5	0.4	0.7
Interfamily transfers (remittances)	1.6	1.4	1.4	1.5	1.4	1.4	1.5	2.0	2.4	5.2	2.5
Other income	1.0	0.8	0.8	0.7	0.7	0.9	0.9	0.9	1.3	2.6	1.3
Total disposable income	100	100	100	100	100	100	100	100	100	100	100
1997											
Wages and salaries	16.7	27.2	32.6	35.8	39.5	40.4	43.3	46.3	49.6	44.6	40.8
Non-agricultural self-employment	7.4	4.7	3.9	3.0	2.6	2.8	2.7	3.0	3.2	10.4	4.9
Income from agriculture	43.1	36.2	32.5	30.3	27.7	26.6	24.7	23.8	23.1	23.9	27.1
Income from capital	0.1	0.1	0.0	0.1	0.2	0.1	0.3	0.4	0.6	2.7	0.8
Pensions	13.1	18.3	20.2	21.0	21.8	22.3	21.5	19.2	16.3	6.8	16.7
Unemployment benefits	3.1	2.1	2.0	1.6	1.0	0.8	0.7	0.6	0.4	0.3	0.9
Family benefits	11.3	6.6	5.0	4.1	3.4	2.9	2.4	2.0	1.6	0.9	3.0
Other social benefits	2.3	2.0	1.6	1.4	1.2	1.1	0.9	0.8	0.6	0.4	1.0
Interfamily transfers (remittances)	2.3	1.8	1.5	1.6	1.6	1.6	1.9	2.2	2.2	4.2	2.4
Other income	0.7	1.0	0.7	1.1	1.1	1.4	1.5	1.6	2.4	5.8	2.4
Total disposable income	100	100	100	100	100	100	100	100	100	100	100

Source: IHS 1995, 1997.

223

Table RO1: The structure of household income sources, by income deciles (horizontal structure)

	D1	D2	D3	D4	D5	D6	D7	D8	D9	D10	Total
2001											
Wages and salaries	10.5	19.9	27.2	29.8	35.5	38.1	42.9	47.3	51.9	57.0	42.0
Non-agricultural self-employment	13.0	7.4	4.8	4.4	3.2	3.2	2.3	2.8	2.4	4.3	4.0
Income from agriculture	44.0	38.8	33.2	29.7	26.7	25.0	22.8	21.1	19.5	17.7	24.6
Income from capital	0.1	0.1	0.1	0.0	0.1	0.1	0.1	0.2	0.4	1.3	0.4
Pensions	14.5	21.2	24.1	26.2	26.0	25.5	24.8	21.5	18.6	9.9	19.9
Unemployment benefits	3.2	2.9	2.4	2.2	1.7	1.4	1.0	0.6	0.5	0.2	1.2
Family benefits	9.8	5.2	3.8	3.0	2.3	1.9	1.6	1.4	1.0	0.6	2.2
Other social benefits	1.5	1.4	1.2	1.2	0.8	0.8	0.8	0.8	0.8	0.5	0.9
Interfamily transfers (remittances)	2.2	1.9	2.4	2.2	2.0	2.3	2.0	2.5	2.7	4.7	2.8
Other income	1.1	1.2	0.9	1.3	1.5	1.7	1.6	1.8	2.2	3.7	2.0
Total disposable income	100	100	100	100	100	100	100	100	100	100	100
2004											
Wages and salaries	12.5	21.6	27.4	32.4	36.1	38.7	42.2	48.4	53.7	56.2	42.9
Non-agricultural self-employment	11.8	9.1	6.2	5.2	4.3	3.9	3.6	3.0	3.8	6.4	5.2
Income from agriculture	34.1	30.9	28.2	24.8	22.6	20.2	19.6	17.1	15.8	14.7	20.1
Income from capital	0.1	0.0	0.1	0.1	0.1	0.1	0.2	0.3	0.3	2.7	0.8
Pensions	17.3	23.1	25.4	25.8	26.6	27.1	24.2	20.6	15.6	7.6	19.1
Unemployment benefits	1.3	1.2	1.9	1.7	1.5	0.9	0.8	0.8	0.5	0.2	0.9
Family benefits	7.4	3.9	2.6	2.2	1.7	1.4	1.2	1.0	0.8	0.4	1.6
Other social benefits	10.2	4.9	2.7	1.9	1.5	1.3	1.0	1.0	0.8	0.5	1.7
Interfamily transfers (remittances)	2.6	2.4	2.4	2.6	2.5	2.7	2.6	2.3	3.2	5.1	3.2
Other income	2.6	2.9	3.0	3.2	3.2	3.7	4.6	5.4	5.5	6.1	4.6
Total disposable income	100	100	100	100	100	100	100	100	100	100	100

Source: FBS 2001, 2004.

Table RO2: The distribution of household income sources across income deciles (vertical distribution)

	D1	D2	D3	D4	D5	D6	D7	D8	D9	D10	Total
1995											
Wages and salaries	1.5	3.6	5.0	6.3	7.6	9.0	11.0	13.5	18.0	24.4	100
Non-agricultural self-employment	5.7	5.3	4.4	4.6	4.6	4.2	4.7	6.3	9.1	51.1	100
Income from agriculture	6.9	8.0	8.3	8.4	8.6	8.5	9.1	9.6	11.1	21.5	100
Income from capital	1.2	3.1	1.4	3.9	4.5	2.8	5.5	7.2	11.4	59.0	100
Pensions	3.3	6.5	8.7	10.3	11.9	13.1	14.0	13.5	10.5	8.2	100
Unemployment benefits	15.6	15.6	14.5	14.0	10.1	7.7	7.1	6.1	5.9	3.4	100
Family benefits	16.1	14.3	12.1	10.5	9.5	8.4	8.3	7.7	7.4	5.9	100
Other social benefits	9.8	11.2	10.9	11.1	9.2	9.8	7.8	9.2	9.1	12.0	100
Interfamily transfers (remittances)	2.4	3.1	3.6	4.4	4.5	5.0	6.2	9.5	13.2	48.0	100
Other income	2.9	3.4	4.1	3.8	4.5	6.3	6.9	8.5	13.8	45.8	100
Total disposable income	3.9	5.6	6.6	7.5	8.3	9.1	10.3	11.7	14.0	23.0	100
1997											
Wages and salaries	1.8	4.0	5.4	6.8	8.2	9.2	11.0	13.1	16.4	24.2	100
Non-agricultural self-employment	6.4	5.7	5.3	4.7	4.5	5.3	5.6	7.0	8.7	46.7	100
Income from agriculture	6.8	7.9	8.2	8.6	8.7	9.1	9.4	10.2	11.5	19.5	100
Income from capital	0.5	0.6	0.4	0.8	1.8	1.5	3.8	5.9	10.2	74.5	100
Pensions	3.4	6.5	8.2	9.7	11.1	12.4	13.3	13.3	13.2	8.9	100
Unemployment benefits	13.9	13.4	14.2	12.9	9.4	8.0	8.0	7.0	5.5	7.8	100
Family benefits	16.2	13.1	11.3	10.7	9.7	8.9	8.3	7.8	7.2	6.7	100
Other social benefits	9.8	12.0	10.8	10.7	10.2	10.1	9.5	9.6	8.7	8.7	100
Interfamily transfers (remittances)	4.1	4.5	4.3	5.1	5.7	6.3	8.3	10.9	12.5	38.4	100
Other income	1.3	2.4	2.0	3.4	3.9	5.3	6.6	7.8	13.6	53.7	100
Total disposable income	4.3	5.9	6.8	7.7	8.5	9.3	10.3	11.6	13.5	22.1	100

Source: IHS 1995, 1997.

Table RO2: The distribution of household income sources across income deciles (vertical distribution)

	D1	D2	D3	D4	D5	D6	D7	D8	D9	D10	Total
2001											
Wages and salaries	1.0	2.7	4.3	5.4	7.1	8.4	10.8	13.5	17.4	29.4	100
Non-agricultural self-employment	13.3	10.4	7.8	8.3	6.7	7.4	6.1	8.3	8.4	23.3	100
Income from agriculture	7.4	9.0	8.9	9.2	9.1	9.5	9.8	10.3	11.2	15.7	100
Income from capital	1.2	0.8	1.8	0.8	2.7	3.0	2.0	4.6	13.1	69.9	100
Pensions	3.0	6.1	8.0	10.0	10.9	11.9	13.1	13.0	13.1	10.8	100
Unemployment benefits	11.2	14.1	13.5	14.2	12.3	10.6	8.7	6.5	5.4	3.3	100
Family benefits	18.6	13.7	11.6	10.4	9.1	8.2	7.8	7.6	6.7	6.2	100
Other social benefits	7.3	9.3	9.2	10.4	7.9	8.8	10.0	10.6	12.9	13.5	100
Interfamily transfers (remittances)	3.3	3.9	5.5	5.9	5.9	7.7	7.6	10.6	13.6	36.2	100
Other income	2.2	3.2	2.9	4.8	6.3	7.6	8.3	10.7	14.9	39.0	100
Total disposable income	4.1	5.7	6.6	7.6	8.4	9.3	10.5	12.0	14.1	21.7	100
2004											
Wages and salaries	1.2	2.8	4.2	5.6	6.9	8.2	10.2	13.5	18.0	29.3	100
Non-agricultural self-employment	9.1	9.6	7.8	7.5	6.8	6.8	7.2	7.0	10.5	27.7	100
Income from agriculture	6.8	8.4	9.2	9.2	9.2	9.2	10.1	10.2	11.3	16.4	100
Income from capital	0.3	0.3	1.2	0.6	1.4	1.2	3.3	4.9	6.5	80.1	100
Pensions	3.6	6.6	8.7	10.0	11.4	12.9	13.2	12.9	11.8	8.9	100
Unemployment benefits	6.1	7.8	14.5	14.8	14.0	9.4	9.1	11.5	8.4	4.3	100
Family benefits	18.7	13.6	11.0	10.4	9.0	8.3	8.0	7.6	7.2	6.3	100
Other social benefits	24.3	16.0	10.5	8.3	7.1	6.8	6.4	6.9	7.1	6.5	100
Interfamily transfers (remittances)	3.2	4.2	4.9	6.2	6.4	7.8	8.6	8.7	14.3	35.8	100
Other income	2.2	3.4	4.3	5.2	5.8	7.3	10.4	14.2	17.3	29.8	100
Total disposable income	4.0	5.5	6.5	7.4	8.2	9.1	10.4	12.0	14.4	22.4	100

Source: FBS 2001, 2004.

Table RO3:   The structure of household members, by socioeconomic status and income deciles (horizontal structure)

	D1	D2	D3	D4	D5	D6	D7	D8	D9	D10	Total
1995											
Employees	7.6	14.3	19.3	23.7	27.6	31.8	35.6	40.6	47.6	50.5	28.6
Non-agricultural self-employed	2.7	1.5	1.2	1.2	1.2	1.1	1.1	1.4	1.7	3.8	1.7
Active in agriculture	20.6	15.8	12.6	11.0	8.6	6.7	5.7	4.5	4.1	4.6	10.0
Unemployed	9.6	8.6	7.6	6.6	5.1	4.1	3.6	2.8	2.9	1.7	5.5
Pensioners	13.4	18.0	21.3	23.8	25.5	26.8	25.8	23.2	17.4	14.5	20.8
Dependants 0-17 years	34.0	30.5	27.1	25.1	23.4	21.5	21.3	20.7	20.1	18.1	24.7
Dependants 18+ years	12.0	11.4	10.9	8.7	8.6	7.9	6.9	6.7	6.2	6.8	8.8
All population	100	100	100	100	100	100	100	100	100	100	100
1997											
Employees	8.6	15.6	21.2	24.9	28.8	31.3	35.6	38.6	42.8	46.1	28.2
Non-agricultural self-employed	2.8	1.8	1.7	1.4	1.3	1.3	1.3	1.5	1.4	3.7	1.8
Active in agriculture	20.2	15.5	11.2	9.5	7.2	6.8	5.6	4.4	4.5	5.0	9.5
Unemployed	10.5	7.9	6.5	5.5	4.4	3.7	3.0	2.9	2.1	2.1	5.1
Pensioners	11.2	18.4	22.0	23.5	25.3	26.5	26.9	25.6	24.0	16.4	21.6
Dependants 0-17 years	33.3	27.6	25.6	24.5	23.2	21.9	20.7	19.9	18.6	18.7	23.9
Dependants 18+ years	13.5	13.2	11.7	10.6	9.9	8.5	7.0	6.9	6.5	7.9	9.8
All population	100	100	100	100	100	100	100	100	100	100	100

Source: IHS 1995, 1997 and FBS 2001.

Table RO3: The structure of household members, by socioeconomic status and income deciles (horizontal structure)

	D1	D2	D3	D4	D5	D6	D7	D8	D9	D10	Total
2001											
Employees	4.4	9.8	15.1	18.0	23.8	26.7	31.8	36.5	41.4	49.1	24.3
Non-agricultural self-employed	3.8	2.6	2.2	2.4	1.9	2.1	1.8	1.9	1.8	3.4	2.4
Active in agriculture	23.9	18.7	13.2	10.2	7.7	6.8	4.9	4.6	3.6	3.1	10.4
Unemployed	11.4	9.5	9.1	8.1	7.0	6.2	4.9	3.3	2.9	2.1	6.7
Pensioners	11.4	20.4	24.4	27.9	29.2	30.2	30.3	27.5	25.5	17.9	24.0
Dependants 0-17 years	32.8	26.4	24.0	22.2	20.2	18.9	18.1	18.1	16.9	16.2	21.9
Dependants 18+ years	12.3	12.6	12.0	11.2	10.3	9.2	8.2	8.1	7.9	8.3	10.2
All population	100	100	100	100	100	100	100	100	100	100	100
2004											
Employees	4.8	10.8	15.7	21.0	24.9	28.6	32.8	38.8	44.6	51.2	26.0
Non-agricultural self-employed	5.3	3.2	3.4	2.9	2.6	2.7	2.7	2.3	2.8	4.8	3.3
Active in agriculture	19.0	17.2	13.1	8.7	7.5	5.8	5.4	3.7	3.5	3.8	9.3
Unemployed	11.4	7.5	7.2	5.5	4.7	3.7	3.5	3.1	2.5	1.7	5.4
Pensioners	12.1	21.6	25.5	28.0	30.0	31.5	29.5	26.4	22.4	15.5	23.9
Dependants 0-17 years	32.4	25.6	22.1	21.9	19.5	18.5	17.4	17.4	16.1	15.7	21.2
Dependants 18+ years	15.0	14.0	12.9	12.0	10.7	9.2	8.8	8.2	8.2	7.4	10.9
All population	100	100	100	100	100	100	100	100	100	100	100

Source: FBS 2004.

Table RO4:   The distribution of household members (by socioeconomic status) across income deciles (vertical distribution)

	D1	D2	D3	D4	D5	D6	D7	D8	D9	D10	Total
1995											
Employees	3.3	5.6	7.2	8.4	9.4	10.4	11.7	13.2	15.4	15.3	100
Non-agricultural self-employed	19.6	9.9	7.6	7.0	7.0	6.1	6.1	7.9	9.3	19.5	100
Active in agriculture	25.4	17.8	13.4	11.1	8.5	6.3	5.4	4.2	3.8	4.0	100
Unemployed	21.3	17.5	14.7	12.1	9.0	7.0	6.2	4.8	4.9	2.7	100
Pensioners	7.9	9.7	10.9	11.6	12.0	12.0	11.7	10.4	7.8	6.1	100
Dependants 0-17 years	16.9	13.9	11.6	10.3	9.3	8.1	8.1	7.8	7.5	6.4	100
Dependants 18+ years	16.8	14.6	13.1	10.0	9.5	8.4	7.4	7.1	6.5	6.6	100
All population	12.3	11.3	10.6	10.1	9.8	9.3	9.4	9.3	9.3	8.7	100
1997											
Employees	3.8	6.2	7.8	9.0	10.0	10.5	11.9	12.7	13.8	14.4	100
Non-agricultural self-employed	19.0	10.9	9.7	7.7	6.7	6.9	6.7	7.6	7.0	17.9	100
Active in agriculture	26.6	18.2	12.2	10.1	7.4	6.8	5.5	4.3	4.3	4.7	100
Unemployed	25.7	17.1	13.2	10.8	8.3	6.7	5.5	5.3	3.8	3.7	100
Pensioners	6.5	9.5	10.6	11.0	11.5	11.6	11.7	10.9	10.1	6.7	100
Dependants 0-17 years	17.5	12.9	11.1	10.4	9.5	8.7	8.1	7.7	7.1	6.9	100
Dependants 18+ years	17.3	15.0	12.4	10.9	9.9	8.2	6.7	6.5	6.0	7.1	100
All population	12.6	11.2	10.4	10.1	9.8	9.5	9.4	9.2	9.0	8.8	100

Source: IHS 1995.

229

Table RO4: The distribution of household members (by socioeconomic status) across income deciles (vertical distribution)

	D1	D2	D3	D4	D5	D6	D7	D8	D9	D10	Total
2001											
Employees	2.4	4.5	6.4	7.4	9.4	10.3	12.3	14.0	15.4	17.9	100
Non-agricultural self-employed	20.4	11.7	9.2	9.9	7.4	8.0	7.0	7.4	6.6	12.5	100
Active in agriculture	29.7	19.8	13.1	9.8	7.1	6.1	4.5	4.1	3.1	2.6	100
Unemployed	21.8	15.7	13.9	12.0	10.0	8.7	6.8	4.5	3.9	2.8	100
Pensioners	6.1	9.4	10.5	11.7	11.7	11.8	11.9	10.7	9.6	6.6	100
Dependants 0-17 years	19.3	13.3	11.3	10.2	8.9	8.1	7.8	7.7	7.0	6.6	100
Dependants 18+ years	15.6	13.7	12.2	11.1	9.7	8.5	7.6	7.4	7.1	7.2	100
All population	12.9	11.1	10.3	10.1	9.6	9.4	9.4	9.3	9.1	8.9	100
2004											
Employees	2.4	4.6	6.3	8.1	9.2	10.3	12.0	14.2	16.0	17.1	100
Non-agricultural self-employed	20.4	10.6	10.7	8.8	7.5	7.6	7.6	6.6	7.7	12.5	100
Active in agriculture	26.1	20.1	14.6	9.4	7.8	5.8	5.5	3.7	3.5	3.5	100
Unemployed	27.1	15.2	13.9	10.2	8.5	6.5	6.1	5.5	4.4	2.8	100
Pensioners	6.5	9.9	11.0	11.7	12.1	12.4	11.7	10.5	8.7	5.6	100
Dependants 0-17 years	19.6	13.2	10.8	10.3	8.8	8.2	7.8	7.8	7.1	6.4	100
Dependants 18+ years	17.6	14.1	12.3	11.0	9.5	7.9	7.6	7.2	7.0	5.9	100
All population	12.8	10.9	10.3	10.0	9.6	9.4	9.5	9.5	9.3	8.6	100

Source: IHS 1997 and FBS 2001, 2004.

Chapter 6

The Transition Process and Changes in Income, Income Inequality and Poverty: The Case of Slovenia

Tine Stanovnik / Mitja Čok

1 Changes in wages, pensions and social protection expenditures

The economic transformation and even more the political disintegration of Yugoslavia resulted in a very large decrease in real wages from 1989 to 1991. Following independence, formally declared on 25 June 1991, the economy was quickly stabilized, so that wages in 1992 remained almost at their 1991 level in real terms. Since 1992, wages were continuously increasing, as can be seen from Table 1; unfortunately, this table does not include the very turbulent years between 1989 and 1991. The income source second in importance – pensions – have also been steadily increasing (in real terms) during the 1992-2003 period (Table 1).

Concomitantly with the large drop in real wages during the 1989-1992 period, employment also experienced a very large decrease. However, unlike wages, employment kept on falling till 1996. In view of these negative developments, it seems quite extraordinary that the social protection system functioned in a very "business as usual" manner, in spite of the vast increase in the exigencies placed on it. That the system did not snap was mostly due to a very well organized system of social security contributions collection, which prevented a serious deterioration of contribution revenues.[1]

---

1   A detailed assessment of contribution collection in Slovenia is presented in Vezjak and Stanovnik (2004).

Table 1:   Changes in average real pension, average real wage and share of wages in GDP, 1992-2003

	Index of average real pension (1992=100)	Index of average real wage (1992=100)	Share of wages in GDP[1]
1992	100.0	100.0	53.6
1993	108.1	111.2	50.1
1994	117.9	115.3	48.7
1995	124.5	120.3	48.8
1996	126.8	126.2	47.5
1997	129.8	130.2	46.9
1998	132.1	132.2	54.6
1999	138.6	136.5	45.2
2000	139.7	138.7	47.1
2001	139.9	143.1	47.6
2002	142.0	146.2	46.6
2003	141.3	148.9	46.1

Note: 1) Not reliable before 1999 due to changes in methodology.
Source: Yearbook of the Statistical Office (2003, 2004, 2006).

After 1992, the economy was on the rise, with high growth rates of GDP, and a somewhat lesser growth of wages and household income. This can be observed in Table 2. However, one must point out that the high growth rate of GDP, as measured in Euros, is also the result of a strong appreciation of the Slovene Tolar, which occurred in the early 1990s. This appreciation was mostly caused by strong capital inflows into the country.

Table 2:   Changes in household income, real wages and GDP p.c. (1993=100)

	Median household equivalent income	Real wage	GDP per capita
1993	100	100	100
1998	124	119	174
2002	136	131	218

Note: For median household equivalent income, the data are based on the HES for 1993, 1997-99 and 2001-2003. For GDP p.c. the index is computed from data on GDP p.c. in euros (for 1993 in ecus). It is not based on purchasing power parity.
Source: 2005 Statistical Yearbook for Slovenia and HES for 1993, 1997-99, 2001-2003.

The social protection system proved to be remarkably "accommodating" in adapting to the large increase in beneficiaries, without any sizeable decrease in social protection rights. Expenditures increased, though unfortunately the most critical period, i.e. from 1989 to 1992, is not well documented, due to large political and economic changes, which also entailed statistical and methodological changes. Thus, data on social protection expenditures according to ESSPROS methodology are not available for years prior to 1996. Nevertheless, in order to at least grasp the basic trend of the most important expenditures within the system of social protection, in Table 3 we present some of the more important expenditures (pensions, unemployment cash benefits etc) according to national statistics. Clearly, data on expenditures for health care are not presented.

Table 3:   Social protection expenditures, as percentage of GDP

	Social protection expenditure as percentage of GDP	Unemploy-ment cash benefits as percentage of GDP	Pensions as percentage of GDP	Cash social assistance as percentage of GDP	Family benefits as percentage of GDP
1992		0.83	13.8	0.05	1.23
1993		1.17	14.0	0.17	1.36
1994		1.14	14.4	0.20	1.43
1995		0.78	13.7	0.25	1.32
1996	23.9	0.71	13.6	0.29	1.48
1997	24.3	0.90	13.5	0.32	1.52
1998	24.5	0.81	13.5	0.28	1.45
1999	24.4	0.79	13.6	0.26	1.59
2000	24.3	0.56	13.7	0.25	1.73
2001	24.7	0.58	13.7	0.23	1.70
2002	24.6	0.48	13.7	0.33	1.64
2003	24.0	0.45	13.4	0.48	1.62

Notes: "Unemployment cash benefits" include unemployment benefits, which is a social insurance benefit and unemployment assistance, which is a means-tested benefit targeted at unemployed persons.
"Pensions" also include pension-related expenditures, health insurance for pensioners and administration costs of the pension system.
"Cash social assistance" does not include national educational grants.
"Family benefits" include parental compensation, child allowance, birth grant, parental allowance, allowance for nursing a child, large family allowance, partial compensation for foregone income and payment of social contributions.

Source: Pension Insurance Fund (2006); Statistical Office (2006, 2005, 2003); Ministry of Labour, Family and Social Affairs (2006).

Table 3 does show considerable stability of pension expenditures since 1992, decreasing expenditures on unemployment cash benefits and increasing expenditures on cash social assistance and family benefits. Fairly stable expenditures on pensions resulted from a gradual decrease in the ratio between pensions and wages. This was mostly caused by the pension reform introduced in 2000, which not only decreased the pension rights of new entrants – pensioners, but also for old pensioners.[2] This can be seen in Figure 1.

Figure 1:   The pension/wage ratio, 1992-2003

Source: IPDI (2006): Annual Report 2005; Yearbook of the Statistical Office (2003, 2004).

2   Income structure at the household level

The socioeconomic structure and the income structure of Slovenian households experienced large changes in the early transition years. The most important shifts were in the size of the active and inactive population. Large decreases in labour activity and increases in unemployment occurred in this period. The number of labour-active decreased from 943.5 thousand in 1989 to 766.4 thousand in 1993. After 1993, the decreases were much smaller. The number of registered unemployed also experienced a large increase – from 28.2 thousand in 1989 to 102.6 thousand in 1992, reaching its peak in 1993, with 129.1 thousand registered unemployed persons. On the part of the in-

---

2   This is a rather unique feature of the Slovenian pension reform, as pension reforms usually involve the decrease in pension rights only for the active population. For a detailed account, see Stanovnik (2002).

active population, the number of pensioners increased from 365.1 thousand in 1989 to 448.8 thousand in 1992, i.e. an increase of 23% in only three years! After 1992 the increases were much more modest, also due to the fact that pensionable cohorts were smaller. One must mention the large increase in the number of students (see Chapter 1, Table 1), as this contributed to the decrease in the active population.

It would be interesting to analyse these large socioeconomic and income changes using data from the Household Expenditure Survey (HES) and starting with a pre-transition year sufficiently close to the beginning of transition. Unfortunately, the 1988 HES is of poor quality, due to the very high inflation in that year (199%) and inadequate preparations, so that it cannot be used as a reliable statistical source. We have refrained from using the other large survey, i.e. the 1983 HES, as the time span between this survey and the 1993 HES is too large.[3] So, our analyses will be based on HES surveys for 1993, 1997-1999 and 2001-2003. The 1997-1999 and 2001-2003 surveys refer to three annual surveys, suitably merged.

Table 4 shows the structure of current household disposable monetary income[4] in the first decile, tenth decile and overall (i.e. all households) for the three cross-sections: 1993, 1997-99 and 2001-03.

The structure of income sources differs markedly across income deciles: for poor households, the main income sources are pensions, family benefits and social transfers (unemployment benefits and other social benefits). For these households, the share of labour income is much smaller than for the average household; in 2001-2003 the share of wages in current disposable monetary household income was 59.8% for all households, whereas for households situated in the first decile wages represented only 25.6% of household income. A fairly high share of income from agriculture, pensions and unemployment benefits in the first decile simply means that farmers, pensioners and unemployed persons are somewhat more concentrated among poor households.

The changing structure through time is also revealing. The share of wages has remained stable, representing close to 60% of total household disposable income. However, the shares of self-employment income, income from agriculture and income from occasional work have decreased. While increased under-reporting of self-employment income cannot be ruled out,

---

3   Actually, the 1983 HES will be used in just one instance, comparing incomes and educational attainments (section 4).

4   Though technical and methodological issues are described in the Technical Annex, we note here that households are ranked according to equivalent (disposable) income, using the OECD equivalence scale. Each decile contains 10% of all households.

the decreasing share of income from agriculture is also confirmed by macro data, which show the decreasing share of agriculture in GDP; in 1990 agriculture amounted to some 5.5% of GDP, decreasing to 3.2% in 2001. The share of the second most important income source – pensions – has been increasing, from 21.1% of household disposable income in 1993 to 25.2% in 2001-2003. Interestingly, the largest increase in the share of pensions in household disposable income occurred at the top of the income distribution, in the tenth decile. For these households, pensions represented "only" 11.5% of household income in 1993, increasing to 20.3% in 2001-2003. How can this be explained? Table 10 shows that the composition of households situated in the tenth decile was very different in 1997-99 as compared to 1993. The share of pensioners has increased considerably, with a concomitant large decrease in the share of children in the high-income households. Does this mean that high-income earners are having less and less children? Some other analyses seem to confirm these findings: the analysis of personal income tax returns shows[5] that the number of high income taxpayers making use of the tax allowance for children is decreasing, meaning that they have less children. Pensioners are thus taking their positions, and the share of pensioner households – mostly pensioner couples collecting two pensions – has increased considerably between 1993 and 1997-99 in the top income decile.

Though income from capital is still a modest income source, its increasing share is due to privatization, with a large number of shareholders receiving their first dividends. The decreasing share of unemployment benefits – from 1.4% of household income in 1993 to 0.9% of household disposable income in 2001-2003 is also confirmed by data published by the National Employment Service: in 1993 these benefits amounted to 1.25% of GDP, decreasing to 0.58% in 2001. The quite large increase in family benefits, from 0.7% of household disposable income in 1993 to 3.0% in 2001-2003 can be explained by two factors: a very large expansion of child benefits and definitional changes. With regard to the latter, parental wage compensation was included in wages and salaries in the 1993 survey;[6] following the new survey design in 1997, parental wage compensation was treated as a separate income item and included in family benefits. As for child benefits, this was probably the only social and family programme that experienced a vast

---

5   The analysis is presented in Vales (2006).

6   The reason for this is that the employer disbursed these benefits and was later recompensed by the social insurance institution.

Table 4:   The changing structure of household income

	Wages & salaries	Income from oc-casional work	Self-em-ployment income	Income from ag-riculture	Income from capital	Pensions	Unem-ployment benefits	Family benefits	Other social benefits	Inter-family benefits	Other income	All
First decile												
1993	33.5	2.3	0.9	7.3	0.2	37.6	4.8	4.9	6.4	1.4	0.7	100
1997-99	31.8	2.6	2.7	8.1	0.0	32.1	6.1	8.1	7.0	1.3	0.1	100
2001-03	25.6	3.5	3.2	6.3	0.3	35.7	4.9	10.5	9.0	0.5	0.5	100
Tenth decile												
1993	58.2	5.0	14.3	1.5	0.5	11.5	0.1	0.0	0.5	4.2	4.1	100
1997-99	66.3	3.1	7.5	0.1	1.0	20.1	0.3	0.9	0.7	0.0	0.1	100
2001-03	67.2	3.1	5.8	0.0	1.1	20.3	0.2	1.1	0.8	0.0	0.3	100
All												
1993	59.2	3.2	6.3	2.8	0.1	21.1	1.4	0.7	1.4	2.0	1.7	100
1997-99	60.4	2.0	4.8	1.5	0.4	24.9	1.4	2.5	1.7	0.3	0.1	100
2001-03	59.8	2.2	5.1	1.1	0.4	25.2	0.9	3.0	1.7	0.3	0.2	100

Source: HES 1993, 1997-99, 2001-03.

expansion in the 1990s, paved by a resolution on family policy passed by Parliament in July 1993. This resolution stated that universal child benefits were a national goal, and national legislation quickly followed in step, with the Family Benefits Act passed in December 1993. Though this act put the universality ideal "on hold", it nevertheless expanded child benefits, with further important increases promulgated in 1995 and 1999. Expenditure on child benefits amounted to 0.53% of GDP in 1993, increasing to 0.64% in 1995 and to 1.02% in 2000.[7]

The relatively low share of interfamily transfers in the two last surveys, the 1997-99 and 2001-2003 surveys, as well as the low share of other income is quite plausible. Namely, the relatively high values of these two income sources in 1993 are difficult to explain, particularly since it appears that rich households were the largest recipients of interfamily transfers! A possible explanation for this aberration is that, due to the required balancing of incomes and expenditures, the underreporting of some income sources in 1993 could have been "compensated" by inflated statements of the more "innocuous" ones. A further explanation could be that, due to the 1991 Housing Act, which offered the sale of the public housing to sitting tenants, large cash transfers occurred between households.

3 The coverage of social benefits and the socioeconomic status of household members

The structure of household income has experienced large changes in the period from 1993 to 2001-2003. In this section we focus on income transfers, in particular, social benefits. As seen from Table 4, social benefits other than pensions represented some 3.5% of household income in 1993; this increased to 5.6% in 2001-2003. In this same period, the share of the largest social benefit – pensions – increased from 21.1% to 25.2% of household income. We explore to what degree these increasing shares are due to increased coverage, meaning that relatively more households received these benefits. Toward the end of this section, we analyse the overall socioeconomic structure of households, with particular emphasis on household members without own sources of income (dependants).

---

7   A detailed account of the changes in family policy and family benefits is described in Stanovnik et al. (2006).

3.1 The coverage of social benefits

"Coverage" denotes the share of the relevant population receiving a given social benefit – for example children receiving child allowances, unemployed receiving unemployment benefits etc. Our analysis is not concerned with persons with a given characteristic, but with households. In other words, we explore how many households with a given member (elderly, child, un-employed) receive a relevant social benefit. With regard to the "elderly", a meaningful definition of coverage would include persons above retirement age who receive a pension (as percentage of all persons above retirement age). However, due to very different types of pensions (old-age, disability, survivors') and the gradual evolution of the retirement age for old-age pensioners, such a comparison is fraught with difficulties. For this reason, we somewhat tautologically define coverage of pensions as the share of households with pensioner(s) receiving pension(s), as percentage of all households with pensioner(s). Table 5 shows that the coverage of pensions is now virtually 100%, meaning that all households with a pensioner also receive a pension. In 1993, only 94.8% of households with pensioners re-ceived a pension. This can be explained by the fact that a number of elderly persons, who considered themselves as "retired", i.e. declared themselves as "pensioners" in fact did not receive a pension.

Table 5:   Coverage of pensions

	A	B
1993	50.5	94.8
1997-99	50.7	99.8
2001-03	50.7	99.9

Notes: A: Households with pensioner, as percentage of all households.
         B: Percentage of households with pensioners that receive pensions.
Source: HES 1993, 1997-99, 2001-03.

Table 6 shows a very large increase in the coverage of family benefits, which is a consequence of the aforementioned expansion of child allowances, which occurred in two waves, in 1994 and 1996. Due to the very high in-come ceiling (above which families are not eligible for these benefits), child allowances are an almost universal benefit, though the amount disbursed does depend on family income[8] and birth order of the child. The number

---

8   Changes of various types of family benefits are described in greater detail in Stanovnik et al. (2006).

of children, recipients of child allowances, increased from 147 thousand in 1993 to 401 thousand in 2003. This expansion can be seen from Table 7, which also shows the large shift toward universality, so that in 2001-03 some 88% of households with children received this benefit. Because of the income ceiling, the coverage among high-income households with children is much lower; in 2001-03, in the tenth income decile only some 57% of households with children received this benefit. The further increase in coverage, which occurred in 2001-03, as compared to 1997-99, was due to a decrease in the income ceiling (enacted in May 1999). Also to be noted is an expansion of other existing types of family benefits, as well as the introduction of new ones. For an example of the former, starting in 1994, parental allowance was being granted also to persons not eligible for the insurance-based wage compensation during parental leave; the duration of disbursement of this benefit was also considerably increased. For an example of the latter, a new benefit, the large family allowance was introduced in 2001, for which families with three or more children were eligible.

Table 6:   Coverage of family benefits

Decile	1993		1997-99		2001-03	
	A	B	A	B	A	B
1	28.4	54.4	33.9	87.0	24.8	93.1
2	38.7	42.4	36.5	87.6	31.5	95.1
3	37.8	30.8	32.5	86.1	30.5	91.7
4	45.1	22.0	36.1	88.5	34.8	95.1
5	43.4	16.0	41.7	82.4	36.2	88.3
6	38.0	14.4	34.0	84.9	29.2	94.1
7	38.3	14.3	37.7	84.4	30.9	90.5
8	39.0	4.3	33.4	82.0	27.5	87.1
9	41.1	4.8	27.5	70.8	20.2	68.4
10	36.5	4.6	21.5	47.3	18.7	57.2
All	38.6	19.8	33.5	81.7	28.4	88.0

Notes: A: Household with child, as percentage of all households in income decile.
           B: Percentage of households with child, receiving family benefits
Source: HES 1993, 1997-99, 2001-03.

The coverage of unemployment benefits has considerably decreased in this period of time; this is hardly surprising, as we have already observed the large decrease in these expenditures. As seen from Table 7, in 1993 14.1% of all households were households with unemployed member(s), with 52% of these households receiving unemployment benefits. In 2001-2003, the share of households with unemployed member(s) has remained about the same (14.5%), but only 30.2% of these households were receiving unemployment benefits. The decrease in coverage mostly concerned households with unemployed persons in lower to middle deciles. This decreasing coverage is confirmed by data from the National Employment Service:[9] in 1993, 43.1% of all registered unemployed persons were recipients of an unemployment benefit, whereas in 2003 the share decreased to 24.9%.

Table 7:   Coverage of unemployment benefits

	1993		1997-99		2001-03	
Decile	A	B	A	B	A	B
1	24.5	35.2	45.2	35.1	39.7	23.9
2	23.4	64.9	35.5	34.0	25.1	27.2
3	16.5	48.9	21.1	33.1	20.8	33.2
4	13.6	61.0	17.8	43.9	14.7	29.7
5	17.9	58.5	18.6	48.0	12.0	38.5
6	13.4	61.4	11.8	54.5	8.2	25.8
7	10.5	41.9	11.7	57.5	10.3	29.3
8	6.8	47.8	9.2	41.6	7.0	45.4
9	9.1	57.6	4.9	48.4	4.1	57.6
10	4.9	27.8	3.3	58.7	3.2	29.9
All	14.1	52.0	17.9	40.7	14.5	30.2

Notes: A: Household with unemployed member, as percentage of all households in income decile.
          B: Percentage of households with unemployed member, receiving unemployment benefit.
Source: HES 1993, 1997-99, 2001-03.

The decreased coverage of unemployment benefits resulted from the reform of the unemployment benefit system in October 1998. The most significant changes were a shorter period of disbursement of unemployment benefits, a lower minimum amount of benefit and a changed base for benefit calculation. Following the "reform year", the replacement rate for unemployment benefit dropped, as seen from Figure 2.

9   2003 Annual Report of the National Employment Service.

Figure 2: **Replacement rate for unemployment benefit (average unemployment benefit as per cent of average wage), 1992-2002**

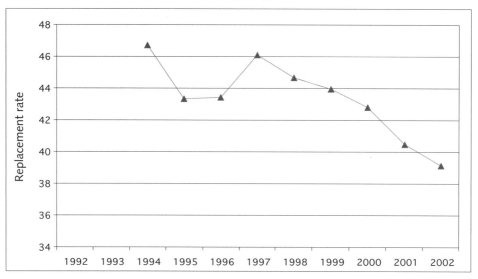

Note: Average unemployment benefits refer to December average of each year.

Source: Employment Service of Slovenia, Annual Report 1992-1992; Yearbook of the Statistical Office (2003, 2004).

Table 8: **Share of households receiving other social benefits (as percentage of all households)**

Decile	1993	1997-99	2001-03
1	36.4	55.0	48.3
2	37.9	54.4	52.8
3	30.1	49.3	51.1
4	27.7	57.0	54.0
5	27.1	56.5	53.9
6	20.0	52.6	48.6
7	18.9	52.8	47.0
8	12.6	43.1	41.1
9	14.1	33.5	31.3
10	8.8	24.2	22.3
All	23.4	47.9	45.1

Source: HES 1993, 1997-99, 2001-03.

As for other social benefits, these include a rather eclectic set of benefits, such as social assistance benefits, scholarships to high school and university students as well as some benefits disbursed by the Institute for pension and disability insurance. Table 8 shows that an expansion of coverage occurred, due to the very large Increase in the number of recipients of social assistance benefits. These were a new group: the unemployed who have exhausted their insurance-based unemployment benefits, being directed to centres for social work for social assistance.[10]

3.2 *The socioeconomic structure of households*

Changes in the socioeconomic structure of households since 1993 have been rather modest, as seen from Table 9. However, one must bear in mind that very large changes occurred in the early years of transition, from 1990 to 1993. Quite understandably, there are large differences between income deciles. Households in the poorest income decile are characterized by a low share of labour-active persons – in particular low shares of employees and non-agricultural self-employed persons. The large share of agricultural self-employed persons in the lowest decile simply reflects the fact that most farms in Slovenia are subsistence farms: in 2000 some 73% of all farms had an estimated annual income of less than 4,800 EUR.[11] The share of unemployed, pensioners and dependants in the poorest decile is similarly quite above the average share in the whole population.

From Table 9 we see that the overall share of labour-active persons (excluding self-employed in agriculture) has slightly increased. This is also confirmed by other statistical sources. According to the 2003 Annual Report of the Institute for Pension and Disability Insurance (IPDI), the total number of labour-active insured persons[12] was 664 thousand in 1993 and 699 thousand in 2003. The largest group of labour-active persons are employees and they represent a very heterogeneous group, with widely differing labour market status: part-time or full-time employed, temporary employed or those with a permanent labour contract. There are those with a single job and those with multiple jobs. Part-time employment[13] in Slovenia is rare, amounting to 5.5% of the labour-active population in mid-2002. High shares of part-time employment are typical for agriculture. Temporary employ-

243

---

10   A description of these changes is provided in Stropnik and Stanovnik (2002).

11   Kum (2006).

12   This refers to pension-insured employees, pension-insured (non-agriculture) self-employed persons and pension-insured self-employed persons in agriculture.

13   Rapid reports of the Statistical Office of the Republic of Slovenia, no. 33, 2003.

ment is more widespread, as some 14.8% of all employees in mid-2002 were employed according to such a labour contract.[14] Such employment is more concentrated among the young. The 2001-2003 Household Expenditure Survey also shows that this type of employment is considerably more concentrated in low-income households, which is quite what one would expect. Unfortunately, there are no published data on multiple job holders; it is, however, legal to have two jobs in the formal sector, with the proviso that the time spent on the second job cannot exceed 20% of the time of a full-time job.

According to the Statistical Registry, the number of self-employed (other than agriculture) slightly increased from 47 thousand in 1993 to 50 thousand in 2003, whereas the number of self-employed in agriculture dropped from 55 thousand in 1993 to 28 thousand in 2003.[15] The HES data imply a somewhat smaller figure for self-employed in agriculture (some 20 thousand in 2001-2003) and a larger figure for self-employed other than agriculture – some 65 thousand in 2001-03.

According to the HES data, the share of the largest group of social benefit recipients – pensioners – has steadily increased throughout this period: from 21.9% in 1993 to 23.6% of household members in 2001-2003. This is also confirmed by data from the IPDI: in 1993 there were 458 thousand pension recipients, increasing to 518 thousand in 2003.

Somewhat surprising is the high share of unemployed persons. From Table 9 one can compute the unemployment rate according to the HES data. It was 11.5% in 1993 and 12.7% in 2001-03. However, according to the Labour Force Survey (LFS), the unemployment rate was 9.1% in 1993, decreasing (though not monotonically) to 6.6% in 2003. In the HES the unemployment status is based on self-declaration. This simply means that a large number of persons consider themselves as "unemployed", though they are not counted as unemployed according to LFS criteria (i.e. they have not been actively seeking work or they have been gainfully employed for at least one hour in the reference week). Who are these persons? The LFS shows that a large number of persons would like to have work, but are not actively seeking employment; it seems that this group of persons consider themselves as "unemployed", but they are not unemployed according to the LFS methodology, which means that they are likely to be "discouraged unemployed".

---

14   Rapid reports of the Statistical Office of the Republic of Slovenia, no. 33, 2003.
15   2004 Annual report of the NES.

Table 9:   Changes in the socioeconomic structure of households

First decile	Employees	Active in agriculture	Other self-employed	Persons with occasional income	Unemployed	Pensioners	Dependants	Other	All
1993	14.0	8.6	0.6	1.8	11.5	26.2	34.9	2.5	100
1997-99	12.5	3.9	1.4	0.2	21.1	21.0	37.5	2.3	100
2001-03	10.2	3.7	1.5	0.7	20.3	24.0	38.6	1.2	100
Tenth decile									
1993	46.9	1.0	7.2	1.2	1.8	15.2	26.3	0.3	100
1997-99	50.4	0.0	5.5	0.3	1.2	22.9	19.5	0.1	100
2001-03	52.3	0.0	4.6	0.2	1.4	21.9	19.4	0.2	100
All									
1993	35.2	2.5	2.3	0.8	5.2	21.9	31.1	0.9	100
1997-99	34.9	1.1	3.2	0.2	7.1	22.6	30.3	0.5	100
2001-03	36.0	1.0	3.4	0.4	5.9	23.6	29.3	0.4	100

Source: HES 1993, 1997-99, 2001-03.

The number of dependants has been gradually decreasing. In 1993 they represented 31.1% of all household members, in 1997-99 some 30.3% and some 29.3% in 2001-2003. Table 10 provides a basis for explaining this overall trend, by subdividing dependants into four age groups. The decreasing share of younger dependants (i.e. less than 18 years old) is clearly caused by falling fertility rates; whereas these younger dependants represented 23.3% of all household members in 1993, their share shrank to 19.1% in 2001-2003. On the other hand, the share of dependants in the age group between 18 and 29 years is increasing – a consequence of the large increase in university enrolment. Here, the share of women is somewhat greater than men, due to the fact that more women are enrolled in university education. As for the two other age groups, from 30 to 59 years and 60 years and above, we observe that there are virtually no men-dependants in these age groups. Also, the share of women-dependants decreased in both of these age groups. In 1997-99 women-dependants aged 60 and over represented 1.7% of all household members, with their share dropping to 1.1% in 2001-2003. This is not only a consequence of the increased employment rate of women, which causes a gradual movement of higher labour-active cohorts into older age. This decrease was mostly caused by a new social benefit, the state pension, introduced by the 1999 Pension and Disability Insurance act. It is a benefit earmarked for elderly persons without a social insurance pension and with only modest own income sources.[16] Some 94% of state pension beneficiaries are women.

Table 10: The share of dependants, by age groups and gender (as percentage of all persons)

	Less than 18	18 to 29	30 to 59	60 +	All
	1993				
Men	12.0	1.8	0.1	0.0	14.0
Women	11.3	2.0	2.1	1.7	17.1
All	23.3	3.8	2.2	1.7	31.1
	1997-99				
Men	10.7	2.7	0.1	0.0	13.6
Women	10.2	3.1	1.7	1.7	16.7
All	20.9	5.8	1.8	1.7	30.3
	2001-03				
Men	9.8	3.6	0.0	0.0	13.4
Women	9.3	3.8	1.6	1.1	15.9
All	19.1	7.4	1.6	1.1	29.3

Source: HES 1993, 1997-99, 2001-03.

4 Income inequality

Milanović (1998: 40) has shown that income inequality increased in virtually all European countries during the transition from a centrally planned to a market economy. In most cases, the increase was abrupt and large; however, in Central European countries (where Milanović includes the Czech Republic, Hungary, Slovakia and Slovenia), changes in income inequality were less dramatic than in other parts of the former Communist bloc.

Though we shall not explore the causes for this increase, we do note that the returns to education increased considerably in the very early years of transition. This is well documented for a number of countries; Rutkowski (1996) for Poland, Orazem and Vodopivec (1994) and Stanovnik (1997) for Slovenia, Kertesi and Köllö (2001) for Hungary, Vecernik (2001) for the Czech Republic. The increasing returns to education in Slovenia can be observed from Table 11, which shows equivalized household income by education

16 In other words, means-testing does not apply for total family (or household) income, but only for one's own income sources.

levels. We observe that the relative equivalized income of labour-active persons with attained primary education level experienced a sharp drop in the early years of transition (i.e. early 1990s), whereas those with attained tertiary education level improved their relative position.

Table 11: Relative equivalized income by education levels of labour-active persons aged between 25 and 64 years

Education level	1983	1993	1997-99	2001-03
Primary	0.83	0.70	0.75	0.76
Vocational	1.05	0.90	0.85	0.85
Secondary		1.11	1.03	1.02
Tertiary	1.32	1.39	1.41	1.37
All	1.00	1.00	1.00	1.00

Source: HES 1983, 1993, 1997-99, 2001-03.

Table 12: Attained educational level, by income deciles (all labour-active persons aged 25 to 64)

	Primary	Vocational	Secondary	Tertiary	All
			1993		
Decile					
1	71.4	21.2	5.5	2.1	100.0
2	48.8	34.2	14.9	2.1	100.0
3	35.6	42.8	18.0	3.6	100.0
4	28.7	39.2	24.2	7.9	100.0
5	28.2	35.0	27.9	8.9	100.0
6	24.2	32.1	36.5	7.0	100.0
7	20.9	27.9	38.3	12.9	100.0
8	13.6	23.6	37.9	24.9	100.0
9	7.9	21.5	39.0	31.7	100.0
10	3.9	16.9	32.4	46.9	100.0
All	23.9	28.8	29.7	17.7	100.0
			2001-2003		
Decile					
1	42.2	36.2	14.6	7.1	100.0
2	34.0	38.0	22.2	5.8	100.0
3	33.4	36.5	27.3	2.8	100.0
4	23.6	40.4	30.9	5.0	100.0
5	25.0	36.6	31.5	6.9	100.0
6	15.3	39.0	35.8	9.9	100.0
7	16.6	29.3	37.2	17.0	100.0
8	9.6	24.9	42.7	22.8	100.0
9	4.7	15.8	41.4	37.9	100.0
10	2.0	7.4	29.2	61.3	100.0
All	17.1	28.5	33.5	20.8	100.0

Source: HES 1993, 1997-99, 2001-03.

These broad conclusions are further corroborated by a more detailed table, showing the attained educational level by income deciles. As seen from this table, the overall percentage of labour-active persons who have attained the tertiary educational level increased from 17.7% in 1993 to 20.8 in 2001-2003. The increases in the shares of persons with tertiary education were particularly large in the higher income deciles: in 1993, 46.9% of labour-active persons in the tenth income decile had attained a tertiary educational level, increasing to 61.3% in 2001-2003.

The large increases in the returns to education can be explained by unleashed market forces, with the rapid social and economic transformation causing a decompression of wages and salaries, hitherto strongly regulated and compressed. Persons with higher educational attainment were now being paid more, and wages were better aligned with workers' marginal productivity. Also noteworthy is the relative deterioration of the income position of persons with vocational and secondary education, as seen from Tables 11 and 12.

248

4.1 Inequality of household income

What happened to household income inequality during the 1990s and early 2000? A very crude measure of income inequality is to compare the top quintile (the 20% of households with the highest equivalent income) with the bottom quintile (the 20% of households with the lowest equivalent income). Table 13 shows the shares of total household disposable income accruing to each income quintile, as well as the ratio of income accruing to the top and bottom quintile. According to this measure, inequality in 1997-99 decreased and then remained approximately constant.

Table 13:   Income distribution, by quintiles

Quintile	1993	1997-99	2001-03
1	8.95	9.44	9.15
2	14.28	14.56	15.33
3	18.05	19.78	19.22
4	22.46	23.48	23.98
5	36.26	32.73	32.31
All	100	100	100
5/1	4.05	3.47	3.53

Source: HES 1993, 1997-99, 2001-03.

Following this crude measure,[17] a more detailed analysis of the sources of income inequality is possible using the well-known decomposition first derived by Rao (1969). This decomposition is given by the following expression:

$$G = \sum s_k C_k$$

where G is the Gini coefficient, s_k the share of income source k in total income, and C_k the coefficient of concentration of income source k. The results of the Rao decomposition are shown in Table 14.

The Gini coefficient of income inequality attained its highest value in 1993, significantly decreasing by 1997-99, with a further decrease in 2001-03. The concentration coefficients are also quite revealing. Thus, the most important household income source – wages – is more unequally distributed than overall household income. This is due not only to the increased dispersion in the distribution of wages, but also to the fact that wage-earners are more concentrated in higher (household) income deciles. In spite of the overall decrease in household income inequality, the concentration coefficient for wages and salaries[18] increased from 0.299 in 1993 to 0.317 in 1997-99.

Income from occasional work includes two different income sources: income from contractual work and income from "property rights". Recipients of income from contractual work were (and are) mostly (a) persons with no other form of labour remuneration and (b) persons with high wages and salaries. Obviously, these two groups of labour-active persons are wide apart in terms of total income received: for the first group income from contractual work represents the only income source, whereas for the other group it represents a supplement to the already high labour incomes from regular salaried work. With regard to income from "property rights", this refers to property rights very broadly defined; recipients are mostly cultural workers, free-lancers and high-skilled professionals. It is in fact a form of contractual work subject to very favourable tax treatment. Tax privileges for

249

---

17   This is a very crude measure, as it compares the aggregate incomes of the top 20% of households with the bottom 20% of households, without taking into account different household size. Taking into account household size may result in different conclusions on income inequality; see the chapter on Hungary in this volume.

18   "Wages and salaries" also include wage-related benefits, some of which have a very egalitarian distribution among wage-earners, such as the vacation allowance. Other important wage-related benefits, such as meal and travel allowances, are somewhat less equally distributed.

income from contractual work were reduced in 1994, whereas the favourable tax treatment of income from "property rights" lasted till 2004, when
a new PIT law was passed by Parliament.[19] Both of these income sources,
which are in fact labour incomes, are still not subject to social contribution
taxation.

Table 14: Decomposition of income inequality

	1993	1997-99	2001-03
Concentration coefficients			
Wages and salaries	.2990	.3168	.3145
Income from occassional work	.4660	.3043	.2219
Income from self-employment (non agriculture)	.6399	.3374	.2509
Income from agriculture	-.0297	-.3581	-.3397
Income from capital	.7017	.5733	.5204
Pensions	.1096	.1785	.1617
Unemployment benefits	-.2062	-.1747	-.2158
Family benefits	-.3850	-.0972	-.1598
Other social benefits	-.1180	-.1702	-.1751
Interfamily transfers	.5203	-.0529	.0408
Other income	.6455	.0850	.3347
All	**.2722**	**.2485**	**.2375**
Income shares			
Wages and salaries	.6059	.6185	.6122
Income from occassional work	.0322	.0197	.0222
Income from self-employment (non agriculture)	.0653	.0486	.0524
Income from agriculture	.0295	.0154	.0109
Income from capital	.0014	.0042	.0041
Pensions	.1929	.2314	.2337
Unemployment benefits	.0145	.0140	.0090
Family benefits	.0082	.0274	.0331
Other social benefits	.0143	.0167	.0171
Interfamily transfers	.0196	.0027	.0031
Other income	.0164	.0013	.0021
All	**1.0000**	**1.0000**	**1.0000**

Note: The income shares in this table differ slightly from the income shares presented in Table 1. In Table
          1 the "point of reference" was the household whereas for Table 14 the "point of reference" is the
          household member, so that a three-member household is counted three times.
Source: HES 1993, 1997-99, 2001-2003.

19   It must, however, be stated that the favourable tax treatment of income from "property
      rights" was not completely abolished, as taxation of this income increased considerably
      only for salaried persons.

Table 14 shows a steady decrease in the concentration coefficient for income from self-employment, implying that this income is becoming less concentrated among the rich. An explanation offered is that the number of self-employed increased in the 1990s; for many it was an involuntary switch, caused by redundancies due to enterprise restructuring. The self-employed have become a very heterogeneous group; some were receiving low subsistence income, while some were operating large manufacturing or service units. One must also bear in mind that underreporting of self-employment income is present, so that caution in interpretation of these results is nevertheless warranted.

Income from agriculture is obviously more concentrated among low-income households, simply meaning that most farmers have low monetary income. The high concentration coefficient for income from capital accords to expectations: in spite of massive privatization and dividends disbursed to new small shareholders, most of this income accrues to the rich. The fairly low (but positive) concentration coefficient for pensions also means that pensioners are not "too" concentrated among the poorer households and that there is some inequality in the distribution of pensions. As the concentration coefficient for pensions is much lower than that for wages, this means that pensions are quite redistributive. Namely, in spite of the fact that most pensions are earnings-related, even these social insurance pensions have strong built-in redistributive elements, such as the setting of a minimum and maximum pension. Some pensions, such as state pensions, are means-tested, and thus represent social assistance disbursements.

The concentration coefficients for the three groups of social benefits: unemployment benefits, family benefits and other social benefits are all of the expected (negative) sign. This means that the poor receive (in absolute terms) more of this income source than the rich. The large (absolute) decrease in the concentration coefficient for family benefits, from -0.3850 in 1993 to -0.0972 in 1997-99 is caused by the strong move toward universality of child allowances in 1994, which has been explained in section 3.1.

The (implausibly) large values of the concentration coefficients for interfamily transfers and other income in 1993 and their rather large share in household income is – as we have already surmised – caused by intentional misallocation by the survey respondents (not willing to reveal their "true" income sources). In latter years, i.e. in 1997-99 and 2001-03 the concentration coefficients, as well as the much lower shares of these sources in total household income, are more plausible.

So, what is the final assessment of the income inequality trend? Our results show a decrease in inequality between 1993 and 1997-99, with a further decrease in 2001-03. However, if we would discard the two "dubious" income sources in 1993 (interfamily transfers and other income), the decrease in inequality between 1993 and 1997-99 would have been quite small.[20] Taking into account other studies,[21] which have shown that the Gini coefficient for household disposable income was about 0.23 in the mid-1980s, one can – with considerable confidence – state that the Gini coefficient for household disposable income increased (but not dramatically) in the first years of transition, i.e. in the early 1990s, followed by relatively small changes.

4.2 Wage inequality

The study of wage inequality and its causes is important, in order to ascertain to what extent trends in income inequality have been driven by trends in wage inequality. To quote Alan Blinder (1993: 308): "If you want to understand the rise in income inequality in the 1980s, the place to start is with the rise in wage inequality". Though this quote refers to the United States, it is also quite valid for other countries. Anthony Atkinson (1998: 19) commented on Blinders' remark, stating: "I agree, but one should not stop there". This point has to be stressed, as the increased inequality in the distribution of primary incomes can be countervailed by an increasing role of social transfers (including pensions) and more progressive taxation, resulting in little overall change in the distribution of disposable household income.

As seen from Table 4, wages are the major household income source, accounting for some 60% of monetary disposable household income in 2001-2003. Needless to say, the share of wages in gross household income would be much higher, as most other income sources are taxed at lower rates or not taxed at all. Taxation includes not only personal income taxation, but also the payment of social contributions. Thus, only high pensions are subject to personal income tax, whereas family benefits, unemployment benefits and other social benefits are not taxed at all. Income from capital and income

---

20   Considering the concentration coefficients and income shares of these two sources, the decrease in Gini with the elimination of these two income sources would be about 0.02, bringing the Gini for 1993 close to 0.25. This is to be compared to the value of the Gini coefficient based on the 1997-99 HES, which was 0.25 (see Table 14).

21   See for example Milanović (1998: 41) and Stanovnik and Stropnik (1998).

from occasional work is subject to personal income tax but not to payment of social contributions.

Wages are also the major type of factor income, as the sum of all other factor incomes (income from occasional work, self-employment income, income from agriculture and capital income) did not exceed 13% of household disposable income. The study of wage changes and wage inequality is therefore important per se; it is also important to establish whether the "story" of household income inequality is consistent with the "story" of wage inequality, i.e. whether the trends in household income inequality have been driven by trends in wage inequality. For the analysis of wage inequality we will use administrative data, which have a certain advantage over HES data.

A detailed analysis of the development of wage inequality is presented in Stanovnik and Verbič (2005). Their analysis was performed using two different data sources. The first was obtained from the administrative dataset of personal income tax (PIT) returns, by matching the identification of the taxpayer with data from the registry of the working population.[22] Only persons fulfilling the following criteria were considered: (1) employed full-time (meaning that information in the registry stated that they worked at least 36 hours per week) and (2) employed with the same employer throughout the year. The Statistical Office of the Republic of Slovenia (SORS) provided grouped data with 15 groups being formed. Data for each income group contained the number of wage-earners and the group sum of gross income per income source. The income sources referred to are income sources subject to tax, so that social transfers are not included. The second statistical source contains data obtained from enterprise surveys. These data are published by the SORS for March and September. The distribution of wages is provided using 20 income groups, and only employees who worked full-time in the given month (March or September), meaning from 139 to 200 hours per month are included. Employees in small firms (with one or two employees) and employees working for self-employed persons are not included in these surveys.[23] Wages include all compensation paid and borne by the employer (for example, sick leave compensation for up to 30 days), but do

---

22   This registry is with the Statistical Office of Slovenia; the Statistical Office is also responsible for its continuous updating.

23   These omissions are important, as both groups of employees have low wages, quite possibly because of underreporting, i.e. receiving part of their remuneration in cash. Employees with the self-employed represented some 9% of all employees in 2003.

not include vacation allowance and cost compensations such as travel and meal allowance.

The reason for including all incomes subject to tax in the first dataset is that for wage-earners the whole remuneration package is relevant: this includes not only wages, but also various work-related benefits, such as vacation allowance, various cost reimbursements (for travel and meals), fringe benefits (payment of rents, cars, supplemental health insurance etc). PIT data show that for wage-earners, wages represent some 91% of total (gross) taxable income, with vacation allowance trailing at second place, accounting for some 5%.[24] This allowance is important for income equalization, as all employees receive virtually the same amount of this wage-related benefit.[25] Income from contractual work accounted for some 0.7%, and income from "property rights"[26] accounted for 1% of total taxable income of wage-earners. These two types of supplemental income are strongly concentrated among high-income wage-earners.

Labeling the first dataset with "A" and the second dataset with "B", we provide some basic measures of the income distribution of wage-earners ("A") and distribution of wages ("B") in Table 15. We must reiterate that series "A" includes only those incomes of wage-earners, that are subject to tax, so – strictly speaking – it would be more appropriate to use the long-winded expression "income subject to tax (of wage-earners)", instead of "gross income (of wage-earners)". Similarly, "net" income of wage-earners is defined as income subject to tax minus social security contributions minus withheld personal income tax.

---

24   Figures refer to 2002.
25   This benefit is taxed with the PIT; however, disbursed amounts surpassing the limit set by government regulation are also taxed with social security contributions (both the employee and employer part).
26   See discussion in section 4.1.

Table 15: The distribution of gross income (of wage-earners) and distribution of wages, Slovenia, 1993-2002

	Bottom 20 per cent		Top 20 per cent		Top 10 per cent		Top 5 per cent		The Gini Coefficient	
	A	B	A	B	A	B	A	B	A	B
1993	0.0990	0.0992	0.3724	0.3677	0.2325	0.2263	0.1461	0.1374	0.2718	0.2638
1994	0.0980	0.0961	0.3776	0.3854	0.2424	0.2418	0.1577	0.1496	0.2794	0.2823
1995	0.0916	0.0973	0.3859	0.3905	0.2492	0.2491	0.1610	0.1556	0.2950	0.2859
1996	0.0921	0.0969	0.3896	0.3888	0.2538	0.2475	0.1653	0.1515	0.2988	0.2831
1997	0.0906	0.0940	0.3922	0.3943	0.2550	0.2524	0.1666	0.1577	0.3024	0.2946
1998	0.0909	0.0956	0.3954	0.3915	0.2581	0.2511	0.1686	0.1576	0.3053	0.2913
1999	0.0902	0.0923	0.4014	0.3985	0.2633	0.2568	0.1724	0.1631	0.3119	0.3009
2000	0.0911	0.0903	0.4003	0.3994	0.2606	0.2551	0.1708	0.1603	0.3109	0.3038
2001	0.0907	0.0900	0.4032	0.4009	0.2617	0.2562	0.1711	0.1613	0.3131	0.3073
2002	0.0927	0.0899	0.4006	0.3983	0.2581	0.2526	0.1681	0.1570	0.3083	0.3045

Source: A – Statistical Office of the Republic of Slovenia, data from the PIT database. Refers to distribution of gross income of wage-earners.
B – Statistical Office of the Republic of Slovenia, Rapid Reports (The distribution of wages of employees in firms and other organisations, in September).
Refers to distribution of gross wages. See section 4.2 for more details.

Figure 3: **The Gini coefficient for gross income and wages and concentration coefficient for "net" income, 1993-2002**

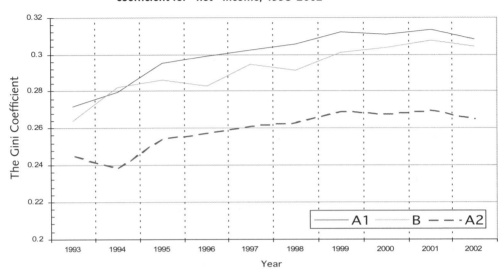

256

Source: A1 – Statistical Office of the Republic of Slovenia, data from the PIT database; gross income.
B – Statistical Office of the Republic of Slovenia, Rapid Reports (The distribution of wages of employees in firms and other organisations, in September); gross wages.
A2 – Statistical Office of the Republic of Slovenia, data from the PIT database; "net" income.

Figure 3 shows that the two datasets are broadly congruent, i.e. that the changes of income and wage inequality are similar. Quite predictably, curve A is smoother, as it refers to annual data; curve B is based on monthly (September) data. Obviously, "the big action" in terms of wage inequality occurred in the early 1990s and was completed by 1995. However, we note that even after 1995 wage inequality did not stop its upward-creeping trend.

Whereas the Gini coefficient gives an indication of the overall trend in income inequality, it is perhaps more revealing to observe what has been happening at the lower and upper ends of the income distribution. From Table 15 one observes that the income share accruing to the bottom 20% of wage-earners has considerably decreased in a short time period: from 9.9% in 1993 to 9.2% in 1995. The income share accruing to the top 20% of wage-earners increased, but this was almost completely picked up by the top 5% of wage-earners: their income share increased in the same period from 14.6% to 16.1%!

In analysing the changes in income inequality, one must consider not only the influence of market forces and their effect on the decompression of wages, but also the institutional setting and other possible relevant factors.

First, an important finding relates to the "fractal" nature of income dispersion[27] in that a similarly large increase in income dispersion from 1993 to 1995 was observed in the private as well as the public sector, though wage inequality (measured by the Gini coefficient) in the public sector was smaller.

Second, the period up to 1995 was marked by the absence of wage regulation. Only in late May 1995 did the National Assembly of the Republic of Slovenia (*Državni zbor*) pass a law with the long-winded title "On Enforcing the Agreement on Wage Policy and Other Payments to Employees and the Social Agreement for 1995, and the Minimum and Maximum Wage" (Official Gazette of the Republic of Slovenia, 29/95). This law endeavoured to stem the tide of rising inequality. Though inequality did abate in 1996, it would be difficult to "pin the credit" on the "cooling down" and subsequent incremental increases solely on this legislative act.

Third, "damage control" introduced by the legislative acts stated in the previous paragraph might have been a consequence of another piece of legislation which, in its turn, might have triggered an increase in income inequality. We refer here to the PIT act,[28] introduced in late 1993 and applied from 1 January 1994. This act caused a large increase in tax progressivity, as compared to the 1991 PIT act; it also came as a complete surprise. Due to this large increase in tax progressivity, the concentration coefficient for "net" income in 1994 was even lower than in 1993, as seen from Figure 3! We recall that this "net" income is defined as income subject to tax ("gross income") minus social security contributions minus withheld personal income tax (PIT). The decrease in the inequality of "net" income did not last long, as the backlash came in the following year. In 1995 income inequality considerably increased, and not only gross income, but "net" income as well.

So, what is the bottom line on wage inequality? Obviously, wage inequality has increased during the 1990s; however, the increases were quite modest after 1995. The personal income tax dataset shows that the Gini coefficient for gross income of wage-earners increased from 0.272 in 1993 to 0.295 in 1995 and 0.308 in 2002; the increases in the concentration coefficient for "net income"[29] were smaller, from 0.245 in 1993 to 0.255 in 1995 and 0.265

---

27 This expression was used by Krugman (1994), when describing the phenomenon of observed increased inequality even in very narrowly defined groups.

28 The first PIT legislation was passed in 1990 and applied from 1 January 1991.

29 Recalling that net income is defined here as gross income minus social security contributions minus withheld PIT.

in 2002. As already mentioned, the values of the Gini coefficient of income inequality for net income would be even smaller, because withholding PIT does not mean final PIT liability. Analyses of the annual reports by the Tax Administration show that high wage-earners have to pay additional tax, whereas low wage-earners mostly received a tax refund. To conclude, in spite of this increase in "net" income inequality of wage-earners, there is no strong evidence of increasing inequality of household disposable income, taking the early years of transition as the point for comparison.

5   Risk of poverty

In the previous section we observed that income inequality, measured at the household level, has actually decreased from its 1993 level. The trends in wage inequality are different, as wage inequality has been increasing since 1993, though increases in the inequality of net wages were fairly modest. In this section, we focus our attention on measures of the overall income position of several broad population groups, as well as measures of the income position of these population groups at the lower end of the income distribution. First, we present the average relative income position of four population groups in Table 16.

Table 16:   Relative average equivalized income of some population subgroups

Socioeconomic groups	1993	1997-99	2001-03
Unemployed	0.79	0.69	0.69
Pensioners	0.93	1.01	0.99
Labour-active	1.11	1.12	1.12
Children (<14 years)	0.99	0.93	0.99
All persons	1.00	1.00	1.00

Source: HES 1993, 1997-99, 2001-03.

Table 16 shows that the relative income position of unemployed persons deteriorated significantly in the mid- and late 1990s, as their average equiv-alized income in 2001-03 represented only some 69% of the overall average equivalized income (of all persons). The relative income position of pension-ers has improved since 1993, though the pension reform enacted in 1999 might – quite possibly – produce a gradual downslide. The relative income position of children (less than 14 years old) has slightly deteriorated between

1993 and 1997-99, followed by a rebound, so that their average equivalized income in 2001-03 was quite close to the overall average equivalized income (of all persons).

Table 16 provides a very broad measure of the income position of these population groups, which we complement with an analysis of poverty incidence, i.e. risk of income poverty. This is defined as the percentage of persons with a given characteristic (pensioners, elderly, unemployed etc) who live in households with household equivalent income below a given income threshold. Three income thresholds are used, i.e. 40, 50 and 60% of the median household equivalent income. The results for the whole population and some population subgroups are presented in Table 17.

Table 17:   Risk of income poverty (in per cent)

Poverty line as % of median equivalent household income	1993	1997-99	2001-03
All persons			
40	3.6	4.2	3.7
50	7.1	8.4	7.1
60	13.0	14.0	11.6
Pensioners			
40	3.9	3.9	4.3
50	8.4	7.2	7.6
60	15.7	12.5	12.2
Children < 14			
40	3.5	4.6	3.2
50	6.5	9.3	6.9
60	12.5	16.3	11.5
Unemployed			
40	9.1	16.0	16.3
50	17.3	27.2	25.4
60	26.6	39.2	36.8
Persons 60+			
40	6.2	5.2	5.8
50	12.2	9.8	9.8
60	21.3	16.4	15.4

Source: HES 1993, 1997-99, 2001-03.

As seen from Table 17, poverty incidence, i.e. risk of income poverty, has remained fairly stable for the whole population. If we set the poverty threshold at 60% of the median equivalent income, we observe that in 2001-03 only

11.6% of all persons lived in households whose equivalent income was be-low the poverty threshold, which represents even a slight improvement in comparison to 1993. Comparing the results for 1993 and 2001-03, we see that the risk of income poverty has decreased for pensioners and persons aged 60 and above. However, if we compare the results for 1997-99 and 2001-03, we can observe that poverty incidence for pensioners and persons aged 60 and above has increased in relative terms. The similar trend for these two groups is due to considerable overlapping between them. The risk of income poverty increased for the unemployed; this is not surprising, in view of the decrease of coverage of unemployed persons and the decrease in the value of unemployment benefit disbursed. The risk of poverty for children is about average: this is in stark contrast to other Central and Eastern European countries that were undergoing transition (Milanović, 1998). Even more recent findings for Hungary, Poland and the Czech republic have shown that the income position and poverty among children have deteriorated during the 1990s (Förster and Tóth, 2001).

Table 18: Risk of income poverty for persons aged 60 or above (in per cent)

Poverty line as % of median equivalent household income	1993	1997-99	2001-03
Married women			
40	6.2	4.1	5.6
50	13.0	8.9	9.6
60	20.8	15.4	15.0
Unmarried women			
40	6.3	6.7	6.6
50	12.0	10.9	10.1
60	23.5	18.8	17.1
Married men			
40	5.7	3.9	4.5
50	11.7	8.0	8.7
60	18.5	13.5	13.2
Unmarried men			
40	6.6	3.8	7.2
50	11.4	10.3	11.7
60	22.0	16.6	16.2

Source: HES 1993, 1997-99, 2001-03.

Table 18 shows the poverty incidence for four elderly subgroups, i.e. subgroups of persons aged 60 and above. As seen from this table, marital status is important, and the poverty incidence is typically higher for unmarried (divorced, single, widowed) women than for married women. The same also holds for the comparison between unmarried and married men. However, these differences are not large if the poverty threshold is taken to be 60% of the median household equivalent income.

Child poverty is much lower in two-parent households than in single-parent households; one must, however, note that there are relatively few children living in single-parent households, so that the high poverty incidence among these children does not translate into a high overall child poverty incidence (Table 19).

Table 19: Risk of income poverty for children (less than 14 years old), in per cent

Poverty line as % of median equivalent household income	1993	1997-99	2001-03
Children in two-parent households			
40	3.0	4.0	3.0
50	6.2	8.6	6.1
60	11.6	15.5	10.5
Children in single-parent households			
40	8.3	13.2	5.5
50	9.1	18.4	15.3
60	20.6	27.8	22.7

Source: HES 1993, 1997-99, 2001-03.

6   Concluding remarks

In comparison with other Central and Eastern European countries, the story of Slovenia appears rather dull, devoid of dramatic deteriorations of social and economic conditions and subsequent upswings. Though income inequality has increased in the beginning of the 1990s, data on income inequality since the mid-1990s do not all point in the same direction. Wage inequality increased rapidly during the early 1990s, and the increase persisted even after 1995, but was more moderate. In contrast, household income inequality shows a decrease in the late 1990s, as compared to its peak value, which was reached in 1993. It must be stated that if we were to exclude two transient income components – interfamily transfers and other income (which includes gifts, lottery gains and other windfall gains) from total household disposable income, the high value of household income inequality in 1993 would decrease and be quite close to the values attained in the late 1990s and early 2000s.

The income position of some groups has deteriorated during the 1990s and early 2000s. This is particularly true for the unemployed and those with low skills (and low attained levels of formal education). Though the role of the social protection system was very important in cushioning a large part of the population from the consequences of withdrawal from the labour market into retirement, its performance is less satisfactory for those who have temporarily withdrawn from the labour market – i.e. the unemployed. The pension reform of 1999 not only severed eligibility conditions and decreased pension rights for new entrants, but also introduced less favourable indexation for existing pensioners. It is thus not surprising that the risk-of-poverty for pensioners and the elderly has increased in relative terms (as compared to the population at large). The income position of this large population subgroup will have to be closely monitored in the future.

7 References

Atkinson, A. (1998) 'The Distribution of Income in Industrialized Countries', pp. 11-32 in: *Income Inequality: Issues and Policy Options*, A Symposium Sponsored by The Federal Reserve Bank of Kansas City Kansas City, Federal Reserve Bank of Kansas City.

Blinder, A.S. (1993) 'Comment', in: Papadimitriou, D.B. / Wolff, E.N. (eds.), *Poverty and Prosperity in the USA in the Late Twentieth Century*. Basingstoke: Macmillan.

Borak, N. / Pfajfar, L. (2002) 'Inequalities in Income Distribution in Slovenia', *Post-Communist Economies* 14 (4): 455-468.

Cazes, S. / Nesporova, A. (2003) *Labour market in transition: balancing flexibility and security in Central and Eastern Europe*. Geneva: ILO.

Förster, M. / Tóth, I.G. (2001) 'Child poverty and family transfers in the Czech Republic, Hungary and Poland', *Journal of European Social Policy* 11 (4): 324-341.

Kertesi, G. / Köllő, J. (2001) Economic transfromation and the revaluation of human capital – Hungary, 1986-1999, Working papers on the Labour Market, Institute of Economics, Hungarian Academy of Sciences, Budapest.

Krugman, P. (1994) 'Past and Prospective Causes of High Unemployment', in: *Reducing Unemployment: Current Issues and Policy Options*. Papers and proceedings from a symposium sponsored by the Federal Reserve Bank of Kansas City in Jackson Hole, Wyoming, August 25-27.

Kum, T. (2006) *Posredni davki v kmetijstvu* (Indirect Taxes in Agriculture). Ljubljana: Faculty of Economics.

Kump, N. (2002) 'Porazdelitev dohodkov in neposrednih davkov v letih 1991 in 2000 v Sloveniji' (Distributions of Income and Direct Taxes in 1991 and 2000 in Slovenia), *IB revija* 36 (2-3): 66-73.

Milanović, B. (1998) *Income, Inequality, and Poverty during the Transition from Planned to Market Economy*. Washington, D.C.: The World Bank.

Milanović, B. (1999) 'Explaining the Increase in Inequality during Transition', *Economics of Transition* 7 (2): 299-342.

Oražem, P./Vodopivec, M. (1995) 'Winners and Losers in Transition: Returns to Education, Experience and Gender in Slovenia', *World Bank Economic Review* 9 (2): 201-230.

Rao, V. M. (1969) 'Two Decompositions of Concentration Ratio', *Journal of the Royal Statistical Society* 132: 418-425.

Rutkowski, J. (1996) 'High Skills Pay Off: the Changing Wage Structure During Economic Transition in Poland', *Economics of Transition* 4 (1): 89-112.

Stanovnik, T. (1997) 'The Returns to Education in Slovenia', *Economics of Education Review* 16 (4): 443-449.

Stanovnik, T./Stropnik, N. (1998) 'Vpliv socialnih transferjev na revščino in dohodkovno neenakost v Sloveniji: Primerjava let 1983 in 1993' (Impacts of Social Transfers on Poverty and Income Inequality in Slovenia: Comparison of Years 1983 and 1993), *IB revija* 32 (8-9-10): 69 82.

Stanovnik, T. (1999) 'Analiza virov dohodnine v Sloveniji v letih 1991 in 1996' (Analysis of Personal Income Tax Sources in Slovenia in 1991 and 1996), *IB revija* 33 (4): 22-30.

Stanovnik, T./Kump, N./Čok, M. (2006) 'The gender dimensions of social security reform in Slovenia', in: Fultz, E. (ed.) *The gender dimensions of social security reform*. Volume 2, Case studies of Romania and Slovenia. Budapest: ILO.

Stanovnik, T./Verbič, M. (2005) 'Wage and Income Inequality in Slovenia', *Post Communist Economies* 17 (3): 381-397.

Stropnik, N./Stanovnik, T. (2002) *Combating Poverty and Social Exclusion: A Case Study of Slovenia*. Budapest: International Labour Organization.

Vales, J. (2006) 'Analiza dohodnine v Sloveniji v letih 1995 in 2000' (Analysis of the Personal Income Tax in Slovenia in 1995 and 2000), undergraduate thesis, Faculty of Economics, Ljubljana.

Vecernik, J. (2001) 'Earnings Disparities in the Czech Republic: Evidence of the Past Decade and Cross-National Comparison', WP no.373, The William Davidson Institute, University of Michigan, Ann Arbor.

Vezjak, K./Stanovnik, T. (2004) 'The Collection of Pension Contributions in Slovenia', in: Fultz, E./Stanovnik, T. (eds.), *Collection of Pension Contributions: Trends, Issues, and Problems in Central and Eastern Europe*. Budapest: ILO.

Annex

Table SI1: The structure of household income sources, by income deciles (horizontal structure)

Deciles	1	2	3	4	5	6	7	8	9	10	Total
						1993					
Wages & salaries	33.5	46.6	53.5	60.3	64.2	62.0	60.4	65.6	62.2	58.2	59.2
Income from occasional work	2.3	1.6	1.7	1.8	2.7	2.7	2.7	2.5	4.3	5.0	3.2
Self-employment income	.9	2.4	1.4	2.9	2.1	2.3	4.6	5.2	8.6	14.3	6.3
Income from agriculture	7.3	6.6	3.7	5.1	3.6	2.7	2.0	1.2	2.4	1.5	2.8
Income from capital	.2	.0	.0	.0	.0	.0	.0	.0	.0	.5	.1
Pensions	37.6	30.7	31.1	22.8	21.2	24.8	24.7	20.8	17.5	11.5	21.1
Unemployment benefits	4.8	4.7	2.5	2.3	2.2	1.8	.7	.5	.9	.1	1.4
Family benefits	4.9	2.7	1.7	1.2	.7	.5	.6	.0	.1	.0	.7
Other social benefits	6.4	3.2	2.2	1.9	1.8	1.0	1.9	.8	.7	.5	1.4
Interfamily transfers	1.4	.8	1.0	1.4	1.0	1.3	1.6	1.8	1.5	4.2	2.0
Other income	.7	.5	1.1	.3	.6	.9	.7	1.5	1.7	4.1	1.7
All	100.0	100.0	100.0	100.0	100.0	100.0	100.0	100.0	100.0	100.0	100.0
						1997-1999					
Wages & salaries	31.8	41.4	49.5	57.1	60.0	59.6	63.0	68.6	66.1	66.3	60.4
Income from occasional work	2.6	2.3	1.7	2.0	1.6	1.5	1.6	1.4	1.8	3.1	2.0
Self-employment income	2.7	4.9	4.6	3.9	4.3	3.6	4.1	5.1	3.7	7.5	4.8
Income from agriculture	8.1	5.2	2.4	2.1	2.3	1.9	.6	.4	.4	.1	1.5
Income from capital	.0	.1	.2	.2	.2	.2	.4	.4	.4	1.0	.4
Pensions	32.1	31.8	32.5	26.1	24.8	27.2	24.6	21.1	24.7	20.1	24.9
Unemployment benefits	6.1	3.6	2.0	1.8	1.8	1.4	1.5	.9	.6	.3	1.4
Family benefits	8.1	5.7	3.6	3.9	2.9	2.5	2.8	1.3	1.2	.9	2.5
Other social benefits	7.0	4.3	3.1	2.4	1.6	1.4	1.3	.7	.8	.7	1.7
Interfamily transfers	1.3	.4	.2	.3	.3	.4	.0	.1	.5	.0	.3
Other income	.1	.3	.2	.3	.1	.2	.0	.0	.1	.1	.1
All	100.0	100.0	100.0	100.0	100.0	100.0	100.0	100.0	100.0	100.0	100.0
						2001-2003					
Wages & salaries	25.6	41.5	51.1	54.8	55.9	58.8	66.4	64.0	67.4	67.2	59.8
Income from occasional work	3.5	3.2	2.7	2.2	1.5	1.9	1.5	2.0	1.7	3.1	2.2
Self-employment income	3.2	7.4	4.0	4.8	5.2	4.2	4.7	5.0	5.5	5.8	5.1
Income from agriculture	6.3	3.0	2.2	1.5	1.0	1.0	.8	.5	.4	.0	1.1
Income from capital	.3	.2	.3	.2	.1	.2	.3	.3	.4	1.1	.4
Pensions	35.7	31.1	29.2	27.8	28.5	28.1	22.0	24.5	22.3	20.3	25.2
Unemployment benefits	4.9	2.2	1.5	1.2	1.2	.7	.6	.6	.5	.2	.9
Family benefits	10.5	6.8	5.5	5.2	4.0	3.0	2.2	1.7	.8	1.1	3.0
Other social benefits	9.0	3.9	3.0	1.9	1.8	1.4	1.0	1.0	.9	.8	1.7
Interfamily transfers	.5	.6	.3	.3	.4	.4	.4	.2	.3	.0	.3
Other income	.5	.1	.1	.2	.3	.1	.2	.2	.3	.3	.2
All	100.0	100.0	100.0	100.0	100.0	100.0	100.0	100.0	100.0	100.0	100.0

Source: HES 1993, 1997-99, 2001-2003.

Table SI2: The distribution of household income sources across income deciles (vertical distribution)

Deciles	1	2	3	4	5	6	7	8	9	10	Total
1993											
Wages & salaries	1.9	4.4	5.9	7.9	9.5	9.7	10.6	13.4	15.7	21.0	100.0
Income from occasional work	2.5	2.8	3.4	4.5	7.4	7.7	8.9	9.3	20.1	33.5	100.0
Self-employment income	.5	2.1	1.4	3.6	2.9	3.4	7.5	10.0	20.2	48.4	100.0
Income from agriculture	8.8	12.8	8.5	13.9	11.0	8.8	7.3	5.2	12.5	11.1	100.0
Income from capital	5.7	.6	3.7	2.3	.0	2.5	2.2	2.3	3.2	77.5	100.0
Pensions	6.1	8.1	9.6	8.4	8.8	10.9	12.2	11.9	12.4	11.7	100.0
Unemployment benefits	11.4	18.3	11.2	12.7	13.8	11.8	5.4	3.9	9.4	2.1	100.0
Family benefits	22.6	20.4	15.0	12.6	7.9	6.1	8.3	1.6	2.8	2.8	100.0
Other social benefits	15.2	12.2	10.0	9.9	11.2	6.2	13.6	6.6	7.6	7.6	100.0
Interfamily transfers	2.5	2.3	3.3	5.5	4.4	6.1	8.3	10.9	11.7	45.0	100.0
Other income	1.4	1.8	4.5	1.2	3.2	5.1	4.5	10.9	14.8	52.5	100.0
Total income	3.4	5.5	6.5	7.8	8.8	9.2	10.4	12.1	14.9	21.4	100.0
1997-1999											
Wages & salaries	1.9	4.0	5.4	7.5	9.7	10.0	11.9	13.8	14.7	21.2	100.0
Income from occasional work	4.8	6.8	5.5	7.9	7.6	7.8	9.0	8.5	12.0	30.1	100.0
Self-employment income	2.0	6.0	6.3	6.5	8.7	7.5	9.7	12.8	10.4	30.0	100.0
Income from agriculture	19.7	20.3	10.6	11.0	14.9	12.9	4.5	3.2	1.3	1.5	100.0
Income from capital	.7	1.5	3.6	3.5	5.6	5.0	10.0	10.6	13.5	46.0	100.0
Pensions	4.7	7.4	8.6	8.4	9.7	11.0	11.2	10.3	13.3	15.5	100.0
Unemployment benefits	15.4	14.8	9.3	10.1	12.1	10.1	12.1	7.4	5.3	3.6	100.0
Family benefits	11.7	13.1	9.4	12.6	11.3	9.9	12.9	6.1	6.2	6.9	100.0
Other social benefits	15.2	15.0	12.3	11.2	9.5	8.4	9.0	5.2	6.4	7.8	100.0
Interfamily transfers	17.4	7.5	5.7	8.8	12.3	16.4	2.3	6.4	22.3	.8	100.0
Other income	3.7	10.7	8.8	16.1	8.3	16.3	3.9	4.0	13.7	14.6	100.0
Total income	3.6	5.8	6.6	8.0	9.7	10.1	11.4	12.1	13.4	19.3	100.0
2001-2003											
Wages & salaries	1.5	4.0	6.0	7.6	8.7	9.8	12.5	13.6	16.0	20.4	100.0
Income from occasional work	5.3	8.2	8.6	8.0	6.2	8.7	7.5	11.4	10.6	25.4	100.0
Self-employment income	2.2	8.3	5.5	7.8	9.5	8.2	10.4	12.4	15.3	20.5	100.0
Income from agriculture	20.4	16.2	14.9	11.7	9.2	9.8	8.4	6.6	1.4	1.4	100.0
Income from capital	2.1	3.4	5.0	4.2	3.0	4.9	8.2	9.4	12.2	47.6	100.0
Pensions	4.8	7.1	8.1	9.1	10.5	11.1	9.8	12.4	12.5	14.6	100.0
Unemployment benefits	18.3	14.0	11.5	10.9	11.7	7.4	6.8	8.0	7.5	3.7	100.0
Family benefits	11.9	13.0	12.9	14.3	12.2	9.9	8.3	7.1	3.8	6.6	100.0
Other social benefits	18.0	13.2	12.5	9.3	9.6	8.4	6.3	7.4	7.1	8.1	100.0
Interfamily transfers	5.2	10.5	7.0	9.2	13.4	14.2	15.5	9.4	12.4	3.3	100.0
Other income	7.5	2.8	3.6	6.3	11.0	4.8	7.9	10.5	19.7	25.8	100.0
Total income	3.4	5.7	7.0	8.3	9.3	10.0	11.2	12.7	14.2	18.1	100.0

Source: HES 1993, 1997-99, 2001-2003.

Table SI3: The structure of household members, by socioeconomic status and income deciles (horizontal structure)

Deciles	1	2	3	4	5	6	7	8	9	10	Total
						1993					
Employees	14.0	23.6	30.0	34.7	37.5	39.9	38.0	44.8	42.6	46.9	35.2
Active in agriculture	8.6	4.4	2.3	2.8	2.3	1.8	.9	.6	1.1	1.0	2.5
Other self employed	.6	.9	.5	1.3	.8	1.4	2.1	3.0	5.4	7.2	2.3
Persons with occasional income	1.8	.5	.9	.8	.7	.5	.9	.3	.7	1.2	.8
Unemployed	11.5	8.3	6.3	4.7	5.7	4.6	3.7	2.3	3.0	1.8	5.2
Pensioners	26.2	24.5	26.0	19.7	19.7	23.9	24.3	21.8	18.3	15.2	21.9
Dependants	34.9	35.9	33.9	35.3	32.4	27.5	29.4	27.0	27.9	26.3	31.1
Other	2.5	1.9	.2	.7	.8	.5	.7	.3	1.1	.3	.9
All	100.0	100.0	100.0	100.0	100.0	100.0	100.0	100.0	100.0	100.0	100.0
						1997-1999					
Employees	12.5	19.9	27.3	33.8	35.2	38.2	41.5	45.5	47.3	50.4	34.9
Active in agriculture	3.9	2.6	1.3	.9	1.2	1.0	.2	.0	.0	.0	1.1
Other self employed	1.4	3.2	2.9	2.7	3.5	2.6	3.1	4.3	3.4	5.5	3.2
Persons with occasional income	.2	.1	.3	.2	.3	.4	.3	.1	.0	.3	.2
Unemployed	21.1	13.8	8.2	6.1	6.2	4.0	3.9	3.3	2.0	1.2	7.1
Pensioners	21.0	22.6	24.4	21.9	21.7	24.8	22.3	20.6	24.2	22.9	22.6
Dependants	37.5	37.4	35.2	33.8	31.8	28.7	28.5	26.0	22.7	19.5	30.3
Other	2.3	.4	.4	.6	.2	.3	.3	.0	.3	.1	.5
All	100.0	100.0	100.0	100.0	100.0	100.0	100.0	100.0	100.0	100.0	100.0
						2001-2003					
Employees	10.2	20.4	28.3	32.7	35.2	39.3	44.2	46.9	49.8	52.3	36.0
Active in agriculture	3.7	2.2	1.2	1.1	.7	.6	.7	.4	.0	.0	1.0
Other self employed	1.5	3.9	2.6	3.2	3.5	2.9	3.4	4.0	4.5	4.6	3.4
Persons with occasional income	.7	.7	.5	.4	.3	.4	.2	.2	.4	.2	.4
Unemployed	20.3	10.3	7.8	5.5	4.2	3.0	3.6	2.4	1.5	1.4	5.9
Pensioners	24.0	23.5	24.0	23.8	24.5	26.1	20.6	24.0	23.1	21.9	23.6
Dependants	38.6	38.2	34.9	33.0	31.2	27.4	27.2	22.0	20.6	19.4	29.3
Other	1.2	.8	.7	.4	.4	.4	.0	.0	.2	.2	.4
All	100.0	100.0	100.0	100.0	100.0	100.0	100.0	100.0	100.0	100.0	100.0

Source: HES 1993, 1997-99, 2001-2003.

Table SI4: The distribution of household members (by socioeconomic status) across income deciles (vertical distribution)

Deciles	1	2	3	4	5	6	7	8	9	10	Total
1993											
Employees	3.7	6.8	8.5	10.4	11.4	11.1	10.7	12.8	12.5	12.2	100.0
Active in agriculture	31.5	17.7	8.9	11.6	9.7	6.8	3.4	2.2	4.5	3.6	100.0
Other self employed	2.3	3.9	2.3	5.9	3.9	6.2	9.1	13.3	24.2	28.9	100.0
Persons with occasional income	20.8	6.0	10.5	10.6	9.0	5.9	11.3	3.5	8.4	14.0	100.0
Unemployed	20.7	16.2	12.1	9.6	11.8	8.7	7.1	4.5	5.9	3.2	100.0
Pensioners	11.2	11.3	11.8	9.5	9.6	10.7	10.9	10.0	8.6	6.4	100.0
Dependants	10.5	11.7	10.9	12.0	11.1	8.7	9.4	8.7	9.3	7.8	100.0
Other	25.9	21.9	1.8	8.7	9.5	5.9	7.6	3.1	12.4	3.3	100.0
1997-1999											
Employees	3.6	5.9	7.4	9.9	11.4	11.2	12.3	12.8	12.5	13.0	100.0
Active in agriculture	33.5	23.0	10.7	8.4	12.2	9.4	1.7	.7	.5	.0	100.0
Other self employed	4.4	10.2	8.6	8.5	12.1	8.2	10.0	13.0	9.6	15.3	100.0
Persons with occasional income	9.3	6.7	14.5	7.3	12.4	16.4	11.9	4.8	3.1	13.7	100.0
Unemployed	29.9	20.0	10.9	9.0	9.9	5.8	5.8	4.5	2.6	1.6	100.0
Pensioners	9.3	10.3	10.2	10.0	10.8	11.3	10.2	8.9	9.9	9.1	100.0
Dependants	12.4	12.7	11.0	11.5	11.8	9.7	9.8	8.4	6.9	5.8	100.0
Other	47.0	7.5	8.5	13.4	3.5	5.4	5.8	1.3	5.2	2.4	100.0
2001-2003											
Employees	2.6	5.6	8.0	9.7	10.6	11.2	12.7	13.5	13.4	12.7	100.0
Active in agriculture	32.5	20.9	11.6	11.1	7.5	5.7	7.2	3.6	.0	.0	100.0
Other self employed	3.9	11.4	7.8	9.9	11.0	8.7	10.4	12.3	12.8	11.9	100.0
Persons with occasional income	16.0	18.3	14.0	10.2	8.6	9.6	5.5	4.7	8.7	4.3	100.0
Unemployed	31.2	17.1	13.4	10.1	7.8	5.2	6.4	4.2	2.5	2.0	100.0
Pensioners	9.2	9.8	10.4	10.8	11.2	11.3	9.1	10.6	9.5	8.1	100.0
Dependants	11.9	12.8	12.1	12.1	11.5	9.6	9.6	7.8	6.8	5.8	100.0
Other	25.7	17.6	17.7	10.3	9.7	9.0	1.8	1.3	3.7	3.3	100.0

Source: HES 1993, 1997-99, 2001-2003.

Technical Annex

Here, we will briefly describe the main methodological issues and the country sample features.

A1 Equivalence scale

For the purpose of our analysis, we use the OECD equivalence scale, which assigns the value of 1 to the first household member, 0.7 to each additional adult and 0.5 to each child (less than age 14). This scale is sometimes also called the "old" OECD scale, as the more recent OECD scale – "the OECD-modified scale" assigns the values of 1 to the first household member, 0.5 to each additional adult and 0.3 to each child (less than age 14). Equivalized household size ("number of equivalent adults") is obtained by summing the values ("weights") of all household members.

A2 Household income

The analyses in all the country studies are based on the concept of household net income, i.e. income net of social contributions and withholding personal income tax. In the Bulgarian and Slovenian surveys all incomes are recorded "net", whereas in the Hungarian and Romanian surveys incomes are recorded "gross", and "net" income is computed, applying the rules for levying social contributions and withholding personal income tax. In Bulgaria, Hungary and Romania the income concept also includes some types of income in kind, though none of the country studies include imputed rent. Country-specifics are discussed in section A6.

As all analyses are based on household net income, the term "net", or the term "disposable" are frequently omitted. Household equivalent income is obtained by dividing household net income by equivalized household size. This value is also frequently referred to as "equivalized net income".

A3 Analysis based on deciles

The decile analysis was used in describing the socioeconomic structure of households, the structure of household income, the distribution of household members (according to socioeconomic status) and the distribution of household income sources. Deciles[1] were formed taking the household as a unit. Thus, the first (i.e. "bottom") decile contains the 10% of households with the lowest household equivalent income, whereas the tenth (i.e. "top") decile contains the 10% of households with the highest household equivalent income. Therefore, these deciles have equal numbers of households, but unequal numbers of household members; typically, households situated in the lower deciles have more household members than households situated in the higher deciles.

A4 Income inequality

Income inequality is analysed using the quintile share ratio, i.e the ratio of household net income accruing to the top 20% of households to household net income accruing to the bottom 20% of households. Households are ranked according to their equivalent income. Eurostat uses the quintile share ratio as one of the primary "Laeken" indicators, where the quintile share ratios are computed as the ratio of the equivalized net income accruing to the top 20% of persons to the equivalized net income accruing to the bottom 20% of persons.[2] This is also the approach adopted by the Hungarian study, where both quintile share ratios were computed, i.e. one based on households and the other on persons: it was shown that structural changes can cause divergence in income inequality trends using the quintile share ratio, but basing this ratio on (a) households (i.e top 20% households/bottom 20% households) and (b) persons (i.e. top 20% persons/bottom 20% persons).

The Gini coefficient of income inequality is computed using household equivalent income, but basing the computation on persons, so that each household member is taken with his equivalized net income. This is the case for Hungary, Slovenia and Romania; for Bulgaria (and also for Romania), the computed Gini coefficient is based on the household as a unit, i.e. each household (regardless of size) is counted once.

---

1   Throughout the book, we use the term "decile" as a shorthand term for "decile group". There is no "point-usage" of deciles in the book. The same applies to quintiles, which are used as shorthand for "quintile groups".

2   See for example Eurostat (2002).

A5 Decomposition of income inequality

For the purpose of our analysis, we use the following decomposition of the Gini coefficient:

$$G = \sum_{k} \frac{\mu_k}{\mu} C_k \qquad (1)$$

where

μ_k = average income of income source k
μ = average total income
C_k = concentration coefficient[3] of income source k
G = Gini coefficient of total income

This decomposition was first derived by Rao (1969). It is tempting to compute contributions to overall inequality based on the above formula. For example, one could compute

$$\frac{(\mu_k / \mu) \cdot C_k \cdot 100}{G} \qquad (2)$$

and declare this as the percentage contribution of income source k to overall inequality. However, as pointed out by Podder (1993), this procedure does not have any intuitively clear interpretation. For example, a clear interpretation of the contribution of income source k to overall income inequality would be

1. The reduction in inequality if this income source was eliminated.
2. The reduction in inequality if differences in income source k were eliminated, i.e. if all persons (or all households) had the same amount of income source k, namely μ_k.
3. The percentage of inequality that would be observed if this was the only source of income differences and all other income sources were allocated evenly (i.e. all households would have the same – average – amount of income sources, except for income source k).

Expression (2) does not fit into these three – or any other – sensible interpretations. A meaningful interpretation, but not in the sense of "contributions"

---

3   The concentration coefficient is frequently referred to as concentration ratio or pseudo-Gini.

to overall income inequality, can be obtained by differentiating relation (1), to obtain:

$$\mu_k \frac{dG}{d\mu_k} = \frac{\mu_k}{\mu}(C_k - G) \tag{3}$$

and further:

$$\eta_k = \frac{\mu_k}{G}\frac{dG}{d\mu_k} = \frac{1}{G}\left[\frac{\mu_k}{\mu}(C_k - G)\right] \tag{4}$$

showing the percentage change in the Gini coefficient due to a proportionate change in the mean value of income source k. Expression (4) has a plausible interpretation. For a concentration coefficient of income source k that is lower than the Gini coefficient, one can say that a proportionate increase in the value of μ_k will decrease the value of the Gini coefficient. The lower the concentration coefficient and the higher the share of income source k in total income (i.e. the higher the ratio μ_k/μ), the greater will be the proportionate decrease in the Gini coefficient. Conversely, for a concentration coefficient of income source k that is higher than the Gini coefficient, one can say that a proportionate increase in the value of μ_k will increase the value of the Gini coefficient. The higher the concentration coefficient and the higher the share of income source k in total income (i.e. the higher the ratio μ_k/μ), the greater will be the proportionate increase in the Gini coefficient.

In the country chapters, the interpretation of the income decomposition results was in the sense of equation (3), and elasticities from equation (4) were not computed. Secondary income sources, meaning transfer payments (public or private) were labeled income equalizers if the respective concentration coefficient was less than the overall Gini coefficient of income inequality. Two types of income equalizers were defined: (a) relative income equalizers, with positive values of the concentration coefficient, but lower than the Gini coefficient, and (b) absolute income equalizers, with negative values of the concentration coefficient.

It is worth noting that a decomposition of the Gini coefficient, which presents an extension of decomposition (1) was derived by Lerman and Yitzaki (1983):

$$G = \sum_k R_k G_k S_k \tag{4}$$

where R_k is the "Gini correlation" between income source k and total income, and is equal to the ratio between the concentration coefficient of income source k and the Gini coefficient of income source k. G_k is the Gini coefficient of income source k, and S_k is the share of income source k in total income (i.e. μ_k/μ). We have not pursued this "continuation" of the Rao decomposition. We also strongly subscribe to Shorrocks' view,[4] that the calculation of "contributions" of income sources to overall income inequality is not determinate.

A6 Description of the country samples

Bulgaria

The empirical assessment of the dynamics of income inequality and poverty in Bulgaria is based on data from the Household Budget Survey (HBS) conducted regularly by the Bulgarian National Statistical Institute. The HBS contains data on the structure of income, expenditure and consumption of households as well as other aspects of the standard of living of the population. Analysing the household budgets over time allows tracing the changes in the population's income and expenditure patterns. It should be noted, however, that the methodology of the Bulgarian HBS was changed in 1992, so that data after 1992 are not fully comparable with data before 1992. Therefore, our analysis starts in 1992 (it does not include information about the pre-transition years) and is based on three data points: 1992, 1997 and 2002.

The general population from which the sample is selected comprises all households in the country. A two-stage random sampling on a territorial principle is implemented to select the sample as follows: at the first stage the census enumeration areas (clusters) are selected; at the second stage the households to be surveyed are identified. The selection of territorial units is performed on the basis of a probability distribution, with probabilities proportional to the size of units.

At the selected enumeration areas (clusters), the full lists of households are arranged in ascending order, depending on the number of household members (this indicator is closely correlated with the surveyed indicators – income, expenditures, and consumption per capita). Afterwards six house-

---

4   See Shorrocks (1988).

holds from these lists are chosen from each cluster with a selection step. No weighting procedure is performed.

In 1992, the size of the annual HBS sample was 2,508 households. The sample size in 1997 varies: it was 6,000 households until July and 3,000 for the rest of the year. In 2002 the sample covered 4,200 households until July and 3,000 for the rest of the year. Due to consistency considerations, only households that were present in the sample during the whole year were used in our analysis . For 1992 we drew 12 monthly observations for the selected annual sub-sample and for 1997 and 2002, 11 monthly observations.[5]

The HBS questionnaire seeks information on: household composition and socio-demographic characteristics of its members; number of days at work and absence from work due to illness for all employed persons in the household; amounts of monetary and in-kind income by sources; amounts of monetary and in-kind expenditures by type of expenditure; amounts of purchased food products and of some other goods; consumer goods produced and consumed by the household; number of domestic animals and production/consumption related to that.

The HBS concept of income includes seven major sources – wage income and other remuneration from employment, property income, social security reimbursements, welfare benefits, income from sales, other sources of income, loans, credits and savings withdrawals. Income is net of social security contributions and withheld personal income tax. The annual estimates are derived as weighted averages of the monthly figures. The income unit is the household, which includes one-person households, one-family households, and households comprising more than one family who make common provisions for food and other essentials for living.

It should be noted that some of the survey income sources, such as income from sales of property, borrowing and saving withdrawals, do not constitute current income. The inclusion of these sources potentially distorts the income distribution in Bulgaria, as they are typically concentrated in the wealthiest households.

The evaluation of in-kind income is based on retail prices; in-kind income includes the value of food and non-food products obtained from household plots, agricultural enterprises, friends and relatives as well as the increased value of livestock. In-kind income does not include imputed rent. The share of in-kind income in total household agricultural income was 86% in 1992, 83% in 1997 and 89% in 2002.

---

5   Since 1997 the substitution of the households in the sample has been made not at the beginning of the year but in February.

The survey method is based on self-recording by a member of the sampled household, combined with an interview. Households record daily information on: all monetary expenses for food and other products, services and other expenditure; all money income from wages and salaries, social insurance, sale of products from household plot and other sources; in-kind income and consumption of food and non-food products; data on the members of the household and changes in the household or its members. Persons who have left the household to form a new household or to join an institution are not considered members of the initial household. Persons in institutions are not included in the household budget survey.

The selected households are surveyed on the basis of household diaries for a period of one year to eliminate problems associated with seasonal factors. Interviewers pay visits to surveyed households at least twice a month. They execute a detailed interview with members of the household and check the completeness and consistency of the records in the diary.

Hungary

The Hungarian Household Budget Survey (HBS) has been conducted annually by the Hungarian Central Statistical Office since 1993. The survey covers the Hungarian population living in private households, i.e. the population living permanently in institutions is not included. The unit of sampling is the dwelling, the unit of observation is the household. The source of the sampling is the updated census data.

Primary sampling units were selected from the census units (containing about 100 dwellings on average) by a stratified one- or two-stage sampling.[6] For all settlements with 15,000 or more inhabitants, a one-stage primary sampling unit selection was carried out. The smaller settlements were stratified by their size and their county (6 size groups, 19 counties). In the case of settlements with more than 2,000 and less than 15,000 inhabitants in the first stage the settlements and in the second stage the primary sampling units were selected. All census units of the selected settlements with less than 2,000 inhabitants are part of the sample. Four different sampling fractions were applied by size of settlements: in settlements with less than 10,000 inhabitants the sampling fraction was 1%, with 10,000–50,000 inhabitants 0,8%, with more than 50,000 inhabitants 0,6% and in Budapest 0,5%.

In 1993 usually three, later (in 1997 and 2002) six households were selected from every primary sampling unit, decreasing also the number of

---

6   This paragraph is based on the Methodological Remarks of the Yearbook of Household Statistics 1993, 1997 and 2002, published by the Hungarian Central Statistical Office.

the settlements in the sample and the number of primary sampling units. A third part of the sample is rotated each year. The response rate in 1993 was 61%, in 1997 58% and in 2002 57%. The three surveys contain 7,432, 7,066 and 9,297 households, respectively.

The survey is based partly on monthly household records and partly on *post facto* annual interviews. The income data applied in this study stem from the annual interviews. Before 1993 all of the income and the large majority of the expenditure data were based only on two-months household diaries. Inequality measures based on annual income are necessarily lower than those based on monthly income. This distortion is further increased by the different income structure of different months (relatively high year-end incomes, large costs – consequently large negative income – during some months in agricultural activities, large agricultural income in other months, etc.). Another methodological problem was that the stratified samples of the 1980s did not contain all of the social strata (e.g. self-employed). To summarize, the HBS data before and after the transition are not really comparable, justifying the selection of 1993 as the first investigated year.

Because of differences in non-response rates inhabitants of Budapest and larger cities, young adults, higher education graduates, active earners and especially entrepreneurs are underrepresented in the HBS sample. Weighting – using the generalised iterative scaling method – was applied to restore representativity. No weighting will ever solve an important sampling problem of the HBS after the transition, namely that the poorest (homeless, functionally illiterate persons) and the most affluent household are missing, as in many household surveys.

We use the concept of *net* incomes of households throughout the study. The usual kinds of own consumption of self-produced food and beverages, net farm revenue, housing subsidies granted after the birth of children (included into family benefits), cash revenue derived from sales of movable or immovable property and sales of restitution vouchers are all included in income. Although these latter two are not current incomes, we included them into the capital income category, because they usually are the declared substitutes of other, concealed capital incomes. Incomes from capital are still underrated.

Direct taxes and social security contributions are not included. The original HBS data sets contain only the gross value of the different kinds of income and the total amount of taxes and social contributions. Generation of the net income by income sources was performed, applying the rules for withholding tax.

Reported household earnings and informal/hidden income are not checked against tax office or enterprise records. These kinds of income are frequently concealed, consequently we have to be very careful interpreting our results; inequality measures can be underestimated.

Romania

The information on incomes is derived from two comparable, nationally representative surveys: (i) the Romanian Family Budget Survey (ABF, after its Romanian acronym) for the period 2001-2004; and (ii) the Integrated Household Survey (AIG) for 1995-2000.

Both surveys aim for an annual sample of 36,000 households, in fact 12 repeated cross-sections of 3,000 households interviewed for one month during the year. Each month, responses are gathered from 2,600-2,800 households out of 3,000 selected households.

Both surveys use a two-stage sampling scheme. The differences between surveys consist in the number of strata and primary sampling units (PSU) used: in AIG only 2 strata were used (rural/ urban) and around 500 PSUs, while in ABF there are 16 strata (rural/ urban and 8 development regions) and more than 700 PSUs. The PSUs consist of Census sectors. Different weights are assigned to households (because of the differing probability of inclusion in the sample). These weights are actually obtained by multiplication of several different weights.

Surveying[7] is based on the face-to-face interview method. During the reference month the incomes, consumption, and expenditures are recorded in a diary, which is left with the interviewed household at the beginning of the month. The interviewers visit the selected households several times during the month to offer guidance and support to the household members for filling in the diary.

The recall period for consumption, expenses, and incomes is one month. Because the survey is implemented in 12 monthly waves (sub-samples), a one-month recall period provides accurate estimates for the average monthly income/ consumption/ expenditure over the year, but could affect distributional analyses, especially in the case of seasonal incomes. To control for the effects of inflation within the year, all incomes were deflated (see below).

---

7   The information applies to both surveys – ABF and AIG

Incomes are recorded separately for each household member only in the diary. In the questionnaire the incomes are aggregated and recorded at household level, excepting social benefits which are recorded for each individual.

Own consumption refers to consumption of food produced by the household. It does not include imputed rents; about 95% of households own their dwelling and there is virtually no house renting in rural areas. Also, ABF (AIG) does not record the self-consumption of non-food and services. The food consumption module collects information about the consumption of 104 (83) commodities, using a balance approach. The household reports the initial stock of that commodity, the inflows and outflows during the month, and the final stock. The inflows are split between (the value and quantity of) goods bought (Bo), quantities produced on-farm, derived from processing, received in gift or in exchange with other commodities. Outflows consist of the value and quantity of goods sold, processed, given as gifts, used as farm inputs, exchanged and goods consumed (Cs) by members of the household. Own consumption is computed as $Sc = \max(0, Cs - Bo)$, and the amount of food purchased for the household members as $Pc = Cs - Sc$. Own-consumption is included in the category "agricultural income".

The share of own-consumption in total household agricultural income was 78% in 1995, 82% in 1997, 83% in 2001 and 80% in 2004.

To ensure comparability across time during high-inflation periods, each component of current income is inflated with the total CPI; self-consumption is inflated with food CPI, in December 2002 constant prices. For the self-consumption computation, to account for the significant differences in the cost of living across areas of residence, rural consumption is further inflated in urban prices, using a Laspeyres rural-urban price index constructed from the unit-value information collected in the survey. To ensure comparability between the monthly waves of the survey, seasonality in consumption was smoothed using seasonality indices constructed for each month, quintile and area of residence (as the ratio of the predicted value of consumption for that month, quintile and area to the national average).

The income concept used in this study is *household net income*. The income indicator includes own-consumption (computed as presented above), which is considered as being agricultural income. Besides own-consumption, the agricultural income includes cash incomes from sales of food and livestock. In addition, the income indicator includes: a) wages and incomes assimilated with wages, including social security benefits for temporary disability, maternity and child leave, b) income from (non-agricultural) self-employment, c) pensions, d) other social protection cash benefits (including unemployment, family allowances, social welfare benefit), e) income from capital, and f) interfamily transfers (including remittances from abroad). Income is recorded "net", i.e. without social contributions and withheld income tax; this deviates from the net income that is established on the basis of the annual income tax return.[8] Savings and loans are not included.

The bias inherent in surveys is worth mentioning, so that caution in interpreting the results is warranted. It is well-known that in countries in which the informal (and illegal) sector is well developed, which is the case of Romania,[9] the omission or inadequate coverage of informal incomes results in underestimation of total household incomes, wherefrom poverty rates are biased upwards. Income inequality is probably also underestimated by not covering those with high incomes who refuse to participate in the survey, which implies that the relative poverty might also be biased downwards.

Underreporting of income is another bias inherent in surveys. The use of income rather than expenditure data yields underestimates of "true" welfare, because people tend to underreport their sources of income (Milanovic, 1998). In our study annual income estimates were derived from information over 12 months.

Seasonality of income is another source of bias, particularly for short recall period surveys. Non-seasonal, regular incomes, such as pensions or wages, are more accurately measured than the volatile incomes, such as income from farming, self-employment, seasonal work, and casual work. For instance, similarly endowed farmer households might appear rich if surveyed after the harvest, and poor if surveyed before. Consequently, if volatile incomes make up an important part of the household budget (as in Romania), a robust household income indicator is difficult to derive.

The bias against the coverage of the poorest and the richest segments of society happens in virtually all household surveys. The very poor are difficult to survey: institutionalized population, homeless people, emerging urban underclass and the socially excluded, poor ethnic minorities are almost always left out. Also, some sources of income such as property (capital) and entrepreneurship are typically under-surveyed.

---

8   This applies to 2001 and 2004. However, the deviation is relatively small for the employees, since most of them have only one (formal) job.

9   E.g. Duchêne, 1998; Dăianu et al., 2001; Stănculescu and Ilie, 2001; Neef and Stănculescu, 2002; Neef and Adair, 2004.

Beyond all these limitations, income data for Romania allow for a relatively satisfactory measurement of the developments during transition.

Slovenia

The 1993 Household Expenditure Survey is based on a two-stage stratified sampling procedure. There are six strata, differentiated according to settlement type (two for Ljubljana, four for other municipalities). Within these strata, 654 primary sampling units were chosen – these are in effect census units. In the second stage, five households from each sampling unit were chosen, resulting in 3,250 households included in the sample. Because of the differing probability of inclusion in the sample, different weights are assigned to households. These composite weights are actually obtained by multiplication of several different weights. For example, one of these weights "corrects" for the higher probability of inclusion in the sample of larger households (i.e. households with more persons aged 18 or above). Surveying is based on the interview method, which requires detailed entries into questionnaires. Annual expenditures and incomes are recorded, and the interviews were conducted between 10 and 25 December. Income (by income source) is recorded jointly for the household and not separately for each household member. Also, only current cash income is included in the dataset, though the amount of own consumption is recorded in the survey. Income is "net", meaning that social contributions and withheld income tax are not included.

Since 1997, the Household Expenditure Survey (HES) closely follows the Eurostat guidelines. The survey is based on a stratified sample, consisting of 12 regions and 6 settlement types, resulting in 72 strata, of which 25 are empty. These "empty" strata are due to the fact that Ljubljana and Maribor are defined as "settlement types". Within these strata, primary sampling units are chosen – these are in effect census units, which each contain 30 households. From each chosen primary sampling unit, 4 households are chosen, using simple random sampling. Similarly to the previous surveys, different composite weights are assigned to households (because of the differing probability of inclusion in the sample), obtained by multiplication of several different weights.

Some 28 to 40 households are included in the annual sample each week; some oversampling is necessary because of non-response. Care is therefore taken to include at least 1,200 households in the sample annually. Households included in the sample participate during two weeks. During this time, all members of the household record their expenses in a diary (each having a separate one). The recall period for expenses and income varies from two weeks (for expenses recorded in the diary) to 12 months. For example, a 12-month recall period is required for all purchases of consumer durables, own production of agricultural products, self-employment income etc. A 3-month recall period is required for clothing and foot-ware, as well as vacation expenses. Wages, salaries, pensions and other types of regular income are recorded according to the most recent date these incomes were received. This "most recent date" also applies to regular expenses (electricity, water, heating etc). Expenses and incomes are then expanded to an annual level. Incomes are recorded separately for each household member.

In order to obtain larger samples, containing at least 3,600 households, three annual surveys are merged into one, taking as a midpoint the month of May of the middle year; for example, for the merged samples of 1997, 1998 and 1999 the midpoint is May 1998. Expenses and incomes are adjusted, using the cost-of-living index and taking (in this case) May 1998 as the reference point.

Though income in-kind is recorded, our dataset includes only current cash-disposable income. At the individual level four broad income groups are distinguished: labour income, income from self-employment, social benefits (including pensions) and family benefits. At the household level, other income types are recorded: income from capital, interfamily transfers, other income. Income is recorded "net", i.e. without social contributions and withheld income tax. This means that no procedure for deducting social contributions and withholding personal income tax was necessary. The "net" income stated in the surveys somewhat deviates from the true net income, which is established only on the basis of the final annual income tax return.

A7 References

Dăianu, D./Albu, L./Croitoru, L./Tarhoaca, C./Ivan-Ungureanu, C. (2001) *The Underground Economy in Romania*. Bucharest: CEROPE.

Duchêne, G. (coord.) (1998) The informal economy in Romania. Final report on the E.U. ACE PHARE Programme P95-2228-R, September, ROSES, Brussels.

Eurostat (2002) The methodology of calculation of the 'Laeken' indicators of monetary poverty, DOC.E2/IPSE/3-2/02.

Lerman, R.I./Yitzhaki, S. (1985) 'Income inequality by income source: a new approach and applications to the United States', *Review of Economics and Statistics* 67 (1): 151-156.

Milanovic, B. (1998) *Income Inequality and Poverty during the Transition from Planned to Market Economy*. Washington D.C.: World Bank.

Neef, R./Stănculescu, M.S. (eds.) (2002) *The Social Impact of Informal Economies in Eastern Europe*. Aldershot: Ashgate.

Neef, R./Adair, Ph. (eds.) (2004) *Informal Economies and Social Transformation in Romania*. Munster: LIT Verlag.

Podder, N. (1993) 'The disaggregation of the Gini coefficient by factor component and its application to Australia', *The Review of Income and Wealth* 38 (1): 51-62.

Rao, V.M. (1969) 'Two decompositions of the concentration ratio', *Journal of the Royal Statistical Society* 132: 418-425.

Shorrocks, A.F. (1988) 'Aggregation issues in inequality measures', in: Eichhorn, W. (ed.), *Measurement in economics*. Physica-Verlag.

List of Contributors

Mitja Čok, Associate Professor at the Faculty of Economics, University of Ljubljana.

Michael F. Förster, Social Policy Analyst at the OECD Directorate for Employment, Labour and Social Affairs, Paris, and formerly for half a decade Research Fellow at the European Centre for Social Welfare Policy and Research, Vienna.

Viktoria Galla, Research Assistant at the Institute of Economics, Hungarian Academy of Sciences, Budapest.

Nataša Kump, Researcher at the Institute for Economic Research in Ljubl-jana.

György Molnár, Senior Research Fellow at the Institute of Economics, Hungarian Academy of Sciences, Budapest.

Silviya Nikolova, Researcher at the Centre for Economic and Strategic Research, Sofia and PhD student at the Center for Population Studies, Bulgarian Academy of Sciences, Sofia.

Lucian Pop, Associate Professor at the Faculty of Sociology and Social Work, University of Bucharest.

Manuela Sofia Stănculescu, Research Fellow at the Institute for the Study of the Quality of Life, Romanian Academy, and Associate Professor at the Faculty of Sociology and Social Work, University of Bucharest.

Tine Stanovnik, Professor at the Faculty of Economics, University of Ljubljana, and Senior Research Fellow at the Institute for Economic Research in Ljubljana.

Wohlfahrtspolitik und Sozialforschung
Herausgegeben vom Europäischen Zentrum Wien
mit dem Campus Verlag, Frankfurt am Main/New York

Campus Verlag, Postfach 90 02 63, D-60442 Frankfurt am Main
Tel: (069) 97 65 16-0; Fax: (069) 97 65 16
www.campus.de, info@campus.de, vertrieb@campus.de

Public Policy and Social Welfare
A Series Edited by the European Centre Vienna with
Ashgate, Aldershot, Brookfield USA, Singapore, Sydney

www.ashgate.com